MASTERING CHANCE

MASTERING CHANCE

Leila   Wilder

For Nick

Table of Contents

DISASTER

The foot hung in the same position over the threshold in Aunt Hannah's house across the road. It looked just the same as it had at dusk last night. It was a waxen cream color except on the sole which was gray. Surely that was her aunt's foot. It could not be Uncle Harold's, it was too small. Aunt Hannah would be ashamed to be seen like this. She always wore her stockings and leather soled shoes. She was dead now. But where was her stocking? How had she come to die just there, instead of in bed like Papa or Momma?

Lena pulled her eyes away from the foot. She closed her eyes. Everything came flooding back. All the horror of the past few days. Her heartbeats began to race. How could she go on? Would she die here in this locked room? Tears slipped down her sweat-streaked smudged cheeks. There was no hope for her. No, no, she must not give up!

She opened her eyes, looking at every now memorized minute piece of the room. This accounting room was very simple, completely unadorned. Only a stool and small table made up the furniture. Just a week ago she had happily sat on that stool, going over the mill's ledger for her father. She struggled to her knees, and leaned out the window, scanning the other houses in the tiny village that she could see from her prison. It was just after dawn. A beautiful orange sun had started to rise from the horizon. There was not a soul in sight. The little track of a road through the village would normally be alive with voices of the villagers as they greeted each other. Where was everyone? Was everyone dead? She saw no smoke coming through the smoke holes or chimneys in any of the roofs. She smelled smoke, but maybe it was from untended fires.

Sadly, she slipped back down against the wall to sit on the floor. She closed her eyes. The light wind tousled the branches of the big oak next to the watermill, brushing them against the building. The leaves rustled. She heard ducks and chickens in the distance, and an occasional mournful mooing of a cow. If no one was alive, the animals might starve. The cows would surely get milk fever.

She leaned her head against the wall. Was it really the fourth morning she had been locked up here in her father's accounts room? Maybe it was longer. She was quite sure she had been delirious for at least two nights. She had drifted in and out of strange dreams, waking herself with her own shivering. Many times she dreamt of the huge stag with mammoth antlers. He looked into the dark at her, coming ever closer. She held tight to the small dead tree because she kept twirling round and round, and if she did not hold tight she would fly away.

Yesterday morning when she woke up, she was cold, but not shivering. No, maybe it was the day before. Memories were all jumbled. Thankfully, her head no longer ached. Probably she was cold because she wore only her shift. Although it was long sleeved and came down to her ankles, it was a very thin linen cloth. She noticed that her blue dress was balled up on her cloak. When had she taken it off? She could not remember.

She shouted, but only a croak came out. Her throat was sore from many attempts to call for help. She picked up her dress, shook it and turned it around to inspect it. It was filthy from sweat, floor dust, and maybe her own vomit. Shaking her head in disgust, she drew it over her head, struggled to get her stiff arms into the arm holes, and then shook out the skirt so that it fell over her shift. The effort exhausted her, and she sat down on the floor for a few moments. When she had regained some energy, she pulled her rumpled linen dress up and crawled over to the jug. No cider was left! When she felt a little stronger, she crawled to the window and shouted, but could only make a mewling weak noise. She called out until her strength was gone. She got up, no longer dizzy, and banged on the door. She gave up when blood started to ooze again from her knuckles. As soon as she recovered somewhat, she tried again to call out and bang at the door, pausing to listen.

How many days had she been shouting? No one answered. The waterwheel was silent, so the sluice gate was closed. No noises came from her husband Dieter or her baby Michael downstairs in the milling room. Where was that hideous man? Why, oh why, had she married him? He was a sneak, a liar, a user, an adulterer. Her darling baby Michael had made no noise since the day after she was shut up in this room.

Michael! Poor lovely little boy…not even a year old. Would Dieter have harmed him? Surely he could not have hurt his own child. Maybe he took Michael away with him somewhere. Would she ever hold her darling boy again? She must find the strength to hold on. Maybe someone would come and let her out of this room.

She opened one eye to look at the jug and covered jar beside her. She knew the cider jug was empty. There was only one piece of biscuit left in the jar. Her night pot was nearly full. After today, she would have to try to leave the room. Dieter had said she must stay here until she was well, and then had locked the door. She tried to think why she had not fought him when he urged her upstairs. She had been so weak and feverish.

What a selfish hard person she had married. He would not open the door now. Michael must have died, she had to accept that. Where was Margit? Had he shut her up as well? Was Dieter dead too? Or had he run away, probably taking her father's few coins. Why had she not died? She felt all right. She was stiff from sitting, but she had no fever and had not vomited many times like her parents or sister Margit had. She pulled up her sleeves. No lumps. She pulled the skirt of her shift to the top of her legs, unhooked her stockings from her garter, pushed them down to her ankles and checked her legs. No lumps. She felt along her groin, then under her arms. No lumps. She pulled off her head scarf, unbraided her hair and felt her scalp. Nothing wrong with her head, though her hair was matted and sticky from her days of fever. She knew she was sinfully proud of her hair—her mother always said it felt like silk. She was just filthy, but she had no dark lumps anywhere on her body as far as she could tell. Had she survived the pestilence? Or had she had some other illness? She shook out her dress and shift, but tied her scarf around her neck rather than covering her messy hair.

A weak mooing roused her out of her musings. That was Buttercup. She would know her cry anywhere. It wasn't the cry to be milked, was it? It sounded more like her moo cracked from lack of water. She probably had been locked up in the byre since Mamma died. What about the hens? Maybe they were dead. Old Jake, her father's horse, had not whinnied. Why? The mooing she had heard earlier was from farther down the road. Some other cattle were in need of care too.

She must figure out a way to get out of the room. The door was impossible. The great oak bolt on the outside of the door would not break from her weak battering. She got up, so stiff she could hardly stand, and leaned out the window. It was a long way to the ground. She was on the grain hopper floor, the grindstones were on the floor below, and the cogwheel from the waterwheel was on the bottom floor. She looked up. The roof was within reach. If she climbed up on the windowsill she could hold on to the roof's edge with both hands. Then what? If she went hand over hand maybe she could get down to the lower corner of the roof. She could see the branches of the oak tree from her window. Maybe she could grab on to a branch, then climb back to the trunk and down to the ground. Or she might fall down and break her head. When she had been a young girl she would have tried it without fear. Now in her third decade she was not so foolhardy. She went and sat down on her wool cape, her shoulders slumped down, and a tear escaped from her closed eyes.

It seemed like an eternity, but it had been only four weeks ago that the sick stranger had staggered down the dusty track into their tiny village. His clothes were stained from sweat and his own vomit. He could not walk straight and had to stop every few steps. It was a novelty to have anyone come to their village on assarted land, other than the lord's bailiff or his steward. The villagers had all come out to see the man as he stumbled along. They had heard that a terrible sickness was spreading across the land, coming from south of the Nahe River, but they had not seen any signs of it.

The stranger was out of his mind in his fever, and as the villagers asked him questions he crumpled and fell to the ground. Normally jolly Father Johan sympathetically rushed forward, calling for her father to help him. A ladle of water was brought by her mother, which the sick man drank thirstily. His eyes wandered over the villagers' faces, and twitched before they closed. Father and Papa carried him into the priest's house. The sick man died that night.

For over two weeks nothing happened. No one became sick. All the villagers relaxed. They were safe. Harvest was half finished; the days were sunny and dry, and all seemed well with the world. Carts loaded with grain came to the mill, and Margit, Dieter and she helped her father. She now did most of the ledger work. The village bustled with all the welcome activities of harvest plenty.

That world ended suddenly. Father Johan woke feeling weak and then became feverish. In the evening Papa became sick. At first he felt feverish, then he trembled uncontrollably. He could not eat, and vomited again and again. Her mother nursed him lovingly, washing his face, cooling his brow, and holding his hand. He became delirious: he did not even seem to know her or Margit. The sisters sat at the bench by the table. Lena clutched Michael, frozen with dread. Margit's eyes were wide with fear, her beautiful sister… she sobbed silently for a moment thinking of her.

Their mother forbad them to come near Papa. The sisters were caught up in the dreadful drama. Dieter sat silently on the other side of the room. He hardly spoke. What had he been thinking then? Probably planning how to escape.

Three days after he became ill, Papa got large boils on his chest, by his armpits, and they were dark purple. He died the next morning, and Father Johan died that day too. The two leaders of the hamlet died in one day. Without Father Johan, everyone felt lost. Who would say the prayers? What about burial? Auntie seemed to have the most sense that day. She got Uncle to harness the oxen to the cart, got the men to put the dead in the cart, and they all went in procession to the cemetery. They said funeral prayers as best they could, laying the two men next to each other in the cemetery.

Her mother had already been sick then, feverish and delirious, too sick to walk unassisted to the cemetery. Leaning on Lena, she had managed to make the journey. Dieter had stayed in the mill. He had not touched her parents or helped her and Margit as they tried to care for them.

The night after the funeral, in the dark, the family woke to a clatter of hooves and wheels. Gregor Plowman's family, parents and children, were fleeing in the night, their cart piled high with belongings. They hoped to escape death.

When Lena woke early the next morning, her mother was dead. Margit was limp and feverish. Just as she was trying to give Margit some broth, she began to feel dizzy herself. Dieter had looked at her oddly as she complained to him about her aching head. No words of consolation escaped his lips as she tried to lay her mother's body out for burial. He picked up the baby and went out of the mill.

Sometime later--she was so ill by then that she felt confused and weak--he came back in, laid the baby down, sat down and stared at her. What was going through his mind? Then he got up and said, "I think we should all move upstairs. I think the sickness is down here in the cog room. I will get you all upstairs, and then I will come back down and take your mother to the cemetery. Can you walk up the stairs? I will help you up, and then come back down for Margit and the baby."

Somehow she climbed the stairs. He came up behind her with her cloak, and the cider and biscuit jar. He laid her cloak on the floor and she collapsed onto it, exhausted. She was not so tired that she did not hear when the bolt shot closed on the outside of the door. She tried to scream, but only a weak croak came out. She crawled to the door and beat on it. How long did she try? When she next woke, she was shivering, lying against the door.

Lena's thoughts wandered to all the people in the village. Her father was the miller, so she had grown up in the mill, next to the stream. Next to their house, just south of it was Gregor Plowman's family. They might be alive, since they had fled in the night in their cart. South of them, some distance away, beyond the church, was Father Johan's house. He was dead. Then came the two houses that had been empty since the famine years when she was a baby. Just those five houses and the church were on the west side of the track. In her family, if Dieter, Michael and Margit were also dead, only she lived. Gregor's family of five might be alive somewhere. Of the twelve on her side of the road she might be the only one living.

She thought about the seven houses on the other side of the track. Straight across from the mill was her auntie's house. Auntie and Uncle were dead, she was sure. She had seen none of the other neighbors since she became ill. Old Hans and Anna lived north of Auntie but she could not see their house from her window. Karl the Older Plowman and his family lived behind Auntie, just on the other side of the hill, also not within view of her window. Hans the younger

5

Plowman's family was just south of Auntie, then, Lars Plowman's family, and Johan the Younger Plowman's family. Kurt the blacksmith's family was the last house in the village. She counted on her fingers. Twenty-six people on that side of the road. Who was alive? Where were they?

She opened her eyes. She could see the pale autumn sun through the window. She must have slept through the day. She was so thirsty. She tried to make saliva in her mouth so that she could swallow. She opened her jar. No biscuits left.

What had awakened her? Was it the wind tossing the oak branches against the building? No. It sounded like stones scraping against each other: a measured, methodical sound. It was someone walking outside on the road! It was the crunching sound of footsteps. Hope and fear struggled in her heart as she crawled to the window to look out. Cautiously she raised her head just high enough to see over the windowsill. She dropped down quickly. Two men she had never seen before were staggering into town from the south. Sick men? No. They looked drunk. They were dressed in an odd combination of clothes. The tall one wore a velvet jacket over his rough peasant tunic. He had a big plumed burger's hat on his head. The shorter man wore a magnificent cloak over his dirty brown tunic, and he had a priest's cross around his neck. They started to sing some song, but broke into giggles. Where had they come from? What priest had such a fine cloak? And where had the burgers hat come from? They had surely come from a city. They stopped. She strained her ears to hear any sound. They started walking. They were coming this way.

She listened as they came into the house. She could not hear what they said, but she heard sounds of barrels being opened and furniture moving. They were searching on the cog wheel floor, looking for things to steal. Then she heard them come up the stairs to the grinding room. She heard enough to know they laughed as they had poked the dead body of her mother. She covered her ears and cried silently. But she *must* listen! She fumbled with her shoes, and after finally getting them on she rose silently and listened. Finally the footsteps stumbled up the stairs toward the grain hopper floor where she was. She tiptoed to the door and with all the strength she could muster, slid the bolt through the angle irons.

The footsteps now shuffled from the top of the stairs toward her room. She heard the sound of the bolt sliding. The man pushed the door, but it did not budge. He pushed his shoulder into the door. The door held. Swearing loudly, he asked the other man to help him. From the way he spoke, she was sure he was not from this area. She heard shuffling as the second man came up to the door. Together they heaved against the door. Again and again they heaved with all their might against the door. They swore and rested, then started again.

They tried this several more times, when suddenly she heard a scream and a low guttural groan. A moment later she heard the sliding of something moving down against the door. Then someone screamed again in fright. There were several loud sounds, like someone falling down or bumping into the wall. She could hear blows and cries of fear and pain. This was followed by the crack of a piece of wood and a strangled cry. What other sound was that? Someone out there was breathing very heavily. She could not make out what was happening. For long moments nothing happened, then it sounded like a sack was being dragged away from the door.

"Lena? Margit? Are you in there?"

"Liebhard, Karl Plowman's son? Is that you?" She jumped to her feet and put her ear to the door.

"Lena, are you all right? We thought all of you had died," Liebhard said.

Lena fumbled with the heavy bolt, her bruised knuckles barely bending. She was so weak that she trembled from the effort of trying to pull it back. At last it moved. Liebhard pushed the door open. He looked like Archangel Michael standing there, great huge Liebhard. Giant Liebhard, the largest man in the village, even bigger than his brother Mark. She flew to him, putting her arms around his hard muscular torso. He had never seemed so tall to her as he did now. His strong arms wrapped around her and he stroked her head. The heavy weight of fear and despondency lifted from her heart. She pressed her face into his chest and wept.

"Lena, poor Lena. Your mother and your baby Michael are lying down there all alone," he blurted out. "Where is Dieter?"

Lena leaned into his chest. Michael was dead then. She struggled not to howl with grief. All her family was now gone. She was alone in the world. Never in her wildest fears and imaginings had she thought she would face such a plight.

Liebhard did not speak, but continued to stroke her hair. She felt his lips touch the top of her head several times. It gave her comfort to know this rock of a man, this perfect specimen of a man—maybe slow minded but kindest of hearts-- had come to find her. She opened her eyes. The two strangers lay on the floor. One's head lay open, the other's head hung strangely to one side.

"Liebhard, you have killed them," she whispered, almost choking from the sight of all the blood and brains spilled on the floor.

"I didn't mean to, but they had cudgels." She looked up and saw he had a tremendous welt across his cheek. She wondered how many times he had been hit. He turned slightly so that his shoulder hid the grotesque scene of the broken bodies from her.

She looked up at the gentle giant, and decided she would not try to explain that his actions went beyond self-defense or protecting her or Margit. Even in these strange times he could be in grave trouble for killing these two. She knew him so well that she knew he did not have a mean bone in his body. She put the thought aside, to be pondered later.

"Let us get Margit. Where is she?" he asked, perhaps unaware of any ambivalent thoughts she might have about the death of these strangers.

"Liebhard, she is dead, I think. If she is not downstairs, Dieter must have locked her in too. Maybe she is in that room," she said, as she pointed to the storage room beyond the grain hopper. She saw that the door was bolted. She started to walk, but staggered weakly. Liebhard caught her from falling and held her against him to support her. When they reached the door, she was unable to pull the bolt back. Liebhard leaned forward, pulled the bolt, and pushed the door. It slowly opened. Margit had tried to get out! She lay there on the floor, crusted in her own vomit and blood. Her darling sister, that perfect chiseled face, and blond flowing hair, had come to this horrible lonely end. Lena howled, grabbed Liebhard's tunic and hid her face in his chest. He held her, quieting her, and pulled the door closed.

"Come, I will take you to my mother."

"Are you all alive?" she asked.

"Yes, all."

"I watched from the window after I got well, but saw no one move. Auntie…"

"Your auntie and uncle are dead. Mother said I was to take them out of the house just now and to the graveyard. We have been very quiet and come out at night because of all the commotion. When I came to do as Mother asked, I heard the noises in here."

"What commotion, Liebhard? I have heard nothing. I have listened with all my might and heard nothing."

"Beyond the hills behind us," he gestured east behind his father's house, "my brother Mark and I climbed up the hill to see down in the valley. Fires are everywhere. What is happening, I don't know. Mother says the people are crazed from the sickness. Even the lord's fortress is burned."

Lena leaned against Liebhard as they walked toward the stairs. He was such a kind man. She was momentarily ashamed that when she was a child she had joined the other children and often baited this big slow man, two years older than her, but always seeming a simple soul.

When they reached the grinding floor, the horror she had anticipated became real. Her mother lay sprawled on the floor. A bundle that must have been Michael lay in the cradle. The smell of vomit and death was overpowering. She turned her face into Liebhard's side and closed her eyes as he walked them toward the last flight of stairs.

"Mark and I will come back and take Margit, your mother and Michael to the graveyard. We will lay them in the ground and then you can come to say goodbye to them."

The cog wheel room was a jumble because the drunken men had checked all the barrels and spilled some of the grain on the floor, but Lena saw it could be quickly put to rights.

She walked over to the cider keg, unstopped the cork and poured cider into a cup. She drank thirstily.

"Do you want some, Liebhard?"

"Yes, please, I would."

She poured out a full cup for him.

"I was afraid for you," he said. "I have worried about you."

The outer door stood ajar, but after they went out, they closed it behind them. Liebhard turned toward the road, but Lena held back.

"I must see to Buttercup, Jake and the hens."

Liebhard jerked his head with his surprise. "Mother did not tell me to do anything about them. I am sorry, Lena, I did not check them."

"I think Dieter probably cared for them until he disappeared. Did you see him leave, Liebhard?"

"He left very early some mornings ago. He took your father's horse. He had a bag on his back," Liebhard answered, scuffing his feet back and forth.

"Which direction did he go?"

"He went up toward the cemetery. I followed him awhile. He fell off the horse a couple times, so he was sick or he was drunk. I stopped following after he went beyond the cemetery."

She cursed Dieter silently. Less than three years ago he had seemed so loving and supportive. He had helped her father run the mill, and had tried to learn how to keep the mill's books. She had stopped liking him months ago, after Michael was born. He was a sly selfish brute. She knew that he was spending stolen time with some girl from Lord Conrad's village. He must have thought marrying her and eventually replacing her father as the miller was his best chance for prosperity after he lost his place in Lord Conrad's household.

She opened the byre door. Buttercup mooed mournfully as she came over to Lena. The chickens glared down from the rafters, Henny and the three others. Lena stepped back and Buttercup walked out to the first blade of grass she could find. She was obviously famished. Liebhard had already picked up two buckets and headed down to the river's edge. Lena went back to the mill and got a bucket of grain from the grain barrel. This would be a rare treat for the hens. She gave some to Buttercup too, who had already drunk half of Liebhard's first bucket. Liebhard and Lena squatted on either side of Buttercup and stripped each teat multiple times into the empty bucket to relieve the bulging tenderness of the cow's udder. When the bucket was half full, they stood and waited while the animals drank and ate.

"We must put them back in the byre now for the night," Lena said. "I will let them out early in the morning."

After they had lured the hens and Buttercup back into the barn and closed it, Lena asked Liebhard to wait while she went in to change her dress. She had brought in half a bucket of water left after Buttercup had drunk her fill. She looked at her dress and shrift before she threw them on the table. They were smeared with blood, some vomit and dust and smelled of acrid old sweat from her long sojourn in the locked room. She had only one other dress and shift, the shift made of linen, which after many washings was now very soft and nearly white, and the dress of lightweight natural brown wool cloth. She hurriedly washed her body with a cloth from the cupboard. She dunked her head into the bucket, soaped it up with lye soap, and then rinsed it. After she had dried herself with another cloth, she pulled her shift over her head and buttoned it at the neck, then the square necked dress. This would be warm to wear, but she had no other summer dress. She changed her stockings too. She pulled her hair back quickly into a ponytail and tied it with a string. She found a clean cap and put it over her hair. Feeling more presentable, she walked out and joined Liebhard. She found she needed to lean on his arm as they walked across the road. Lena looked at Auntie's foot a moment and then averted her eyes. So many had died. They walked the short distance over the hill beyond Auntie's house to Liebhard's home.

There was no visible activity, but when Liebhard opened the door, Lena saw the whole family was busy working. Hilda stood up from her sewing and hobbled over to Lena.

"Lena girl! You are alive! Your family?" Hilda put her arm around Lena and gave her a hug. "There, there. These are trying times." Karl the Older, very quiet as usual, tapped her shoulder and made a little bow in sympathy. Mark, two years older than Liebhard, nodded to her. Hilda's round face beamed at the sight of the half pail of milk.

After Hilda had settled Lena on a bench at the table and put a bowl of porridge in front of her, Lena told the family how she and Margit had been locked upstairs by Dieter, how she had become desperate to escape, then told them about the two drunkards, and the bravery of Liebhard. They all listened in rapt attention, smiling proudly when they heard of Liebhard's actions.

"What about the rest of the village, Hilda?" Lena asked.

"Well, we have been very careful not to be seen. The world has gone crazy. The boys saw fires over the hills behind us. I have Karl and the boys go out at night, but just to look after the animals. I cook at night so as not to let our smoke be seen."

"But have you not gone to look into the other houses? Since you are all well, I think you have some special protection against this sickness. I think I might too, since the rest of my family died and I didn't."

"Well, that may be. We can go out tonight and see inside the houses."

Lena knew that in the Karl the Older Plowman family, Hilda thought for all four, and made the decisions. She decided she must insist that they check on everyone and all the animals.

"At dawn tomorrow, Hilda, your sons and I will go and check on everyone and the animals. We will come back then and decide what we must do." She held her breath, afraid that the old woman would not like this idea.

"Yes, Lena, you are right," Hilda agreed.

The neat cottage was small, and another person in the house made it crowded, but Lena was more than happy to be with this family. The main room had the kitchen and one or two chairs to sit down in the evening. On the far side in a nook, was a bed. A ladder led to a loft. Unlike the mill, it was heated by a stube, so that the room was warm and smokeless. It was cozy here. When Hilda insisted she stay with them, she did not refuse. She could not go back to the mill tonight. Hilda gave her a quilt and laid out a small straw filled mattress on the floor for her. The candles were put out and soon the family was asleep. The sons had climbed the ladder to the loft above her, and Karl and Hilda slept in the bed in the nook.

Lena lay awake listening to the reassuring sound of the regular breathing of the others. Her thoughts wandered to her family. How Margit and her mother must have suffered in their sickness, with no one to console them. Little Michael was so young when he died, he was already with the angels. Her mother was a good woman, a patient but fun-loving mother who was firm but understanding. She went to heaven too. Even Margit, who sometimes was a handful, would be in heaven. She was so beautiful: her soft blond hair, large blue eyes, clear skin and ample figure. Everyone said she was beautiful. She was a tease, but if she made Lena cry, she was immediately sorry.

And Papa: he made everyone happy they were alive. Each morning he was full of joy. He saw life as good with just a few rough bumps. Not a big man, his expansive friendliness made him seem large. People liked to tell him their stories and their woes, and he was glad to listen.

They were all together, and she was alone. She turned on her side and closed her mind to her own plight. She made herself listen to the rhythmic sound of the breathing of the others. The sound became more and more indistinct as she drifted off to sleep.

Before dawn, the brothers had come down from the loft and gone outside. After dawn she sat up and saw that Hilda was getting up too. After she had pulled her dress over her shift and gone out to relieve herself, she came in and helped Hilda lay breakfast on the table. Five at the table was very snug, but the Karl Plowman family seemed comfortable with her presence. Hilda had set aside a cup, bowl and spoon for Lena to use, as her own were at the mill. They ate their porridge and bread in silence. She had so many questions to ask, but felt that the easy silence while they ate was the way of the house. This was so different from her family, where there was always lots of talk and commotion when the family gathered together. Breakfast was also the time when Papa read them a few words from the prayer book. He had taught Margit and her to know their letters too, and she could read a little bit. Breakfast was a happy time of day in her family.

"Mark and Liebhard have taken your family to the cemetery, Lena, and buried them by your papa," Hilda said as they finished their meal.

"You are so kind. I want to go, after we put away the breakfast things, to see their graves. Mark and Liebhard, will you come with me? Then we can go to see the rest of the families."

Both nodded yes.

After Lena had helped to clear the table and clean up, the three walked up the road to the graveyard. Mark said nothing, but nodded his head in agreement when Liebhard talked. Mark had not spoken a word for years. She remembered that when she was very small he used to talk all the time when the village children played together. The whole Karl the Older Plowman family acted a bit differently. Even with all of her own sadness and troubles she mulled over in her mind what could possibly have made the father silent and humble, Mark speechless, and Liebhard seemingly simple. Hilda had always been warm and welcoming to Lena, yet she commanded these three men in every detail. She was drawn out of her reverie by Liebhard.

"We buried your family this morning, in a single grave: your mother, Margit and little Michael. We buried your aunt and uncle together next to them."

"How did you do all of that this morning? I saw you go out just before dawn," she said.

"Oh, we got up in the middle of the night and gathered the bodies. There was a full moon, so we were able to find everyone and load them in the cart. We had already dug the graves, so we just had to fill the holes," Liebhard explained.

Lena stopped and turned to the two young men. "I don't think we need to go out only at night. We must try to catch up taking care of our neighbors. They might be in desperate need. And all of the animals need to be tended. And what about our crops? We need to be ready for the cold season," she explained.

Mark nodded in agreement, but she wondered if he took it all in. Did he understand what she said? Liebhard knitted his brows.

"Our mother has not told us to do these things, but you think we should?"

"I think so, but I will talk to Hilda and see if she agrees," she said diplomatically. Although these were full grown men--Mark was over thirty years old--they usually did as their mother directed. As they nodded in agreement she studied them. She did not really know them well. She had not had much interaction with them since she was a teenager. They were big strong men, both blond and fair skinned. Liebhard was bigger and had sinewy muscles that were much admired by the village men. All praised their work, especially during plowing and harvest. Liebhard led Mark, who seemed happy to do as his brother bid.

The graveyard, which Lena had always thought of as a peaceful place, seemed filled with foreboding now. She saw the fresh earth where the brothers had buried her family, aunt, and uncle. She walked up to the graves, knelt down, and started to pray silently. Mark and Liebhard knelt down behind her. She leaned forward and put her hands on the bigger grave, assuming it was her mother's, and Margit's and Michael's. She turned and looked at Liebhard inquiringly. He nodded yes.

Why had this happened, she wondered. In her twenty-eight years she had only seen young children die or very old people. Here lay her healthy mother, sister, son, aunt and uncle, next to her father. How was she ever going to go on alone? What could be her place now? Who would be the head of the village without Papa and Father Johan?

Lena stood up and turned around, the brothers copying her. They walked together, one brother on each side, out of the graveyard and down the road the short way to the village. It was a clear breezy day, a perfect early autumn day that made her think that nothing should be so wrong in the world as it was.

"When we get back to the village we will look in at all of our neighbor's homes, and see how everyone is, just as I said to Hilda last night," she said, forestalling any worry Liebhard might have. "We know that there is no one else to check on my side of the road, so let's stop first at Hans Plowman the younger's house."

After just a few minutes Hans' cottage was in sight. There was not a movement around the house. The cottage door was closed. The byre at the back of the cottage stood open, and the chickens and geese were scratching in the grass, looking for insects and seeds. A cow and calf she knew to be Hans' grazed in the distance. A few of Hannah's chickens clucked as they approached. Liebhard stepped ahead of Lena and knocked at the door. They waited, but heard no sound.

"Hans? Hannah?" Lena called. There was no answer. Liebhard looked at her inquiringly. She nodded, and he opened the door. The burst of putrid air that escaped from the house was almost more than she could bear. She leaned over and vomited. Mark and Liebhard hovered over her though both seemingly were unaffected by the stench. Lena bolstered her nerve and stepped into the door opening. Hans, Hannah and the two little children lay on the bed, partly covered by a bed covering, their bodies bloated and yellow. Lena walked back out and breathed in fresh air.

"What sad days these are," she said. "What a grim death for the dear little ones and their parents. I hope we find better stories in the next houses. We will look into all the houses and then come back and bury the dead." Liebhard put his arm on her back, turning her away from the house.

They walked on to the house of Lars Plowman. Just as before, Liebhard went up to the door and knocked.

"Lars? Hannah?" she called. Voices and noises could be heard.

"Is that Lena?"

"Yes, it's me. I am here with Liebhard and Mark. We wanted to know if you are all right."

The door opened. Lars stood in front of them, wild eyed and disheveled. Behind him was Margit from next door, holding Hilde, Lars's daughter. Margit and Lars came out of the house hesitantly and stared at Lena.

"Where are Hannah and your children?" she asked, and turned her eyes to Margit. "Where is your husband Johan and your two babies?"

Margit's eyes were wide with fear, but she whispered, "My Johan and babies died two days ago. Lars pulled them out of the house and took his Hannah and two babies out too. We laid them all over there," she gestured toward the mound of dirt visible behind the byre. "I could not be alone in my house, and I came to be with Lars and Hilde."

Lena saw that Lars and Margit could hardly comprehend that anything so normal as a visit by Mark, Liebhard and her was occurring. She decided to tell them all that she knew had happened, so that they could begin to feel that they had actually survived. They listened like little children as she told them that she and the boys were checking on all the neighbors and that those who were still alive would take all of their dead to the graveyard this afternoon and bury them. She directed them to dig up their dead from the mound and load them onto a cart, and that she and Liebhard and Mark would help them later to bring them to the graveyard. Both nodded, so she hoped they understood and would do what she said.

She bade them goodbye and walked on with Liebhard and Mark to Kurt the blacksmith's cottage. Her heart pounded. Kurt had married her best friend Marta. She timidly knocked on the door. She heard some kind of scuttling sound and whimpering. She hesitated, frightened herself. Liebhard stepped forward and opened the door. At first they could see nothing. Then they saw the eyes staring at them from under a quilt on the floor. It was the children, Greta and Klaus. On the bed were their parents, probably they died in the last two days. Kurt had died first, because Marta had laid out his body for burial. Kurt's aged mother, who had been an invalid for the past two years, sat dead against the far wall. She might have died just that morning.

Anger and despair fought each other in her emotions. Her beloved Marta! The one person in the village to whom she had told all her secrets. There was no one left for her. Then her eyes fixed on the frightened eyes of Marta's children.

"Come Greta and Klaus. It's me, Lena. Come," she said, and opened her arms. Klaus, who was eleven, stood up and helped his crying little sister to get up. They clung to each other as they came to her. She pulled them to her and cried with them. They had lost their family like she had. Liebhard and Mark put their arms around her and the children. She felt security and strength flow from them, and she hoped the children did as well.

"I am so sorry, children. We will take you with us now, and we will take care of you. Mark and Liebhard will lay your parents and grandmother out properly and we will bury them. You know though that God has taken them already into his arms." The eyes of both children looked trustingly into hers. She took each by the hand, and left this place which must have brought such terror for them.

When they got back to Karl Plowman's, Hilda hugged the children and gave them each a bowl of porridge as Lena explained what they had found in the rest of the village. Hilda covered her mouth in disbelief.

"You mean to say that all of Hans the Younger's family is dead? Lars and his daughter Hilde, Margit, and then little Klaus and Greta are the only ones you found alive? What about old Hans and Anna?"

"We have yet to go there. So, yes, that means we have four men, three women—counting me—and three children alive that we know of. Gregor Plowman and his family might be alive, but they may never come back. And Dieter….he has run away too." She continued to look into Hilda's eyes, wondering if she too were trying to imagine how any of them could survive with so few hands to harvest crops.

After they had had some bread and peese porridge, Lena, Liebhard and Mark walked to the little cottage of Hans and Anna. Now that Father Johan and her father were dead, Hans was the elder in the village. Their house lay just beyond the brow of a small hill, past her aunt's empty house. When the house came into view, they were surprised to see Anna outside, tossing grain to her geese. It seemed like another world, a homey world with no cares. When Anna noticed them however, she dropped her bowl of grain and ran into the house.

Lena called to her and walked down the hill to the door. She knocked, but Anna shouted, "Go away! We don't want to die!"

"Anna, open up. The sickness has passed. We are trying to make sure everyone is all right. Is Hans well too?"

After a long silence. Anna whispered through the door: "He is acting very strange. He just sits and stares wide-eyed. Ever since he walked over to your aunt's house, he has not spoken a word."

"Anna, please open the door," she said, and slowly Anna did so. She stepped back and they all entered the room. Hans did not look up. He was like a statue in the church up at Lord Conrad's manor. Lena leaned down and tried to catch his eye. She slowly explained all that she knew had happened in the village, leaving out no detail. Hans Plowman the Younger was their son, and he was now dead, with all of his family. Liebhard came forward and put a hand on Hans' shoulder.

The old man continued to stare in front of him, but tears gathered in his eyes. Lena knew he had understood. Why did he not speak?

Anna sobbed at the news of the death of her son and grandchildren. She slumped down onto a chair, pulled her apron up over her head and cried. Lena went behind the chair, leaned over and put her arms around her. She whispered words of sympathy into her ear. Finally Anna lowered the apron. Lena walked around in front of her.

"Anna, maybe Hans just had such a terrible fright. People have acted in strange ways, seeing all of this sickness around them. Liebhard says Lord Conrad's manor was ablaze the other night. Look how Gregor ran away with his family. And Dieter. And those drunken robbers who broke into the mill." She went on to tell Anna everything that she had seen.

"What shall I do, though?" the distraught old woman asked plaintively.

"Now that we have found you, we will help you. Tomorrow we will be able to plan better how we can all help each other," she said, hoping she was not promising what they could not do.

The rest of the day was a sad and tiring one. All of the dead bodies were carried out of the houses, loaded into Karl's oxcart and taken to the cemetery. Everyone followed behind except for Hans. All the dead villagers were laid to rest. Everyone knelt down and Lena read a prayer from her father's prayer book. When she finished, she bowed her head and tried to pray for her family. No prayers came. She felt as though she could not get up. Then Liebhard tapped her shoulder. She looked up and saw his smile. He helped her get up. They had made it through a dark day.

After they had a small supper with Hilda and Karl, she put the two children to bed on her mattress. Then she spoke softly to Hilda. "We still have the problem of the two dead men up in the mill. Hilda, you know that Liebhard can be charged with killing them, even though it was in self-defense. I know he acted to protect me, but what would happen in the courts? I have been thinking we should take them out of the mill tonight and bury them outside the cemetery. Do you agree?"

Hilda nodded. "It is the best thing to do. But we must all understand that we tell no one."

After dark she went with Mark and Liebhard to complete their grizzly task. The men lugged the bodies down the stairs. She lifted the ember she carried to make sure that no belongings of the men remained. She would have to scrub up the awful remnants of the fight later. They loaded the bodies into the cart and encouraged Plowman's draft horse as quietly as possible out to the cemetery. Mark and Liebhard quickly dug a grave and dropped the bodies in. After they had filled the grave, they patted down the ground to make it level with the surrounding area. No one spoke as they returned to Karl Plowman's house. Lena found she was trembling. What kind of trouble could this bring on all of their heads? Then she felt Liebhard's arm around her. He was such a considerate man.

That night she slept in Karl Plowman's house again, snuggling with Klaus and Greta on the straw mat. Before she fell asleep, she decided she would go to the mill in the morning and clean. Then she and these little orphans would move there. They had no one else. They could be like a new family.

Lena was awakened at dawn by the sounds of Liebhard and Mark as they came down the ladder from the loft. She opened her eyes, and saw that Liebhard was looking at her. He smiled. She wondered if he comprehended the depth of despair that she and others who had lost family members experienced. He seemed to feel very sorry yesterday that she had lost her family. Now he smiled brightly, as though he did not remember yesterday's horrors.

After the men went outside, she carefully freed herself from Klaus and Greta, stood up and tucked the blanket around them. She hoped they would sleep for hours more. They must be exhausted from their ordeal. Hilda and Karl were awake now too. They quietly got up and began the day's chores. Soon Liebhard and Mark had joined Lena, Karl and Hilda as they silently ate their porridge. Lena wanted to talk about all the things they needed to do, but ate in silence as they did.

When breakfast was over, she said to Hilda, "We must make plans for the village. So much must be done, and we are so few. Without Papa and Fr. Johan, we must work out for ourselves how we will go on, how we will harvest so many things. And we must go down to see if Lord Conrad is alive. We must let him know the troubles of our village."

Hilda look startled. "But what can we do? Fr. Johan and your father always knew when we should do each thing and how. Your father was Lord Conrad's trusted man. We are so few."

Lena closed her eyes and tried not to cry. Suddenly she had no energy, no desire to go on. Was there no one who would step forward and help her? She herself was not sure what steps should be taken next. Harvesting? Going down to Lord Conrad's castle for direction? Clean out the stinking mess in the houses? Check on the livestock and make sure all were cared for? "God, give me guidance," she said to herself. When she opened her eyes, Hilda was staring at her.

"Did you have a vision?" she asked. "You were still for so long."

Lena started to answer, but stopped. She could see how she thought things should be done. Hilda might feel more inclined to follow her lead if she did let her think she had some kind of vision. She was loathe to speak an untruth like that. It seemed like it might be a grave sin. But perhaps it was not necessary to answer her question. What else would she have to do to get through this time?

"I don't know what happened. I closed my eyes and prayed, and then I seemed to see what would be the things we should do. We are so few, but we must work together to finish the harvest, care for our animals and come together to get through the winter."

"We are only twelve alive, Hilda. We have five men, four women, and three children. Little Hilde is only three and will not be able to help us in this effort. Klaus is eleven and Greta is eight. They will have to take care of our animals in the morning, milking the cows, feeding the animals, gathering eggs, taking the cows to the meadow and in the evening we will be back from the fields to do the chores and shut up the animals at night. I think three of us women will have to work in the fields with the men, and one will cook for all of us. With the three women working with the five men, we will be able to reap most of the grain and sheave it."

"We must go through the village and find what animals we have, and go out in the fields to see what grain is still worth harvesting. We have lost two weeks with everyone sick and dying."

Hilda's brow furrowed as she listened. Liebhard behind his mother sat quietly, looking at Lena. Could she count on him and Mark to work with her? They were the two strongest men in the village. She thought about old Hans. If he could overcome his sadness he would be a great help in organizing.

"I am going up to see how old Hans is. Perhaps now he will begin to speak again," she said, hoping silently that he had gotten over his extreme fright or sadness, whatever had stopped him from speaking.

"I will go with you," Liebhard said, with no prompting from his mother. Lena tried not to show her surprise and great relief.

"I would like that, Liebhard."

She and Liebhard got up and went of the cottage. Mark did not come with them. This too was unusual. They walked silently up the hill and started down toward Anna and Hans' home. Liebhard caught her hand when she tripped, and held it until they got to the bottom of the hill. Lena did not know what to make of his behavior, but welcomed his help and support. When they reached the cottage, he tapped on the door. Anna opened the door immediately.

"He has not talked yet. He has been weeping," she said.

Lena nodded, walked across the room and sat down next to Hans. He was looking down, tears sliding down his worn cheeks. Lena tried to think how old he was, maybe two years older than her father. He must be nearly fifty. In his sadness he looked much older. He was the most experienced villager left among them. He had been a steady friend and supporter of her father.

"Hans, we are trying to think how to work together now that we are so few. There are twelve of us left in the village." She paused, wondering if he was listening. He looked up.

"We are so few. So many dead. My son and his family. I am struck deep with this grief." He wiped his eyes.

Lena breathed a sigh of relief. He was ready to listen to her ideas. She explained how she and Hilda had been talking, and she had prayed for help. Once again, she just explained how the ideas had come to her. He nodded and accepted, just as Hilda had, that Lena had been given God's help. Lena finished her ideas and waited for him to answer.

"Your ideas of how we should harvest are good. Anna is a good cook and can cook for all of us while she takes care of little Hilde. She will be here in the village to help Klaus and Greta with the animals. We will bring our milk, eggs and flour together for her to use. Liebhard and Mark are the strongest of the rest of us, so they will lead in the fieldwork. You, Hilda and Marta will find the fieldwork hard, but all will have to work. Lars, Karl and I will all help Mark and Liebhard with the heavier work. Tomorrow morning early we will all go out and decide which of the fields to harvest. I do not think we will be able to harvest everything in time. On the other side, what we cannot harvest can be used as winter fodder fields for the cows, horses and sheep."

Lena jumped up and cried with joy. She hugged the surprised Hans. A smile momentarily replaced the deep sorrow lines of his face.

"Have you checked on all of the animals?" he asked. Lena marveled that he had jumped ahead of her own thoughts.

"Not yet," she started to say, but Liebhard butted in.

"Some of the animals are dead too, just like our families. All of the dogs are dead. I have checked on the cows, horses and sheep." He went on to count off whose animals were alive. They had five cows, three calves, two oxen, three sows, eleven young pigs and fifteen sheep. There were three field horses and the priest's horse.

"Very good, Liebhard! You have done well." He too was surprised that Liebhard had acted on his own in this situation. "That means the children will have two horses, the cows and sheep to bring to pasture. We will use the oxen and two of the horses in the harvest. What about chickens, ducks and geese?"

"I did not think of that," Liebhard said, crestfallen.

"Liebhard and I will count them now. We will get them together here at your hen house and Anna will care for them," Lena volunteered. Liebhard smiled.

"Off you go, then," Hans said, sounding almost like his old self.

They bade Hans and Anna goodbye, saying they would be back with the poultry. Anna said she planned to go down to see Magrit and arrange to bring Hilde back to stay with her and Hans, which Lena realized was a good idea. She and Liebhard walked silently back toward the village. She waited for Liebhard to speak, but he said nothing. She must lead, she decided.

"We will go to the south end of the village and combine the flock as we come back this way." Liebhard nodded.

Gathering the chickens, ducks and geese was much harder than they had planned. In the end, they put the noisy difficult geese in Hilda's byre. She would have to care for them. In total they had twenty hens, two roosters, nineteen young chickens for the cook pot, eleven ducks, and nine geese. They had a surfeit of poultry for the remaining villagers. What a number of eggs they would all be able to eat! Anna's chicken coup was very full even without the geese.

After agreeing with Hans to have the workers ready at dawn, Liebhard and Lena trudged back to the Karl Ploughman house. Hilda had food ready for them. Mark and his father were back from more burial work. They had burned the dead animals.

Everyone was tired and hungry and they ate in silence. The children, Klaus and Greta, were quiet and tearful. Lena mulled over what to do for tonight.

"Hilda, I had thought to take Klaus and Greta with me to the mill and we will live there. I must clean up first…" she thought with dread about cleaning up after her family's deaths.

"I will help you," Liebhard said. Hilda looked at him in surprise, but nodded.

"You must stay with us until you and Liebhard finish cleaning," she said.

Lena was sure that she had begun to blush. She was now certain that Liebhard had formed a romantic attachment to her. Why now, she wondered. Maybe he had always had a special feeling for her and she had not noticed. She thought about her own feelings toward him over the years. She had pleasant memories of playing with him and the other children. There had certainly been some harmless familiarities between her and Liebhard. Suddenly she remembered that kiss and some fumblings down by the river…but she had always dismissed him as too slow minded for her.

After the meal Lena got Klaus and Greta ready for bed. She scrubbed them thoroughly and washed their hair with strong soap because she saw that they had lice in their hair. She worried that she might now have lice too from sleeping with them last night. When they lay down in bed, Greta clung to her and Klaus nestled on her other side. Lena would have to wash her hair too, she thought, as she drifted to sleep.

The next day was long and arduous, one of many, as they worked to bring in the grain, peas and beans. There were some poorer fields they left unharvested. There was just too much to do for so few. Their division of labor worked better than Lena had thought possible. Everyone was used to Hans' direction, and he deferred to Lena when she made some suggestions. Why, she wondered. Perhaps because she was the miller's daughter and the miller had been the leader in the village.

THE FIND

The morning of the third day of harvest, they found a strange black horse in Lars' barley field by the river. He had on a costly saddle and bridle, and was having some trouble eating with the bit in his mouth. The villagers were awestruck. The horse's trappings were rich. Whose horse was this? Where was his master? Lena screwed up her courage and walked up to the horse, who quietly accepted her hand on his neck. The other villagers edged up to the horse.

"This marking is the coat of arms of Lord Conrad," Hans said excitedly. "Why is he here?" While Lena held the horse, everyone fanned out to see if they could find the rider. After searching for probably an hour, the rider was found. He was more dead than alive. The villagers gathered around. His clothes were of fine cloth, and he had soft leather boots. Hans leaned over and examined him closely.

"This is Lord Conrad's older son! I had heard he was living at his own fief though. My Lord, can you hear me? My Lord!" He fumbled with his brooch, opened his cloak, and then his dark tunic. Crusted blood had turned his fine white cotton shirt brown. With Lena's help, Hans pulled up the tunic and shirt. The young man had several deep gashes across his chest and at least three punctures in his left shoulder. The wounds were red and swollen. The wounds had happened days ago.

"Get water," Lena said to no one in particular. Liebhard ran down to the river. Before he was back, she had lifted the wounded man's head and put a cider jug to his lips. He moaned and his eyelids fluttered. She held the jug to his lips again. He drank! His eyes opened and he looked at her.

"You. Miller's dead-eye daughter," he slurred as he fell into unconsciousness again. Lena was frozen in disbelief. What had he called her? Had the others heard? She tried to cover her embarrassment by taking the water Liebhard had brought.

21

No one said anything as she laid a cold wet cloth on his face. He moaned but did not wake. She looked around. Nobody seemed to have reacted to what he said. They all waited anxiously to see if he woke again.

"We need to take him back to the village," she said. Before she had finished speaking, Liebhard had begun to lift the wounded man up. He placed him astride on the quiet horse, and motioned to Lena. When she came up to the horse, he lifted her up and placed her behind the young man. She put her arms around him to hold him upright.

"Take him back to the village, Lena. Best take him to the mill where there is more room. Liebhard, you help her. We will stay here and work," Hans said.

Lena was still smarting from the name he had called her. Liebhard walked beside the horse and steadied the wounded man. He was not looking at her and she was glad because she felt tears welling into her eyes. Her family had never really told her what her eye looked like. She had always known she had trouble if she tried to look out of her left eye, but her parents had said it was nothing serious. As they rode along, little snippets of memories flooded into her thoughts. She remembered Margit calling her ugly and her parents' punishing Margit. Sometimes other children had said she looked odd. So this was the reason. She had never seen herself in a looking glass, and in still water she had not been able to see how she looked. She had thought she was pretty. She was mortified. Twenty-eight and ugly! No wonder she had had no suitors until Dieter wheedled his way into her life. He must have found her easy pickings.

"Oh, Lena, stop crying over something you can't change!" she told herself. She sighed and shook herself.

"What's wrong? Are you cold?" Liebhard asked. He put his hand on her arm.

"No. No. Nothing is wrong. This has just been a strange morning," she replied.

When they got to the mill, Liebhard lifted the young man off the horse and carried him into the mill. The night before, Liebhard and Lena had cleaned the bottom floor where the fireplace and kitchen table were. They brought two of the newly filled straw mattresses from the second floor down to the kitchen. Liebhard laid the man down.

"I will put the horse in your barn and take care of him," Liebhard said.

"After you do that, please go over and ask Anna to come with her medicines," she said. He nodded and went out.

Lena turned to look at the young man. They must see to his immediate terrible condition, but they had to find out if any of his family was at the manor. They would be in great trouble if he died here and they had not tried to tell Lord Conrad. But now she would have to get these clothes off of him. First she found her father's leather apron and replaced her own linen apron with his. This would be very messy. She set to work. Some of the shirt was stuck to his skin, especially on his back, where there were two more puncture wounds. She soaked the crusted blood until the shirt came free. Occasionally the man moaned, but he did not wake. Finally he was wearing only his leggings and his braies.

She had washed most of the blood from his body by the time Anna arrived. She clucked with concern when she saw the many wounds.

"My, my, this is a very serious case. These punctures are from a pointed knife, I think. The gashes are awful, but I don't think they are dangerous. Hmm. Let me think." She looked at the jars she had brought, mostly healing balms. "If these wounds were fresh, I would have used a hot poker to close them."

Lena knew very little about healing. She had seen wounds mortify, and wondered if this man was already a lost case.

"Do you have any strong soap, Lena? Maybe lye soap? I would like to clean these wounds more. Maybe we should use urine or vinegar."

Lena was shocked at all of these ideas, but did not know if they might be effective. She ran down to the back of the sluice gate and got a jug of vinegar. She found lye soap by the washing buckets. She brought both of these up to Anna.

Anna had already gathered some loose wool from the wool basket. She poured vinegar into a bowl and dipped two pieces of wool into the vinegar, then handed one of the wool sponges to Lena.

"I don't know what else we can try. Let's gently wash the gashes. I think we can try to dribble some into the puncture wounds."

The two women gingerly began their cleaning. The man twitched again and again, but did not wake. After thoroughly cleaning the wounds on his chest and shoulder, they turned him over and worked on the back punctures. Several weak cries escaped from the man's mouth. Anna now folded pieces of linen smeared with lard and placed them over the punctures. She took a length of linen and laid it across his back. When they turned him over, the linen lay on both sides of his body. She then laid folded larded linen squares on his chest and shoulder wounds. She pulled the length of linen from his sides across his chest. Motioning to Lena for help, she pulled the man into a sitting position so that they could wrap the linen around his body twice, then looping once over the wounded shoulder, ripping the ends and tying the dressing in place. They laid him back down.

"Now we wait." Anna said. "Have broth brewing on the fire and offer it to him, often, every hour at least. He must drink hot cider or spirits if you have them. Heat water and milk for him to drink too. I will come back this evening for a few hours to help." She looked at the man's face for a long time. "He looks strong. He might live. I must go now and cook dinner for all of us. Can you manage?"

"Yes. Don't worry. If anything seems very much amiss I will come for you," Lena said.

Alone again with the young lord, she took off the leather apron, wiped it clean, and put her own apron over her blue dress. Then she sat down to watch. He seemed peaceful now. He was younger than her. His long dark brown hair, now combed,

23

framed a strong boned face. He was a tall man, but not heavily built. She laid her hand on his forehead. He was a little hot. She went down to the sluice gate and filled a pitcher with the cold river water. Once back to her patient, she wet a piece of linen, squeezed out the excess water and laid the cloth on his forehead. His lids fluttered. He opened his eyes.

"You're Miller's daughter," he said, barely forming the words.

"That is much more politely said," she replied.

"What? I don't understand..." he mumbled as his eyes closed again.

Throughout the rest of the day and evening Lena frequently put liquid to his lips. He did not wake, but became very restless in his sleep. By the time Anna returned he had a noticeable fever. Lena ran over to Anna and Hans' home and ate. She was famished. She went over to Karl Ploughman's and put Klaus and Greta to bed. Liebhard followed her out of the house saying he would go back with her to help. She decided she would be happy for the company.

The invalid was much the same when they entered the mill kitchen. Anna urged her to give him broth as often as possible. After Anna left, Liebhard and Lena sat down to watch over the wounded young man. Throughout the night they each fell asleep several times, but their patient never opened his eyes. He tossed and mumbled. His skin burned. Each time Lena woke, Liebhard seemed to be awake too. His warm smile was like an enveloping cloud of comfort.

Late in the night, she leaned forward and said softly to him, "We must go to the manor tomorrow to see if any of his family is there." Liebhard nodded. "You will go to Hans in the morning before they go to the fields and tell him we are going over there. We will take the young lord's horse and Father Johan's horse so we can go faster." He nodded again. "Tell Anna to come here to watch over him."

"Yes, yes," Liebhard smiled as he answered. He looked trustingly at her. She wondered if he had substituted her for his mother as the director of his actions.

About an hour after sunrise, Anna had arrived with Hilde in tow. She frowned when she felt the wounded man's forehead. "He has a strong fever. Is he stronger than the fever? We shall know in a day or two. Did he wake?"

"No. His eyelids fluttered when I gave him broth or cider. He drank a little bit each time," Lena replied.

"Good," was all Anna said.

Liebhard had the horses ready and waiting. Lena had put on her clean shift and grey wool overdress as well her clean apron. She wanted to be presentable when she saw Lord Conrad. They mounted the horses gingerly and with a little bit of trouble, since neither had had much experience riding anything but a plow horse. The horses were gentle and patient. They decided to ride cross country to the manor, and they set off at a steady trot. They saw no activity in the fields that belonged to the manor village, which fact struck Lena with foreboding. Was everyone dead or gone? As they neared the village, which lay up against the manor's fortified wall, the devastation was far worse than Lena had imagined. At least half of the village was burned to the ground. The ground was still smoldering in many spots. The keep and manor that were visible from this vantage point were blackened. "So they had fire and pestilence!" she thought. Then they saw someone come out of a house farther up the track.

"You there! Hello!" she called. The woman scurried out of sight. Lena urged her horse forward and stopped at the house the woman had entered.

"Please come out! We are from the assarted village by the river. Please come out and talk to us."

The woman edged into view. Her wary eyes roved over their faces, and she started with astonishment when she saw the black horse's trappings.

"That is young Lord Franz's horse. Why do you have it?"

"Lord Franz is up at our village. He is wounded. Do you know anything about that? Where is his family?" Lena asked.

Others had been watching from other houses, because now several people cautiously edged out toward them.

"We suffered from the pestilence in our village," Lena volunteered. We have only twelve living, but we have gotten together and while we were bringing in the harvest we found Lord Franz lying wounded. We are caring for him but we need to find his family."

Lena waited for an answer, but they all stared at her awestruck. Finally an old woman came forward. Lena recognized her. She was Oona, the village headman's wife.

"We are many dead. There was such frenzy and fear as we tried to take the dead out of the houses and to protect our families, and then somehow a fire started. It burned and burned. Maybe it started at the castle. Many died in the fire here in the village. We are all afraid. We stay in our homes and hope we survive."

Wailing broke out among those gathered in the street. Lena was dismayed by their lethargy. These people had no hope. They needed to draw together for strength.

"Please, quiet. Listen. You are alive! You have survived! But we rode past your fields as we came here, and your crops need to be brought in! You must get together and plan how you can do that. You have to check your animals and decide how you can care for them and harvest your crops. I can see more than four dozen of you here before me. You can do this."

The villagers shuffled about.

"Is the headman here? Dead? Then who is next most respected person who is alive? I am the Miller's daughter. Is your miller here? Dead too? Who can lead then?"

Now the villagers began to look around and talk among themselves. "Good," she thought.

"But please tell us now about Lord Conrad?" she asked.

At first no one seemed to want to speak. Finally the Oona spoke up.

"The servants ran away, those that did not die of pestilence. The lord died, we heard. The young lord sent his new wife away to safety with two knights and her waiting lady. We thought he had died in the fire later, but then there was an awful fight that I could hear, maybe the day before yesterday, or the day before that. I think some hooligans had broken in to steal what they could. We did not dare to go up there."

Lena listened with mounting worry. They themselves would have to go up into the manor and keep. She looked at Liebhard. He showed no fear.

"We will go and see what we can learn," she said.

They turned the horses up toward the manor. Some of the villagers continued to watch them, and a few followed, but most of them remained talking to each other. This was a good sign at least.

They passed through the arch in the fortress wall. Not a living thing stirred. Smoldering debris still filled the air with acrid smoke. The keep door was burned away, so they rode the horses in. On the ground lay three men, dead from wounds. These were probably some of Lord Franz's attackers. One of them looked of the knightly class.

"You stay here with the horses, and I will go up," Liebhard said. He jumped off his horse and picked up a spear and knife from the ground. He moved quickly up the stairs and was soon out of sight. Thank God for Liebhard, she thought. She waited impatiently.

About ten minutes later he came down.

"Two liveried men dead and two more attackers dead up there," he reported. Then he entered the large two-story manor house. He was gone for quite some time. When he returned he had only bad news. "Two more dead of wounds. They look like servants. The Lord's belongings are strewn everywhere, but I don't think there is any damage from the fire." Lena listened but also realized she had not ever heard Liebhard speak so long and coherently.

"There is nothing more we can do here," she said. "Let's go back home. I am so glad you came with me."

His face broke into a sunny smile at the praise. He leaped lightly onto the priest's horse, and they rode back out the gate. They paused at the village and reported what they had found. They said they would come back again as soon as they had news about Lord Franz.

Back at their village, they found no change in the wounded man's condition. Lena told Liebhard and Anna she could handle the nursing, so they left. Liebhard's help was needed in the fields and Anna had her hands full preparing food for twelve people. Lena felt useless sitting there watching. There was so much to do. Care of the animals was a very big job for Klaus and Greta to handle on their own, and

Anna must be overtaxed. She got up, feeling restless. She had already organized her family's belongings and laid them in the family clothing trunk, crying as she thought about each piece of clothing. She opened the trunk and pulled Margit's beautiful dark red dress up to her face and breathed in her sister's scent. After fidgeting for some time she folded it carefully, laid it in the trunk and closed it.

She paced around the kitchen, not liking to be idle. What could she do? Perhaps she could at least bake the bread! She put a fresh cold pack on Lord Franz' forehead, then gathered the flour and other ingredients for bread making. She built up the fire so that it would be a good, even temperature in a couple of hours when she was ready to place the risen loaves in the hearth to bake.

She became so completely immersed in her work that she jumped when Lord Franz started to speak. She whirled around. He did not seem to be aware of where he was. He was talking as if to someone. She went over and sat down beside him, laying her hand on his arm. He looked at her, but did not see her. His words were jumbled and made no sense. He may have been talking to his wife. He started to flail his arms wildly and his spoke urgently about the danger. She spoke softly and soothingly to him, almost crooning as if he were a small child. Gradually his movements became less violent, and finally they stopped. Lena felt his forehead. He was still burning hot.

The rest of the day continued much the same. She was able to make eight loaves of bread somehow, while often returning to Franz's bedside to quiet him. When Liebhard got back from the fields he stopped to check on her and the patient before going to Anna's for dinner. He beamed as he breathed in the wonderful smell of fresh bread, then came over to the bedside to see Lord Franz.

"Is he the same? He asked.

"Yes. Well, no. He has become delirious sometimes and talks and thrashes about."

"Can you manage him?" Liebhard asked. "I can stay with you again tonight."

Lena thought about that. What were the other villagers thinking about Liebhard's staying here last night? She was not quite sure she liked to have him here. Somehow she felt pressed upon by his attentions. She had just become a widow or a cast-off wife. She was a bereaved mother who had just lost her baby boy. She would ask Anna if she thought Lena could manage the situation on her own.

"Go and eat, Liebhard, and take seven of these loaves with you. When Anna comes to be with him while I eat, I will ask her advice."

When Anna arrived, they talked about Lord Franz condition. Anna was not at all surprised that he was delirious. Because of his fever she had expected it.

"He will be delirious on and off now until the fever breaks, or until he dies," she said equably.

"Is there nothing we can do but wait?" Lena asked.

27

"Just wait and try to make him drink," was Anna's response. "Has he passed any water?"

"Yes. In fact, I have tied linen cloth between his legs to save the mattress from getting wet."

"Ha, Ha," Anna chuckled. "That was probably a good idea."

"Can I care for him myself if he gets too violent? I would prefer to be alone, but if you think two should be here, please tell me. Liebhard offered to stay, but I think that looks unseemly to others."

"Pooh. No one will get any funny ideas, Lena. But I think you are fine on your own. I will tell Liebhard to get his rest."

When Lena came back from her dinner and seeing Klaus and Greta off to bed, Lord Franz was thrashing about once again. Anna was unconcerned, but crooned to him just as Lena had done.

The night was a replay of the previous night, interspersed with wild talking by the patient. He drank thirstily several times, which made Lena hope that the illness had turned for the better. As on the previous night, she sat on a chair next to his bed, trying to sleep when he was quiet.

She was running through a field of ripe barley, running away from the black horse, which kept stopping to take mouthfuls of the grain, when suddenly she was wakened out of her dream by someone asking her a question.

"Miller's daughter, where am I?" Franz asked.

"Oh!" she cried, and leaned over to place her hand on his forehead. "The fever is gone!" He was staring at her, and she turned her head away so that he could not see her left eye.

"Where am I? What happened?" His eyes bored into the right side of her face. He was totally himself; she could hear it in his voice. He was a knight, of the lordly class, and he commanded.

"We found you in our assarted fields. Actually, we found your black horse, and then searched until we found you. That was two days ago. You have been delirious until now. You are in our mill."

He made to rise, but moaned in pain, looking down at his bandaged torso. He lay back, his eyes closed, his lips in a hard line to keep from moaning more.

"I need to use the chamber pot." He tried to get up again, groaning in pain.

"Wait, I will help you," said Lena. She pulled back the quilt. As she put her arms around him to help him, he saw the makeshift diaper she had put on him. He almost managed a chuckle as she removed it, set the chamber pot near the bed, and helped him aim into the pot. Between them they managed fairly well, and after she laid him back down she used the linen cloth to wipe up the spilled urine.

Lord Franz had closed his eyes and seemed to be trying to recover from the exertion he had just accomplished. He lay very still and Lena thought he must have fallen asleep. His eyes fluttered again.

"I must get back to the manor. Those attackers must have stripped the place. I must find Elena. I hope my knights are alive and can protect her..." he murmured the last words as he slipped into a deep sleep.

At about dawn he woke again. Lena had been up for about a half an hour stoking the fire and heating water. When she turned away from the kettle to look at him he was watching her.

"What is your name? I can't call you Miller's daughter forever."

"Lena," she said turning her face away.

"Lena, tell me all that has happened since you found me. Have you learned anything about the manor?"

"I will try to tell you all," she said and started from the moment they found him, got him back to the village, sponged off his bloody clothes, cleaned and dressed his wounds, who had cared for him, how they had gone to the manor on the horses and what they had found. Lord Franz had many questions about the damage and looting of the manor, the condition of the village and of his horse.

"Have Liebhard come here so that I can ask him about what he saw in the keep and the manor. As to the villagers, try to remember who you saw and what they all said."

"Liebhard might stop by here before he goes into the fields. He did yesterday. He wanted to see how you were." She then told him every detail she could remember from their visit to his village.

"Turn toward me when you speak," he said.

"No," she answered, lowering her eyes.

"What? Turn toward me."

Lena continued to stand as she was.

"What is wrong? I know what you look like. Turning away will not change that." There was not an ounce of sympathy in his voice.

"You called me Miller's dead eye daughter when we found you," she said.

After a long moment of silence, he said, "You do have a dead eye, is that not true?"

To her mortification, she began to cry.

"What's this? Why are you babbling?" he asked.

Suddenly she was raging with anger, angry that she had not known all of these years that she was so uncomely.

"I did not know I was ugly!" she blurted out. "We folk do not have the luxury of looking glasses. I know there is something wrong with the sight in my left eye, but no one has ever insulted me with a name such as you gave me!" She stormed out of the mill.

"Come back here now! I demand that you come back in here now!" he called.

Lena stood stalwartly outside the door, her shoulders still heaving with anger.

"Lena, come back in here," he called.

After some minutes she decided there was nothing to do but face this bully of a man. She walked into the mill, her face still turned to the side.

"Oh, stop this. Did I not speak the truth? You have a lazy eye. In fact, I might say you are a somewhat pretty woman except for that. I see you are still angry. Let us leave this subject. I must get back to the manor, but I see that will not happen soon. With my father dead, all depends upon me. I must try to reach my brother who is a *ministeriale* with the count. After I talk to Liebhard, I will send him back to look over the situation for me and he can bring messages to my villagers."

"No, he cannot do that," she said.

Lord Franz's face clouded in anger. "Just because you are angry, do not expect that others will not do my bidding."

"He cannot do what you ask, because he is not able," she said as levelly as she could. "He is not a dullard, but his wit is not as others. He is big and strong, he is brave and loyal, but he cannot think what should be done in a situation like this."

"Ahh. I think I might know which one he is now. Karl's son? The one who speaks?"

"Yes, that is Liebhard. His brother is Mark."

"Will he be able to tell me the state of the manor at least?"

"Yes, I think so. He remembers details quite well," she answered.

"Could someone else go with him to direct him? I must be in touch with the villagers. I need to know who is left alive. I can then choose one or two to take charge up there. Damn it" he swore, as he tried to sit up again. "How long will it be I wonder before I can ride up there?"

"We will have to ask Anna. She knows the most about medicines here. It was she who helped me clean your wounds."

"Tell me about my wounds. Hold back nothing. When she comes, I want the dressings changed so I can see them."

"You are the patient here," she said pertly, shocking herself and him. She rushed into a description of his wounds. He interrupted her often, reliving the fighting in the manor, and how he had received each wound. She told him how they had cleaned the wounds with vinegar, which he scarcely seemed to believe.

"I hope you have not killed me with this treatment," he said wryly.

"You don't look dead to me. Now go back to sleep. It is still at least an hour before dawn."

"I am thirsty. I'm hungry too," he said.

"I will get you some broth. We will wait until Anna comes to find out what you can eat," she answered, and she went over to the fireplace, ladled some broth out of the kettle, and brought it back to him.

"You are a tyrant," he said, as she helped him raise his head to drink. She did not answer, but did wonder where this desire to be in charge came from. She helped him lay back, smoothed the quilt and pulled it up over his chest. He closed his eyes, but there was a tiny smile on his lips.

At dawn she woke, stretched and quickly went out to relieve herself. She washed her face and brushed her teeth with a birch twig. Still wearing only her shift, she was just checking the fire when Liebhard arrived. Their whispered good mornings roused Lord Franz.

"Liebhard, there you are. Come over and sit beside me. I understand from Lena, Miller's daughter, that you went inside the keep and manor. Please go through all that you saw." Liebhard looked at Lena. She saw that he did not know how to tell this.

"Liebhard, we walked the horses through the burned door of the keep. You jumped off and picked up a spear and a knife. Oh, and there were three dead men on the ground there. They did not have livery on, but one had costly clothes like you."

"Describe them to me," Franz said. He looked at Liebhard, whose brow wrinkled in perplexity. Lena waited. Franz turned to her. "Well?" She closed her eyes and envisioned that moment. She remembered the scene clearly, and described the men down to the wounds she saw on them.

"Hmm. I think the one you described with dark hair tied back in a tail, and with the faded red tunic, was one of my own villagers. But who was the knight? One of my father's enemies?"

"Liebhard, now tell the lord what you saw after you climbed the stairs. What did you see on that floor?"

"There were no bodies there. There was blood on the floor. Oh, there was a dead dog. He had his throat cut."

"What did the dog look like?"

"Black with a brown belly, and he had a very big head, One of his ears looked like it was only half there. He had a big chain collar." Liebhard answered.

"That was my brave Ajax. He was ferocious during the attack," Franz murmured.

"Then did you climb the stairs to the next level?" She asked.

"Yes. I climbed the stairs. When I got to the top there was blood everywhere. There were four men there. Two had Lord Conrad's badge on them, two did not."

"Close your eyes, Liebhard, and picture what you saw," Lena said. She led him through the scene one person at a time, and he remembered many details. Lord Franz named the servants as Liebhard described them. He thought he knew one of the attackers as well.

"Were there any more stairs, Liebhard? No? Then you came back down all of the stairs and you told me what you saw. Then you went into the manor. Close your eyes again and try to remember how you walked through the rooms, and what you saw." Each time he described entering a different area, she asked him many questions. It was a slow process, as the strewn furniture and tossed clothing distracted him, and he often described these pieces in vivid detail. He remembered the dead servants clearly. The old woman was the housekeeper, while the younger one was a kitchen maid, according to Lord Franz.

"Well done, Liebhard. You have my thanks. I would like you to go up to the manor today and to the village and act for me to give the villagers direction."

"I can't do that. Have Lena go to do that. I will go with her to protect her."

"She cannot do this. The villagers will not listen to her."

"They will. They did when we went before," Liebhard said. He puffed out his cheeks as though he would blow away any demand from Lord Franz. Lena recognized this habit of Liebhard's. It meant he could not be pushed further.

"What's this? What did you tell them that should make Liebhard think they did your bidding?" he asked.

"I was able to coax them out into the street by telling them that we had survived, were harvesting our crops, and that we were caring for you." She tried to remember and paraphrase what she had said to the villagers, and how they seemed to come out of their daze. They had begun to talk together about who should be their leader. She remembered that she had felt hopeful that they would take up their cares again.

"So you told them that you would come back up again to tell them how I did? Well then, I guess you must. Who is the headman of your small village now? I take it Miller and Father Johan are dead?"

"Lena's parents are dead. Her sister Margit died too. And her baby is dead. That Dieter ran away," Liebhard said. "The villagers follow Lena now."

A long silence followed this news, as the young lord took in her situation and her immense personal loss. His eyes flicked toward her and then down.

"Hans Plowman and I are trying to work together," Lena corrected Liebhard.

"Hans, yes, I know who he is. His son is Hans Plowman the Younger, isn't he?"

"Yes. Young Han's whole family died of the pestilence," she murmured.

"Liebhard, go up to Hans' house and tell him I want to see him."

"Lord Franz, his wife is Anna, who has been healing you," Lena interjected.

"Ask Anna to come down too," he said.

After Liebhard left, there was a silence between Franz and Lena. She saw he meant to say something, but was not sure what he wanted to say.

"Lena. You have lost your whole family. I have added to your cares. But did Dieter really run away? He was not a faithful servant to my father, you know. He was in line to be his next bailiff, but the villagers spoke out against his ways. He was a cheat and a liar. Why did you ever marry that man?"

"You know why. I wanted to marry, and he alone asked."

"You could have done better," he said. It almost sounded like a reprimand. She thought she might cry again. She busied herself by the hearth as she tried to think of some answer. When she turned toward him he was asleep. She took her blue dress off the hook and pulled it over her head, adding her apron.

A short time later, Hans and Anna arrived, and the sound of the mill door opening roused Franz from his sleep.

"Come here, right over here. I thank you Anna for your care of my wounds," he said. Anna shook her head.

"It was mostly Lena who cared for you, Lord Franz. I could help her with what to do, but she did most of the work." She nodded toward Lena.

"Hans, Lena tells me that you are the leader of the village now," he began, but both Hans and Anna chortled at the idea.

"Lena has thought what to do and to get us together," Hans said.

Lord Franz turned his eyes on Lena. He had such a quizzical look that Lena almost forgot to turn her face away. He motioned for her to come closer.

"Everyone sings your praises. I might as well ask you what I should do," he said with a bit of a mocking tone in his voice. She could feel her annoyance at him coming back.

"You must do as you please. You are the lord of your village." She turned back to the hearth and ladled some hot cider for him. When she turned back and began to walk toward him, she faced an angry young man. He had not often experienced a lowly villager speak in such a way to him.

"Just do the kindness of helping me," he said in a clipped voice. She realized that he had stopped himself from a far more biting return. Hans and Anna were astounded by the bluntness of these two people.

"Get hold of your temper," she thought. "Lord Franz, if you will think it acceptable, I will go with Liebhard up to your village. Perhaps you can write down a few words that will help me remember all that you want me to say and do."

"You can read?"

"Just a little from my father's prayer book."

"Let me see the book," he said.

She picked up the book from the shelf by the fireplace and brought it over to him. He opened it and turned a few pages.

"So you have learned in Latin. Hmm. Well, I can write you a few words in Latin. Hans and Anna, you may go, but ask Liebhard to come back so he can ride up to the manor and village this morning."

After they had gone, he closed his eyes. She could see the exertion had taxed him. Oh! She forgot to ask Anna about food! She slipped out of the mill and ran after Anna. When she caught up with them they spoke for a few minutes and decided what to feed the invalid. Anna would bring down some food for Lena. When she got back to the mill, Lord Franz was awake.

"Where were you?" he demanded.

She controlled her desire to take offence. "I forgot to ask what you might eat. Anna is bringing some food down for me to prepare for you," she said impersonally.

Lord Franz stared at her for a long time.

"Let's try to work together," he finally said. "Do you have something I can write with?"

Lena went up to the accounts room where she had been a prisoner and got the ledger book and a piece of sharpened charcoal. Incredibly she was so interested in her project to help Lord Franz she did not even think about her days of hopelessness.

Franz had slipped off to sleep again. He was mending, but obviously very weak. She sat down and waited for him to wake. When Liebhard opened the outer door of the wheel room, the sound roused the young man. She held up the ledger and charcoal.

The process of choosing and writing words, going over them several times so that Lena would remember them along with the information Franz was seeking took over an hour. She would have to write a few words and names while she was up at the village to help her remember all that Franz wanted to know. He asked particularly that the villagers identify his people who had been killed and bury them. He wanted descriptions of the invaders, and the knightly crests brought to him, then to bury them in a common grave. He also wanted her to find particular clothes belonging to him.

"I also want to know where Brutus is, and I want him brought up here to me," he said as he lay back tiredly.

"Who is Brutus?" She asked.

"My horse. He is a big black charger. The villagers know him."

We have the horse you rode to our assarted fields. Is that not him?" she asked.

Franz managed a smile. "That's Pisces. He was my learning horse."

A loud commotion attracted their attention. Someone was shouting out in the road. The door swung open and young Klaus ran in, followed by Liebhard. The boy was startled to see the wounded man in the bed, but ran over to Lena.

"There is a great huge grey hound lying out in the fields! He has a cut all the way along his side and he won't get up! We are afraid to go near him. Hans sent me back to get you!" he exclaimed.

"A huge, long-haired dog with a big square nose?" Franz asked.

Klaus, big eyed, nodded.

"That's Smoke, my deerhound. He must have been wounded in the fray too. Lena you will have to go up and get him."

"Me? He will attack me surely!" she remonstrated.

"Saddle Pisces. Take my cloak. Where is it? Put it on. Ride up there, get down off the horse and let Smoke smell my cloak. You probably should not try to touch him. Then say 'Smoke, come.' You must command him."

Lena stared at Franz. She could feel prickles of fear on the back of her neck and arms. She had no experience with such a big vicious dog.

"Don't show him that fear I see in your face. It will make him worse," Franz ordered.

"That makes me feel better, I am sure!" she blurted, wondering how he could ask her to do such a dangerous thing. He showed not a sliver of understanding that he asked too much of her.

"Go. You can do this. Please," he said. She heard almost a pleading in his voice. The dog meant much to him apparently.

"I will go." She said, as she picked up his cloak. She had never had such a richly made cloak in her hands. She carefully put it over her dress. Liebhard had gone outside already, and was just leading the black horse out of the barn. He put the saddle on, tightened the girth, and held the horse while she climbed on.

"I will walk with you," Liebhard said. She smiled down at him in thanks.

When they reached the field where the dog lay, they found the villagers squatting and standing some distance from the dog. The dog was lying exactly where they had found Franz several days before. He must have smelled his master there. Lena pressed her heels into Pisces' flanks. The horse showed no fear of the dog, and walked within steps of the animal. Lena worked up her courage, tried to breathe slowly, and then got down from the horse. She let the cloak trail next to the dog's nose. He immediately raised his ears and sniffed at the cloak, even licking it once or twice.

"Smoke, come," she said with as much authority as she could muster. She mounted Pisces, looked down at the dog and commanded him again. He slowly rose to his feet, swaying a little. He was weak from his wound. She wondered if he could make it to the mill. She turned Pisces back toward the village and checked to see if the dog followed. He walked stiffly with his nose to the ground, but he followed.

She walked the horse slowly all the way so that the wounded dog could keep up. At the mill, Liebhard, who had walked silently beside her horse, held Pisces' head as she dismounted. She turned, commanded the dog to come, and went into the mill. He obediently followed.

The moment he saw Franz, the dog leaped on top of the young man and lay down. He pressed his nose along the side of Franz's neck. He was a huge dog, his body nearly hiding his master. Franz sobbed and hugged the animal, all of his emotions flooding out of him. Lena turned away to give him privacy. When she turned back she saw that Franz had once again slipped into slumber. The dog seemed to be asleep as well. She sat down quietly and waited. It was almost noon.

Perhaps she would have to go to the manor tomorrow, she thought. Liebhard had come in, and sat down quietly.

She got up and checked to see if the porridge Anna had sent up was warm. It would be ready for Franz when he wakened. As she was stirring she heard him murmuring. She turned to see him fondling the dog's head, talking to him. He looked at Lena.

"Can you see to his wound? I would hate to lose such a loyal dog."

"But will he let me touch him?" she asked, looking at the huge fangs as the dog panted.

"We will do it together. He will be quiet for me," Franz answered.

Lena brought the vinegar, bowl, lard and wool swab over to the bed. She dreaded touching the animal. Franz reached over, took her hand and placed it on the dog's side, near the wound. The dog looked up at her, but he did not growl. She took one of the wool swabs, dipped it in vinegar and gave it to Franz. She dipped another for herself. They gingerly dabbed at the ugly wound while Franz talked gently to the dog. Smoke trembled and winced but made no noise. After a thorough cleaning, Lena carefully spread lard over the wound.

"He must be famished and thirsty," she said. "I will get him some water and porridge. You must get him down." As she stood up, Franz pointed to the floor and the dog immediately climbed down from the bed. His eyes followed Lena as she got a bowl of water and brought it back. He drank every drop, and ate every morsel of food she gave him. She concluded he was weak mostly from hunger and lying out in the field. When he was finished, he lay down next to the bed, put his head on his paws and closed his eyes.

"Not too viscous, is he?" Franz asked, the ghost of a smile on his lips.

"Not with you here," she said and sat down to help him eat a bowl of thick pottage. Anna had added small chunks of meat to the stew, and it smelled wonderful. Franz tried to feed himself, but his hands trembled wildly from the effort, so he submitted to being fed by Lena.

"I am so weak," he complained.

"Sleep and eat. You will grow stronger quickly," she answered. She got up and served Liebhard and herself bowls of the pottage.

"It is getting late in the day, but I still want you to go down to the village," he said. He closed his eyes a moment, and then looked at her.

"Yes, I will go, Liebhard and I will ride down together," she said. Liebhard was halfway out of the room before she finished. She picked up the ledger book and charcoal. "You must sleep while we are gone."

The trip to the manor village was a much happier one this time. They found some of the villagers scything the wheat in the fields while others gathered the wheat into sheaves. A few of the workers waved as they rode by, and asked about Lord Franz. A heavy man of about her father's age stepped forward as they reached him. He introduced himself as Matthew Plowman. The villagers had chosen him as headman. Lena told him Franz had many questions and requests, and she took out her ledger book to refresh her memory. Matthew listened patiently to her questions, and answered as many as he could. She printed a few words in the book so that she could report to Lord Franz. She also learned that Brutus had been found in the fields. Matthew said they would bring him up to Miller's village (she was surprised to learn that the manor village called her village this) in the evening. Those questions he could not answer, he suggested she ask the dead headman's wife when she got up to the village.

When she and Liebhard arrived at the manor, the same smell of acrid smoke hung in the air, but they saw no smoldering fires. At least a dozen people were sifting through burned debris. Lena saw Oona, the headman's wife, dismounted and greeted her. Oona was able to tell her who lived and who had died, who had fled and who was injured. Lena tabulated the names as they talked. Five families had fled. All the rest except for fifty-seven were dead. Only one quarter of the original villagers remained. Lord Franz's family had been struck a terrible blow. She told Oona about the young lord's convalescence, her own village's news, and then bade her goodbye.

She and Liebhard rode up to the manor house, dismounted and tied up the horses. Two women were in the manor, straightening up the furniture and putting things in order. One of them was familiar with the household rooms and helped Lena find most of the clothing that Franz had requested. Lena was glad to see that little damage had been done to the belongings of the lord's family. She rolled Franz's belongings into a cloak, tied it and gave it to Liebhard who fastened it behind his saddle. They mounted and rode home under the late afternoon sun. It was a perfect harvest day, she thought. Such beauty after their great calamity.

The village workers were not yet back from the fields when they reached the mill, so Liebhard said he would put away the horses and go out to help them. Lena dismounted, took Franz's belongings from Liebhard and went inside. Smoke stood up and stared at her, making her heart jump.

"This is my house," she thought, and bravely walked over to the table and put the rolled cloak down. Smoke had silently padded over to her side, leaned forward and stretched his nose toward the clothes. He was so tall that he bent his head down to the tabletop.

"Good Smoke. This is my house, and you must be good," she said. From behind her she heard a chuckle.

"Don't worry, he has accepted you as my friend," Franz said. "Lena, can you please come and help me?" He motioned toward the chamber pot. Somehow they managed between the two of them, though his unsteadiness nearly caused them both to fall. When she got him back into the bed he tried to smother moans of pain.

She saw some blood oozing from his chest gashes. She would have to ask Anna how to manage these necessaries.

Franz seemed to fall asleep for some minutes, then he opened his eyes. "How was your visit to the manor? Did you get answers to my questions?"

Lena sat down beside him, motioned toward his belongings on the table, reported that Brutus would arrive in the evening, and then began her long report. Franz listened closely, asking many questions. In the back of her mind she wondered just how old he was. He did not look over twenty, but seemed very mature in this crisis. When she finished her report he closed his eyes.

"Would you like some stew now or would you like to sleep awhile, Franz?" she asked. When he jerked his head and opened his eyes she realized her mistake.

"I beg your pardon, Lord Franz." She said meekly.

He studied her a moment. "I am not offended, Lena. You must not call me by my name when others are here. And yes, I would like more stew. Do you have some bread and cheese? I would like some beer if you have it."

She laughed. He was definitely feeling better. She brought him the stew, which she still had to feed to him. She broke up the bread and cheese into small pieces which he managed to eat by himself. Holding a cup steady was a challenge, but if she held his hand still he did quite well.

He barely finished his beer before his eyelids began to droop. In moments he was asleep.

The evening was quiet. He slept the whole time Anna came to watch over him, and she was confident he would now recover well. For the first time in days, Lena herself lay down to sleep on a mattress by the fireplace. Smoke slept on the floor next to Franz's bed.

A little before dawn she was awakened by Franz, who had successfully sat up and urinated in the chamber pot. He looked up and laughed.

"I am getting better!" he said happily. He lay back on the bed, and after a moment he said, "Lena?"

"What?" she asked. She sat up and waited.

"You have been very good to me. I want to do two things for you. Will you listen and not be angry?"

"I am listening," she said.

"I am going to give you Pisces. That villain your husband stole your horse, so I will give you one of mine."

"Oh! I do not know what to say. This is too generous!" she responded incredulously.

"I will not accept no for an answer. He is mine to give, and I want you to have him."

Lena sat for a moment, thinking. He would not accept or like to hear any more arguments. It was almost mean spirited of her not to accept his liberality. "I willingly accept him! You are very generous to me," she said happily.

"I will write that he is my gift to you for saving my life. The second thing...do not be angry...I want to help you with your eye," he said.

Lena froze for a moment. She had nearly been able to forget his earliest words to her. She turned her face away.

"Please listen to me. I think we can make your eye better. I have a cousin born with this same problem. Are you listening? They covered his good eye with a patch and his slow eye started to work as it should." He fished under his blanket and pulled out an eye patch, holding it up toward her.

"I asked Anna to make this for me. She thought it was odd, but she did not ask any questions," he said laughingly. "Will you come over here so we can try it?"

Lena hesitated. She was embarrassed. She knew he meant well. She got up, went over and took the patch from his hand. She placed the patch over her right eye and tied the string behind her head. The room wobbled. She threw out her hands because she thought she was going to lose her balance. Then her left eye adjusted. Something behind her eye seemed to hurt but she was able to look up. She turned toward Franz who observed her keenly.

"It hurts somehow, behind my eye," she said, but she knew she was looking straight into his face rather than down.

"You are looking straight!" He said enthusiastically. "Please leave it on as long as you can. My cousin wore his patch, when he was awake, for some months. Then he was fine. Well, except when he was very tired. Then the eye would droop again a little bit."

"I will try it," she said. Her feelings were running in every direction. She was angry, elated, upset, sad, happy, and also impressed by Franz's consideration. She pulled her dress over her shift and went out of the mill for her morning necessaries, but also to be alone for a moment. She looked around, moving her eye in all directions. The pain was particularly sharp when she tried to look up. She would not be able to wear the patch very long each day, at least at first.

She went back into the mill, walked over to Franz and smiled. "Thank you for thinking of this. I will use this patch every day, but at first I think I will only use it as long as I can stand the pain."

He nodded and smiled broadly. He was quite a handsome young man in his own way, she thought. His features had been contorted with pain and worry most of the time since she met him. His forehead was perhaps over-high, and he had a square demanding chin, but otherwise his features were good.

"May I ask how old you are, Lord Franz?" she asked diffidently.

"This is my 22nd year," he said laughingly.

"You have been thrown many responsibilities," she said, and smiled.

Franz's recovery once he started to eat was swift. His weakness and trembling subsided, and he seldom slipped off into slumber unexpectedly. Two days after Lena began to wear her patch he began to walk a few steps. The punctures on his back oozed some pus and bloody liquid, which concerned Anna. She made a point of opening these wounds if they started to scab over. The other wounds did not seem to hurt: rather they itched.

From the day Lena had gone down to the manor with all of Franz's questions and demands, Franz had visiting villagers daily. She was present the first days during these visits because she wanted to be sure he did not over-tire himself. She very quickly saw he no longer needed a nurse, so she started spending a good part of each day in the fields. She also moved Klaus and Greta up to the mill as she had promised. Lord Franz was surprised that she wanted to take on the duty of caring for the orphans, but did not discourage her. In fact, they entertained him in the evenings with their energy and questions. Smoke ignored them at first, but soon enough they were lying on top of him as they talked to Franz.

About a week after Brutus was brought up to the mill, Franz broached the subject of moving down to the manor.

"Lena, I think I am well enough to move home, maybe tomorrow."

"What? No, I don't think so. You have hardly walked more than twenty steps at a time, let alone mount a horse. And the jarring would not be good for your wounds. Maybe next week," she countered.

"You are a tyrant. I will ask Anna. Have her come down today."

"Better yet, let's walk up to her house now, to see how you do," she challenged.

Franz made a disgusting sound with his mouth, but got up slowly. The act of standing up was painful.

"Well, hurry up. Let's go!" he commanded.

The walk that should have taken about five minutes took three times that long. The level path was easy enough for Franz, but climbing up the hill and then down to Anna's house taxed his energy and going uphill was visibly painful. Anna saw them coming and walked out to meet them.

"This is too much, Lord Franz! Come in and sit down. You are as white as a sheet," she scolded.

"Don't say that. You support the tyrant here. I need to get back down to the manor."

"What? Then better you should walk than ride! No, it is too early. But walking up and down the village road would be a good thing to do for now." Maybe next week, if all the wounds look good you can ride."

Franz looked dolefully at them, but managed a good-natured grin. After he had had some cider and rested, he and Lena walked back to the mill.

"Lena, since I cannot ride down tomorrow, you will have to go in my stead. I have a problem that only you can solve anyway, I think."

"What is that?" she asked curiously.

"You know that my miller is dead. There is no person living down there that knows anything useful about milling. They have not been able to get the mill started properly. In fact, I think they have somehow gummed up the hopper or the mill stones, from the sounds of it," he said. He went on to describe what the villagers had told him.

"Now they have no grain ground. Tomorrow they wanted to bring grain up here for you and Liebhard to grind."

"We can grind their grain of course," she said. "I know my father ground grain for them on other occasions. I will have to look in the ledger to see what fees we set. If they are coming tomorrow, I would not be able to go down to the manor village."

"All my plans go for naught. Well, get me paper and I will write some notes for you," he said in a mockingly funny imperious tone.

The milling the next day went smoothly. The following day she and Liebhard rode down to the manor. The new headman was waiting for them, and went with them to the mill. The flow of the small stream that ran the waterwheel was quite slow compared to their own stream, so she had to figure out if the gears and cogs were set properly to compensate and then be able to grind the grain. She checked the stones, scraping them as best she could. It looked as though the tentering had been adjusted too loosely, allowing for the grain to build up between the runner stone and the bed stone. Too much grain had been fed into the hopper, and it was too moist. They spent over an hour emptying the hopper and drying it thoroughly and adjusting the tentering on the stones. Liebhard knew little about milling, and she tried to explain everything slowly. Once he saw the effect of the changes she made, he seemed to grasp the mechanics of the mill parts completely. His strength combined with her knowledge worked to solve the problems.

Finally they were ready for a trial run. Liebhard opened the sluice gate. She checked the grain the villagers had brought up to the hopper floor. It was properly dried. She motioned for them to pour it slowly into the hopper. She could tell even from the hopper floor that the runner stone was grinding properly. She ran down the steps and held out her hand to catch the flour as it began to fall out from between the stones. It was a little coarse, so the tentering needed a slight adjustment. The villagers were all beaming as they caught the flour, and the headman patted her back.

She and Liebhard stayed at the mill until the headman was satisfied that enough had been ground that day. They closed the sluice gate and cleaned the mill parts, just as she had always done with her father. The headman asked if Lord Franz had arranged a settlement with them, a question she had not even considered. She said she would settle with the young lord. Several villagers stood and watched as they mounted their horses, thanking them and bidding them good-bye.

They rode along in contented silence. Lena looked over at Liebhard, whose attention was absorbed in the grain fields on both sides of the path. He had a very strong profile. A very pleasing profile. He had been like a guardian angel to her during these incredibly hard weeks. And today he had managed the adjustments very well. She could not have done the work alone.

"Thank you, Liebhard, for all of your help. We will have to ask Lord Franz how we will settle what our pay should be for this," she said as they rode home.

"I do this for you. I want to help you," he answered.

"You are so kind, Liebhard. But you must be paid. It is fair," she said.

"If you say so. I will always help you however I can. And I want to be with you," he said.

Lena rode on in silence. She was beginning to think she was engulfed in a predicament where Liebhard was concerned. With Dieter gone, her baby dead, her whole family torn away from her, she was in a peculiar position. A woman her age should have been surrounded by family cares, not advising the lord of the manor, running a mill, leading a village. Fortunately Liebhard did not seem to expect her to answer him. He guided his horse peaceably beside Pisces.

What was she going to do, she wondered? She had put herself forward to direct the village, and now her position was accepted by everyone, even Lord Franz. She was the only one who knew how to run a mill, and now there were two to run. She had taken on the care of two orphans. Her father was dead with no male heir. He had no brothers or male cousins that she knew of. Was she his heir? Was the position of miller hers? Had she the living of the miller and control of the mill? Was she a widow? What if Dieter came back, could she divorce him or accuse him of murder for leaving her sister, her baby and her to die? Could he be made an outlaw and lose all rights?

When they got back to the mill, she was still pondering all of these questions. Liebhard jumped off his horse and came to Pisces' side.

"You have said hardly anything as we rode, and you look unhappy. I think you did not like to hear what I said," Liebhard murmured.

"He has the kindest face I have ever seen," she thought. He lifted her gently off the horse, sliding her down against his body until she reached the ground and was leaning against his chest. She pushed herself away carefully.

"Thank you, Liebhard, but I can manage to dismount myself. I am not sad, but just thinking about so many things. My whole family is dead. But is Dieter dead? I am trying to think about whether the mill is my responsibility. I must talk to Lord Franz, since the court that will decide this is probably in his hands," she answered. She smiled and stepped away. "Can you come in for a few moments to help me report on his village and mill? Then you will probably want to go up to help in the harvest."

For a moment she thought he was going to disagree. Finally he nodded and followed her in. He had not seemed to react to her mention of Dieter. Perhaps he did not understand the problems of a missing husband whose fate was unknown.

Lord Franz smiled broadly when they entered. He was seated at the table, working on a drawing. She leaned over to see it more clearly, Smoke's nose just inches from hers. It looked like many small squares along several lines.

"I am drawing what I think is left of the village so I can plan what to rebuild," he said. "How was your day at the mill?"

She reported in detail all that happened, even describing the corrections she made on the mill stones and cogs. She knew by now that he wanted every piece of information she could supply. He asked Liebhard about the physical process of making the changes she had described. Liebhard was able to give a fair account of his work, to Lena's surprise. He had understood everything down to the last detail.

"Well, it sounds as though the day went well. What about the other questions I gave you, Lena?" Lord Franz asked.

Lena did not begin her answers immediately. "Liebhard, do you want some dinner before you go up to the fields? Perhaps you can put the horses away and then eat a bite. Or shall I pack some food for you?"

"I should hurry to go up and help. I will see to the horses and then stop by Anna's. She will have made my field food basket for me," he said, and went out.

She picked up her eye patch and tied it in place as she sat down at the table. She took her notes out of her pocket and looked up at Lord Franz to begin her report. He was looking at her oddly.

"What is it?" She asked.

"Start your report. I will tell you later," he said.

Lord Franz had asked her to observe the remaining villagers as closely as possible and give him her thoughts about their capabilities. She ticked off her fingers as she described each villager older than eight years. Lord Franz knew most of them by name, or at least whose family each belonged to.

"I have lost most of my craftsmen, haven't I? I suppose the blacksmith's son, at 14 years, might be able to do some iron work with a man's help I think he has been helping his father for a few years. And the tanner's wife can manage his work, I think, although she will need someone with muscle for the heavy work. My baker is dead too. His wife died years ago. Their eldest daughter is fifteen. We will have to see if she can do the baking. No one seems capable of learning the milling. I will want you to continue to run both mills for now," he decided.

Lena listened to all he said, and these last words defined at least her temporary position.

"What was wrong when you came into the mill?" he asked abruptly.

"Nothing. What do you mean?" She asked defensively.

"Come, now. I know you pretty well by this time. Did something happen in the village that you are not telling me? Or is it Liebhard?"

Lena looked at him belligerently. She was going to say it was not his business, but quelled her anger. He was the only person she could really talk to about this, she realized.

"Everything in the village was as I said. It is how Liebhard thinks of me. I think he wants to be with me. But do I want this? Anyway, am I free? What if Dieter is alive and returns? If that happens I will not accept the murderer of at least my sister, maybe my son, and attempted murderer of me. Could I accuse him and have him ruled an outlaw? And am I my father's heir? He has no sons or grandsons, no brothers alive, and his father is dead. Would I have his miller's position?"

"Whoa! You have been running far afield in your thoughts! But let's go back to Liebhard. I have been the recipient of help from both of you, and you work together like a perfect team. I assumed that you plan to marry. He gives every indication of wishing it. And I think he would be a steady husband."

"Steady! That is not all I would look for! Yes, yes, I made a foolhardy mistake with Dieter. You are responsible for making me see I do not need to accept any man who asks. Liebhard is steady, gentle, loyal, brave and honest…but Franz, he is slow. Could I bear that for years and years? Why do I have to marry if I am now widowed?"

"Lena, don't fret so. No one would expect you to marry so soon after the loss of your family. I think you could remain as you are for some time, maybe a year, before you might find life difficult if you do not marry. But think about this: if you marry soon and start a family, then if Dieter returned and you accused him of being a murderer, you would have your marriage and family to support you in the law. This is a criminal offense and would have to be tried in the count's court. And Lena, there is another thing to think about. Did you not recognize Dieter's mother at the village?"

"I did not hear her name mentioned. I only saw her at our wedding. Dieter did not allow her to come around! I thought there was no love between them," she said

"She married again. Etta is her name. She married Gregor Plowman. He died last year, I think. I expect she has no love for you."

Lena was looking into the hearth, her back to Lord Franz. She took in all of his words. His arguments were sound. Why did this all seem so unfair to her? Perhaps she did not want to marry again at all.

"What about the mill? Am I my father's heir?"

"That would be the court's decision. My court now that my father is dead, since this fief is heritable. So, yes. Had you been his wife, you would have taken over his trade. You are his only living heir, so the trade would most likely go to you, and since there is no other person who can mill, I would expect you will be the miller for both mills. That would be for your lifetime, and then go to your male children. In the case of the mills, Dieter has no claim, as far as I understand the law."

"That is good news at least. What about Klaus and Greta? Can I care for them as my own? They would have their parent's home and goods, of course."

"We will have to look into that. Maybe they have relatives," Lord Franz answered.

A silence fell between them. Lena thought Lord Franz wanted to press her about Liebhard, but he looked down at his drawing and began to draw another square. She rose from her chair and went to the hearth to check the pottage.

"Have you eaten, Lord Franz? She asked.

"Yes, but I will take another bowl. Do you have some boiled eggs or cheese too?"

Lena ladled out stew into two bowls, took some boiled eggs out of the egg jar, and cut fresh cheese. After she had set these on the table, she poured two mugs of beer and brought them with a loaf of bread to the table. As they had become accustomed to do, they sat opposite each other and ate. "How odd and yet comfortable it seems to eat with the lord of the manor," she thought, and smiled wryly.

"What made you smile? He asked.

"Forgive me. I was musing that it seems so easy, so comfortable, to dine with the lord of the estate," she said and smothered an embarrassed chuckle.

"We are comfortable together. And I hope that you trust me as much as I trust you, Lena. I am in your debt, and I expect I will need your help for some time."

"And I will gladly give it," she answered.

They finished their meal in small talk about the winding down of the harvest, and she told him how surprised she had been that his villagers called this village Millers Village. He laughed and said he thought she had known that.

As she cleared the table, he pulled his drawing toward him, but instead of recommencing his work, he leaned back and said, "You know, it is three weeks tomorrow since you found me in the field. Today I walked up and down the road, then up to Anna's. She said I can try to get on a horse tomorrow."

Lena stopped in the middle of cleaning the bowls. Her chest had tightened at this news. She would be here without him. She would miss him. He had become like a substitute family for her, she realized.

She turned around, stood a moment and then walked over to the table. He looked into her eye and she saw he would miss her too.

"It seems hard that you must leave, Franz. It is so strange to me, but I have become dependent upon your being here. You have filled the hole where my family was."

"For me too, Lena. You are like the sister I never had. Like the bossy sister, I might add," and managed a chuckle.

"Tomorrow morning we will saddle Pisces for you. You must just walk at first. All of your wounds have closed nicely except for that difficult one on your back, and we don't want to open them. How fiery is Brutus? Will you be able to handle him?"

"I think we should saddle him, and you ride him with Liebhard leading so that he can get some exercise. We will ride back and forth on the road," he decided.

The next few days were busy for everyone. All of the field work that they would do this fall was complete. Everyone was busy with the threshing of the grain and shelling the peas and beans, and harvesting the crops from their own tiny vegetable gardens. Repair work on the houses started, and additional cleaning of the empty houses had to be done. With the villagers now working at home, everyone enjoyed watching the lord's progress as he rode first the gentle Pisces, and then Brutus,. He was shadowed wherever he went by Smoke, for whom the villagers still held an awed respect. Brutus was full of energy but he was quite biddable and Lord Franz was able to keep him at a slow pace.

RETURN TO THE MANOR

Finally the day came for Lord Franz to ride home. Liebhard and Lena were to ride with him, and see that all was well at the manor and village. Lena would ride home alone, as Lord Franz prevailed upon Liebhard to stay a few days as his temporary retainer. He planned to choose one or two villagers to train for protection of the manor until he could find neighbors who could send sons to be trained by Franz. This might prove difficult, because other knights might have had devastating losses similar to Lord Franz.

The manor village was alive with activity when they reached it. Max, the son of the dead bailiff, ran forward to take their horses as they dismounted. Lord Franz asked Liebhard to go with Max to check out the manor's stable and other outlying buildings. He and Lena went into the manor. Oona came to meet them and greet the young lord. She and Thirza, a young girl of about fourteen, had managed to put the rooms in order. Franz and Lena walked throughout the rooms and Lord Franz took stock of the furniture and belongings of the family. As far as he could tell no pilfering had occurred. He called to Oona and asked her to prepare dinner for him, Lena, Liebhard and to arrange for the headman to come up as well. After she had gone, he and Lena went out to the kitchen building. The food stocks looked adequate, though some sugar, cheeses and smoked meats may have been taken while the lord was gone.

Liebhard came back to the manor just as they returned, and they all sat down at a table in the hall, Smoke curled up beside Lord Franz. Liebhard reported that only one dog was alive in the kennels, and the cows and horses had been taken out to the meadow by the lord's herder. One young boy who described himself as the stable boy told Liebhard that one of the cows had died. He said the dairy looked clean, and there was some fresh milk and butter there, but he did not see a dairy maid.

"Oona and Thirza have been doing that work too for now," Franz said.

After dinner, Liebhard went with Matthew Plowman to learn the perimeters of the fief. Lord Franz and Lena puzzled over work assignments for everyone, and looked at the ledgers for fees due from the villagers and the rents due from Millers Village. Neither was familiar with these ledgers, and Lena had never seen such an account as the one for the fief. She had a basic understanding of the Millers Village account from work she had done for her father. She was startled by the high fees due from the families of the fief's village, usually a third of their harvest, in addition to special fees for milling, marriage, death and, it seemed to her, an endless list. She realized how simple and comparatively easy her village's rental dues were.

According to manor accounts, there was very little ready coin until these harvest fees came in. With the huge decrease in the number of households these fees would be modest indeed. Lena sat back and looked at Lord Franz as he continued to study the figures.

"My future looks grim, doesn't it?" Franz said, as he looked up at her.

"Will you be able to manage? Do you need ready cash just now?" she asked.

"I need to pay for so many things here…messages to be sent to the count for this fief, to the Archbishop of Trier for my fief, I need to locate my brother to find out about that knight who attacked our father's fief—oh, it's very complicated, Lena. I will tell you about it soon. And I need to find my wife and my knights, the cost of journeying to get them and bring them back—and God knows what my knights will need for their equipment—rebuilding the village…aah." And don't forget a priest! For my village and Miller's Village. I wonder how we do that? That is another question for the count."

Franz and Lena sat in silence, thinking of the many problems before them, before Franz particularly.

"The first peddlers and travelers who come by must be used as messengers," Lena volunteered.

"I need to send messengers from here though and as soon as possible. I must learn if my wife is well. I sent her to the archbishop, and must get a message there. You don't think Liebhard could do this? No, I know that he cannot go alone. I cannot send you with him. I cannot spare you and I don't trust the travel conditions for you anyway. We must see if Matthew Plowman thinks anyone from my villagers could go. I might have to go myself, and leave you here to take care of things. Lena, don't look so glum. You are the only person I could trust to do this. But, in the meantime, can you go over the dues lists and match them with the remaining villagers, so we can see who must pay? I am going to write messages that will have to be sent when I have the opportunity to do so."

Hours later, Lena mounted Pisces to ride back to the mill. The sun had not yet set, but she was very tired. Liebhard held her horse, and did not seem to want to let go of the reins. Lord Franz stood at the door of the manor, looking tired and worried.

"Liebhard, you will be fine. I will come back for dinner tomorrow to help Lord Franz. Then you and I will go to the mill here in the village and work for a few hours. Do as Lord Franz asks, as best you can. Will you do that?"

"I don't want to stay," was his reply.

"Lord Franz needs our help very, very much now. Please do this for me too," she said. He looked so dejected she wanted to get off the horse and put her arms around this big unhappy man. This would be the first night in his life he had been away from the village, she thought.

Lord Franz walked up to Liebhard and put his hand on his shoulder. "We will work together, Liebhard, to do things just as Lena would like us to do. Lena, when can you come up again? Tomorrow?"

"I will try to come in the morning."

Liebhard did not shrug Lord Franz's hand off his shoulder, but he puffed out his cheeks. He looked up at Lena for a long time, and then let go of the reins. She turned the horse, looked over her shoulder to smile and wave, and started for home.

When she arrived home, she was relieved to find that Klaus had already milked Buttercup, and Greta had shut the chickens up in the barn. She led Pisces into his stall, Klaus following close behind. He helped her unsaddle the horse, brought water and hay. She wiped the horse down with some straw as she asked the children about their day. They had far more questions for her. They wanted to know about Smoke and Lord Franz, the dinner they had eaten, what she had done all day, and what the castle and village were like.

After all the chores were finished they went into the mill. The children had stoked the fire well, and the porridge was hot. Some freshly boiled eggs were on the table already. Both children were quick to do the things necessary to put the food on the table, leaving only the ladling of the peese porridge for her to do.

"Klaus and Greta, I am very proud of you both. I was so tired coming home that I wondered if I had the energy to make supper and tend to the animals, but you have done everything!"

Both children beamed and Greta put her arms abound Lena's waist. They sat down to eat, talking about the day.

At a pause in the conversation, Greta said quietly, "I miss Lord Franz. I miss Smokey. When shall we see them?"

"It seems like part of our family is missing, doesn't it?" Lena said, hoping instantly that the children would not have their memories pulled back to the terrible death of their parents. Neither child seemed to react to her words other than to agree that they missed Lord Franz.

"I will mention to Lord Franz tomorrow that you miss him. Perhaps he will find the time to ride down. He has so many cares just now that he might not have a chance to come. We will see."

After they had finished eating, Greta helped Lena put away the food and cleaned the dishes. As they had done each evening, they sat down to work. Lena took out her sewing kit and worked with Greta, teaching her how to stitch seams and sew in darts. She had seen that Klaus needed new leggings. She had selected a pair of his father's and they were sewing them to fit the boy. They did not cut any material out, because Lena knew they would need to enlarge them in a year or two. She had also taken Margit's lovely dark red dress out of the clothing trunk. She had decided she would take it in to fit her own less voluptuous figure.

Klaus listened while Lena taught Greta. A little later, he picked up a small knife and began to whittle a small block of wood. Lena looked over at him: he was concentrating so hard! She sighed, and thought "we three survivors have made a start at a new patched together family. If Franz and Smoke were here, we would be complete." She smiled to herself. Not every wish could be a reality.

As though reading her thoughts, Klaus sighed. "Do you think we could have a dog like Smoke?"

"Let's talk to Lord Franz to see if that is possible," she said. She thought to herself that she too would like a big protective dog like Smoke.

After she had made sure both children were safely in bed, she came back down to the wheel room and sat on Lord Franz's empty bed. She lay down and closed her eyes. Where was her life going? Less than a month ago her family had died. Everything in her life had been turned upside down. A wave of sadness washed over her. She could almost feel Michael's little body in her arms, hear her mother's laughing voice, see her father's patient face and imagine Margit's silly tricks.

She slept fitfully, waking several times. The house seemed so empty. Several times when she woke she remembered snippets of a dream. A woman—was it her?—was walking along the river's edge. A man walked behind the woman, often trying to stop her by putting his arms around her. She wanted to stay in his arms, but there was something ahead that she had to reach. She cried, and the man let her loose. This made the woman weep more, and she sank to the ground.

"Lena, wake up!" It was Greta.

"What's wrong?" Lena asked as she sat up. The sun was streaming into the room! She had slept late!

"Are you sick?" Klaus asked, leaning over to touch her forehead.

Poor children. She had given them a scare. "I am fine. I did not sleep well, and I guess I was very tired."

"But why did you sleep down here in the kitchen? We were frightened when you were not in your bed upstairs," Klaus scolded.

"I did not mean to sleep here, but I fell asleep when I lay down here. I like to sleep down here, I think. You would not mind if I slept here would you?"

Klaus shrugged and Greta shook her head. She smiled at the boy and hugged Greta.

"Well, let's have some bread and porridge. We have all the chores to do before I leave to go up to the manor."

Late in the morning, she and Klaus saddled Pisces and she mounted the gentle horse. "I will be back before sunset. If you have time, please go up to your home and clean. Liebhard and I have done a first clean up, and I have cleaned the sheets and quilts." The children nodded solemnly. They had been down to their old home every day to do chores, and she had made sure they spent time in the house while she was there, but she suspected being there would be a sorrowful experience for some time.

She trotted Pisces briskly along the field paths, her mind busy with all the tasks that lay before her both at her mill and at the manor. When she drew near to the manor village, she saw many people busily clearing the rubble from burned cottages. She stopped and talked to several villagers she knew. Finally she reached the manor courtyard. The sound of her horse's hooves brought Max, the bailiffs' son, and then Franz out. As she dismounted and gave her reins to the boy, Franz launched into plans for the day.

"And I greet you too, Lord Franz," she bristled.

He stopped talking, blinked, and laughter overcame incipient anger. "Good morning, Lena, late though you are! It is just that there is so much I need to do!"

"I know. I am tired from a bad night's sleep."

"Me too. It seemed so strange to sleep up here in the manor. No Klaus, no Greta, no mother hen."

They both laughed, caught up with happenings since yesterday, and sat down at the worktable which was covered with papers and ledgers. Franz must have been up late, because he had made good progress. They worked in silence for some time. Lena was trying to make sure which survivors belonged to the remaining families. Franz wanted to know which families had completely died out. Suddenly it occurred to her that Liebhard had not come in when she arrived. She had expected that he would have been awaiting her arrival.

"Where is Liebhard?" she asked.

Franz suppressed a smile. "Liebhard has found a new love," he said. When Lena continued to stare at the paper in front of her, he relented and said, "As it happens, Liebhard is a good carpenter, and loves the work. He worked late yesterday, and was down at the village early this morning with Matthew. Of the two, Liebhard is definitely in charge."

Lena did not reply. She was surprised. She was shocked, in fact. She had not imagined Liebhard able to act independently like this. He had always seemed to be dependent upon his mother for all of his direction, until he had seemed to follow her own lead. She could not understand this. She tried to return to her nearly completed work, but could not concentrate.

"I think I will go down to the village to see him. Do you mind, Lord Franz? I think I have nearly related all of your survivors to any relatives they may have."

"Yes, you may go. Bring him back with you for dinner. I will tell Oona we are ready to eat."

Lena closed her ledger book and got up. Franz looked at her quizzically but did not say anything. It took her only a few minutes to find Liebhard. He was working with half a dozen villagers on one of the partially destroyed houses. She stopped when she saw him and watched the workers. Lord Franz was right, he was directing the work. He did it more by starting to do things and others joined, rather than giving orders. He definitely was planning the process as he went. His large muscular arms glistened with sweat. He was so incredibly strong. The men were enjoying their work, cheerfully talking and laughing. They followed him willingly. She felt proud of him, but strangely deflated herself. What was wrong with her, she wondered?

One of the villagers saw her, and said something to Liebhard. He looked up and saw her. He beamed and waved. He did not stop working. Shifting from foot to foot, she felt almost embarrassed to interrupt him. Somehow--perhaps he was so sharply attuned to her thoughts—he seemed to feel her uncertainty. He put down the board he was lifting, said something to the workers, and walked up toward her.

"Lena, good morning! When did you come?"

"I came a while ago. I have been working with Lord Franz."

"I am sorry I missed greeting you. We have been very busy getting a start on rebuilding the cottages," he beamed. He looked so happy, so satisfied with his work.

"Lord Franz praised your work."

"How was your night? How are Klaus and Greta? Do you have any message from my mother?"

"The children are well, though they miss Lord Franz and Smoke. They had gotten used to having them in the mill. I did not think to look in on your mother this morning. I am sorry. I did not sleep well. I even overslept. The children thought I was sick, and scolded me for sleeping downstairs..."

"You look tired too. I slept very well. At first I could not get to sleep, and Lord Franz suggested I sleep in his room when he found me still awake. It was better for me then. I could hear someone else in the room breathing. I went to sleep right away."

"I did not know that you liked to work with wood, to build," Lena said.

"I have always loved it. I have not had many times when I needed to. I like to make things grow from nothing to something. Lord Franz showed us where to start on rebuilding. We are first rebuilding some of the houses that can be saved. Then we will build the other houses that are needed from the ground up."

"Does this mean you will work at the manor all winter? Has Lord Franz told you how he will pay you? You are not tied to this village, so he must pay…"

"Yes, yes," Liebhard laughed as he interrupted her. "He said you would want to be sure I was fairly treated, and that he would talk to you about my pay."

Lena did not laugh. She felt that Lord Franz presumed too much. She said frostily, "Lord Franz bade me to tell you to come up for dinner."

Liebhard jerked back slightly, almost as if she had hit him. She was immediately sorry. Why should she be mean to him? "I did not mean to be short with you, Liebhard. It is just that sometimes Lord Franz makes decisions without thought of others."

Liebhard looked at her for a long moment. "I will never do anything if I think you will be angry or harmed."

Lena could think of nothing to say, but she smiled and half turned toward the manor. Liebhard called to the workers to say he had to go up to see Lord Franz, and followed Lena as she walked up the hill.

Dinner was a muted affair. Lena found it hard to concentrate on the conversation, and the men were conscious of the fact that she was not paying attention to what they said. Lord Franz made an effort to smooth things over by explaining the building plans. It was certainly going to mean Liebhard would spend several months at the manor. Lord Franz told Lena his plans for paying Liebhard. His offer was more than fair, she knew. On the other hand, the village would be in absolute need of him at planting time.

"It is fall now. You know that we must have Liebhard's help for spring planting," she countered.

"Yes, of course. He must stop building then. I think we will be able to finish most of the work by then."

Somewhat mollified, she tried to overcome her resentment. Then she remembered the fall slaughtering. "But Liebhard, what about the slaughtering? That is planned to start soon. There was a light frost already. Your father has a pig, and Klaus and Greta have one too. Others in the village have a young steer to be slaughtered now.

"Surely you have enough help without Liebhard," Franz answered with finality. Lena had to agree that he was right, but noted Liebhard looked unhappy with that answer. She did not want to upset his work here. He was obviously so content to be here.

"Of course. You are right. But I must take part. I will try to do the parts of the slaughter that Klaus' parents would have done. I do not think I can come up until we are finished. Will that be all right, Lord Franz?"

"I wish it could be otherwise. When do you think you can come back? These lapsed family situations must be settled, and I will need your help at dues collection."

"We should be finished in a week. Do the villagers have enough flour until then?"

"After we finish eating, we will go down to talk to Matthew Plowman about that."

They finished their meal and walked down to the village. Liebhard took her arm several times as they made their way through some of the remaining debris. They found Matthew, who said he thought the flour quantities were enough for about a week.

Liebhard rejoined the workers and she accompanied Matthew, who then spent the afternoon helping her gather the salvageable belongings from the homes of the eleven lost families. All of the items were loaded into a hand cart that one of the young men pushed along behind them.

When this unpleasant work was done, Lena and the young man trudged back up to the manor. Lena found Franz, who directed Oona to help Lena separate all of the belongings. When she was finished she asked the bailiff's son to bring up her horse.

Lord Franz came just as she was ready to mount Pisces. "You are off then. Weren't you going to come to say goodbye?"

"Yes I must get back. Goodbye until I see you again."

"You are still smarting that Liebhard is staying? Be happy for him. This is good for him, Lena. And I really need his help."

"Yes, I know. You are right. I must be off now." She gave the best smile she could muster, urged Pisces and was off. She waved at him briefly.

Lena was lost in thought during the whole trip. What she was thinking about she could not have said. She could have been anywhere and nowhere, not aware of any of her surroundings. She was feeling blue.

She composed herself as she rode up to the mill. She must not be negative about this. Klaus and Greta did no need any more worries in their lives. As she had found the day before, the children had been industrious during their day. The chores were done, the mill was tidy and supper was ready. They were eager for all of her news and full of news themselves about their day at their cottage. She was grateful and pleased. They were dear children, and she was glad that she had their company. If she had not, she would have been crying.

The next week in the Miller's village was bustling with activity. Lena did not have much experience with slaughtering because as miller, her father had not had much livestock, and received payment often in meat and other food. Now she learned about skinning, meat carving, fat rendering, grinding, cleaning out the intestines to make sausage casing, and smoking and salting the meat. Her work was particularly expected because of the pig that belonged to Klaus and Greta. It was a merry time for all, with fresh meat at every meal. She was far too tired every night to feel sorry for herself. Liebhard's family missed him very much, and had many questions about what he was doing. They were proud to hear that his work was very important to the master, but anxious that he would be away most of the time until spring.

Just a week after she had last been up to the manor, she and the children packed a few things and got ready to go up to see Lord Franz. At least they would have a chance to visit him, even if it turned out that she had to bring them home in the evening. She had run the mill the day before with Mark's help, and ground flour for everyone. Mark definitely understood everything she said, but did not utter a word. He listened attentively to every instruction she gave, often nodding in understanding or agreement. He was a puzzle to her. And sometimes when he was working on something or going down the stairs, she thought he could have been mistaken for Liebhard. Though not as muscular and tall he was a giant compared to most men.

In the morning they were to go up to the manor, Klaus saddled Pisces and helped Lena tie their packs onto the saddle. Lena lifted Greta up into the saddle. Klaus was able to climb up behind her, very excited to be riding this big horse. Lena took the reins and walked along beside Pisces. They went along the path through the patchwork of harvested and standing crops in the fields, drawing ever nearer to the big manor. While still a great distance away, they saw the unmistakable silhouette of Liebhard. He was walking to meet them.

When he reached them his face shone with happiness. Before she could react, he had gathered her in his arms and crushed her to him. She felt as though she melted into him, dizzy and lightheaded. She suddenly wanted to cry. She felt anger welling up in her. She pushed against his hard muscular chest and he immediately released her. Before she could think of what to say, he turned to the children and hugged them too.

"I missed you these many days. It is strange to sleep in the manor house."

"I would like to sleep there with Lord Franz," Greta said.

The other three laughed. Lena saw that Greta was crestfallen by their merriment at her expense, and explained, "Lord Franz is the lord and master of all of this land, our village and his village. We are just his renters. The people of his village are his unfree men. We may visit him only at his pleasure and in most things must do as he bids."

"But why did he stay with us then?" she asked.

"You know he was very sick, and we had to make him well. Because of our care, he learned to know us and we became his temporary family."

"But won't he want to see us now?" she asked.

"I think he will be pleased to see you today," Lena said

55

By this time they had drawn close to the keep and the village. Several busy villagers shouted greeting. At the courtyard entrance to the keep, Franz himself stood. He walked forward and took both children off the horse in one movement. He laughed and held them to him.

"I missed you two. No one asks me any questions at night and pesters me. I cannot get to sleep!" he teased. Over their heads he gave Lena a warm smile. "How is my helper?"

"Tired. We have had a very busy week. But Lord Franz, are you not well?" she asked. She had noticed how he staggered and winced as he had put the children down.

He held her eyes for a moment. "You must see to my back. Something has not healed right."

"You have pressed yourself too hard, Lord Franz!" she clucked.

Behind her she could hear the children squealing as Smoke came bounding out of the keep. He literally knocked Klaus down, lay on him and licked his face. Greta jumped on his back and clung to his long grey hair.

"It looks like someone else missed you too," Lord Franz said to the children, as Liebhard picked Greta up and threw her over his shoulder. Once Klaus had been able to scramble out of Smoke's embrace, the whole troupe headed into the courtyard. Lord Franz welcomed all of them into his home.

Lord Franz called Oona and sent the children off for a tour of the house. He also asked her to arrange for all of them to eat with him when they came back. As soon as they were out of the room he directed Lena and Liebhard to the worktable, still covered with ledgers. She stood where she was.

"I want to see your back," she demanded. She stepped closer and gingerly touched his brow. He was burning. "Lord Franz you are very hot. Up you go to your bed chamber." He did not resist, which was a real testament to how ill he felt.

Once they reached his bedchamber, Lena found that he could not lift his arm to take off his shirt himself. With some trepidation she helped him pull his shirt over his head. She was aghast when she saw the old culprit puncture wound that had not healed properly. Around the puncture spread an angry purple swelling. The old wound was suppurating a yellowish material. Inadvertently she cried out. Franz's head drooped.

"It's that bad?" he asked.

"We must send for Anna at once. I will run down to ask Liebhard to fetch her." She raced down the stairs, and found Liebhard still waiting for them at the worktable.

"Liebhard, take the horse, rush to get Anna. Put her on the horse with you no matter how much she argues, and come back as fast as you can!" Seeing her fear, he responded without question. He was galloping away within minutes.

Lena called out for Oona, asked her to bring vinegar, clean cloths, the sharpest knife she had in the kitchen and some loose wool. With all of these items she hurried back up the stairs. Franz was sitting as she had left him. He turned around, staring at all the items she carried.

"I have sent for Anna, but I think I know what she will want to do," she said briskly. Franz managed a weak smile.

"I do have some good news though. I have received a message from my brother Gebhard!"

"Thank goodness, Lord Franz!" Lena answered. "Is he on his way here?"

"A messenger brought a letter from him, asking if we were well. The count's household was struck by the pestilence too, but they suffered deaths of only one in five. I sent him the news that our father had died, and asked him to get leave from the count to come home immediately. I told him about the attack and hope he will bring one or two military servants. Perhaps he will have news that our father's fief is mine. If so, I will ask the archbishop of Trier if Gebhard can inherit my fief."

Lena did not understand the vassalage inheritance system, so she nodded mutely.

"As soon as I have received news of my wife, I hope that I can be off to bring her home. If my brother does not come, Lena, you will have to act as my steward. Don't look shocked. I have confidence you can do the job well. I am sorry to put yet another burden on your shoulders, but I have no one else capable of comprehending these duties."

"There is no chance that you will be going anywhere soon, Franz. Your brother will have to act for you. You know I will help in any way that I can. And Liebhard will too. Now sit very still. I want to examine this swelling more closely." She lightly felt the whole area, trying to see if there was an area that was harder or hotter. Below the old wound there was an area that was so hard it felt like a stone lay below the hot skin. She wondered if the weapon had entered his back in a downward stroke, and this hard spot was where the inside of the wound was. She gathered some wool and dipped it in vinegar. She would wash the area while she waited.

"Lena?"

"Yes?"

"I meant to tell you, your eye looks good. I don't think most people who see you would notice anything different."

Tears came to her eyes. How could he be so considerate when he was in such danger himself? Lena went around to the other side of the bed and looked at him.

"I have you to thank. I have so much to thank you for. I will do everything in my power for you, my adopted brother." She leaned forward and kissed his burning forehead. "Now we must wait for Anna."

As early as could be expected, they heard hurried steps on the stairs. Anna burst into the room, followed by Liebhard..

"What's this I hear? Your wound has gone putrid? Let me see—oh, my. She tisk tisked repeatedly.

"What are your thoughts?" Lena finally asked.

"Lena, I am not experienced in anything like this. Do you think we can express the pus out? What is the knife for? Have you thought of something else?"

"Feel here, Anna, below the puncture. Why is that spot so hard? I am wondering if there is a pocket in there that has gone putrid. Do you think we can make a cut from the puncture down through that area?"

The stunned silence of Anna and Lord Franz unnerved her. What was she thinking? She would be wounding this already weak young man. Suddenly Lord Franz spoke.

"I think you should try it. If nothing else, it may release some of this swelling. I trust you, Lena."

Lena said nothing. She picked up the knife and felt it. It was razor sharp. She thought about how Anna had wanted to cauterize new wounds. She went over to the fire in the grate and put the blade into the flame. She held it there as long as she could bear the heat of the handle.

"Are you ready, Lord Franz? You must not move."

Franz grasped the edge of the bed, his arm muscles rippling. "Cut away." Liebhard went around to the other side of the bed, standing in front of Lord Franz.

Lena lay the knife tip at the center of the puncture wound, pressed down and cut into his skin. At first no blood came, then a mix of blood, pus and colored liquid came out. She pressed through the hard area and a burst of pus flew out, striking her face. She stopped a moment, wiped the mixture away from her eyes and face, and began again. Anna meanwhile was dabbing the blood and other material away as fast as she could. Then she saw something that looked like a fat wiry caterpillar come out.

"What is that?" Lena cried.

Anna gingerly pulled at the dark thing. It was half the length of Lena's middle finger, dense and wiry. Anna laid it on a clean cloth. It did not move. She pressed a cloth on it. When she lifted the cloth, she gasped. Lena leaned closer. It was a piece of cloth! Lena wiped it with the piece of wool wet with vinegar. Now she could see that the cloth was a dark red or brown.

The women sat back and looked at each other.

"Lord Franz, what color was the tunic you wore the day of the fight? Was it a deep red?"

"Yes, why?" he said through gritting teeth.

"Where is it?" Lena asked, but she was already leaning over his clothing chest. She pulled out the tunic, which she now remembered. She sat down next to Anna and they began to examine it. Quickly they found the offending hole.

"Lord Franz, we found a piece of your tunic in the wound. It was in the hard swelling, and the area was full of pus. We are going to try to press out as much more as we can. This will hurt."

Both women worked vigorously, pressing the whole swollen area. So much blood seemed to flow out, but they seemed oblivious, looking hard for any sign of more putrid liquid. Muffled moans came from Lord Franz. They continued to work until only blood seemed to be flowing.

Suddenly Lord Franz pitched over, Liebhard barely catching him before he fell off the bed. Liebhard manhandled him back onto the center of the bed, laying him on his stomach. He looked questioningly at Lena.

"I think he fainted from the pain. Anna, what should we do now? Shall we drip vinegar in again, like we treated the wounds originally?"

"It seemed to work. Let's do that and then put the lard and bandage on. Liebhard, can you go down and get some lard from Oona? Ask if she has some rendered lard she plans to use to make candles," Anna said

Without a word he went out and started downstairs. He returned shortly with a bowl of lard. Klaus and Greta followed close behind. Both children looked solemn and worried: Greta was crying.

"Will Lord Franz be all right?" Klaus asked tremulously.

Lena leaned over and put her arms around the children. "We hope so. We will have to wait and see." Just then Franz's eyelids fluttered. He opened his eyes, saw the worried faces before him. He managed a smile.

"Are you finished pummeling me? Hi, you two little ones. Don't be frightened. You know my old bad wound? It got worse, and Lena and Anna had to try to fix it."

Greta ran up to the bed and hugged Lord Franz, surprising everyone. If her arm hurt him, he did not show it. Klaus sat down at the bed.

"We are not finished treating Lord Franz. Say your goodbyes now and go back down to Oona."

" I hope you will be my guests tonight at the manor, and I will see you tomorrow," he said to them.

Somewhat unwillingly, the two children said goodbye and left the room.

"Lord Franz, we are going to clean the wound with vinegar. This will hurt. Are you ready?"

"Yes, start," he answered.

The worked quickly, very aware of Lord Franz's trembling back. After they had applied the lard, they covered the wound with clean linen cloth and then wound more cloth around his chest and shoulder, Liebhard helping to lift the young man as they wrapped the cloth around him. As they finished, Oona entered the room with some hot mulled wine. Liebhard helped Lord Franz sit up, but the young man was able to drink the wine without assistance.

"I thank you, Lena and Anna. Just knowing what was in that puncture has made me feel better." Anna made a little curtsey and bid Lord Franz take better care of himself. She and Liebhard left the room.

"Now you must rest. No arguments. You may not get up until the fever is gone," Lena commanded, hoping fervently that he would recover from this set back.

"I will do as you say, but only if you work on the project on the table downstairs. I have been studying the villager family lists. There are the eleven families that have been completely wiped out. It is a sad thing, but on the other hand, it may save this estate."

"What do you mean?" she asked.

"The law is like this: if there is no kin to inherit, each family's belongings and land rights go back to the lord. I have talked with the remaining village elders, and these families have no known relatives. The value of the combined belongings that you brought up to the house is small, but it can certainly help with the upkeep of servants and knights through the winter. And the land rights will double the land already in my father's land rights."

"What a sad thing that these families are completely gone. But I do not understand why having more land at your disposal helps you. There are so few to work the land," she said.

"Well, Lena, I had a thought last night that might help me. On my fief from the archbishop, there is a large section of the land that is not good for crops. It is hilly and stony. For that reason, the archbishop's vassals and even the small tenants, have for a long time turned to raising sheep. Only forage crops are needed to feed the sheep, cut once or twice a summer. Each spring the sheep are sheared and the wool is sent to the wool market down on the Nahe River."

"With the belongings from these eleven families I have acquired fourteen sheep. My father already had twenty-nine, so I now have forty-three. That is the beginning of a good flock," he said enthusiastically.

"Have you thought about whether there will be enough land cultivated for grain and other field crops if you take a large part out for meadow and hay? If your farmers turn to sheep as well, where will you get grain and peas and beans?" she asked doubtfully.

Lord Franz did not answer immediately. No doubt he was studying the possibilities just as she was. There was never much coin to be had, so most things were traded. If everyone had sheep, local wool could not easily be traded for foodstuffs. If wool prices were high at the wool market, many farmers would turn to sheep herding, and that would also make food dear.

"Let's not think beyond the next few years. We have too few people and many costly repairs to do. I think we must go with sheep for now." He decided.

"For now, I need you to help me go through the land rights of these families. Will you also check my tally of what fees and payments are due from my remaining families now that the crops are in? And hardest of all, what shall I do about the cases where the head of the household has died? In those cases, I am entitled to a cow I think. With so much loss, I think I want these debts to be noted, but not demand payment now."

Lena stared at Lord Franz. People had lost so much, and he now demanded more. Even if it were the right of the lord, she was disgusted that he could think like this at this time. He stared back. She saw that he felt her disapproval. His neck and then his face reddened, and his big square jaw seemed to jut out. He looked down and said nothing. He was sick, worried and he needed her help.

"This is the way it is. I am bound by law and duty. It must be so." He looked at her.

"I know. But it is so hard!" she whispered.

"These are hard times. Terrible times."

"Be at ease about this, Lord Franz. I will do all that you ask until you can assume these matters again yourself, or until your brother arrives," she murmured.

Franz managed a weak nod, and carefully lay down on his stomach. She felt his brow. It was still very hot.

"I am going down to arrange for broth and beer to be brought up to you. I will come up to make sure you can sit up and feed yourself."

Franz rolled his eyes but did not object.

The rest of the morning was very busy, with trips up to check on the young lord, trying to go through all of the tallies and papers on the worktable, and checking Lord Franz's list of fees and payments due to him.

When Klaus and Greta came back with Liebhard, they sat at the large hall table to eat dinner. It was like a feast without a host. Franz was the missing member of the little quasi-family they had formed in the past weeks, a disparate group with intricate dependent ties.

After dinner, Liebhardt took the children to show them the work he was doing, rebuilding several cottages. Lena worked quietly at her assigned tasks until Matthew the headman came up from the village. He was already aware of the lord's sickness and looked worried. Lena explained what happened, and to assure him, took him up to see Franz. He was awakened by the sound of their footsteps, and greeted Matthew. Lena leaned forward and felt his forehead. He was still too hot, but she thought his eyes looked less feverish. She poured more beer for him, and he drank thirstily, offering the headman some. Franz then asked Lena if she had finished checking his tallies.

"Yes, they look as they should," she said.

"Matthew, I want you to go with Lena and she will read out to you the fees and payments due now that the harvest is in."

"Yes, my lord, and it is in good time. The villagers know their fees but we will announce them and arrange for them to come up to the manor to settle before the next Sunday. Is that acceptable?"

"I do not know what my father arranged in the past, but I think that what you say sounds agreeable," Franz answered.

Matthew touched his forehead and bowed. Lena led him back downstairs and read him the lists. He seemed to know many of these figures from past years, and left a short time later. Lena now turned her attention to the belongings and land rights of the eleven lost families. She determined that she would lay the household items out so that when the villagers came to pay their dues they could see what was available. Perhaps she could sell some of the items for hard coin.

When the children came back, she asked Oona if they might have some supper and decide where they should sleep. Oona said she already had food ready, and that Lord Franz had asked that they be given his father's room while they were at the manor. Liebhard said he would continue to sleep in Lord Franz's room if she thought it was all right.

After dinner, she made sure Klaus and Greta were settled, and then went with Liebhard to see Lord Franz. The young man had fallen into a deep quiet sleep, and did not stir when they entered. Liebhard started to follow Lena as she left the room.

"Aren't you staying here? It's nearly time to go to bed."

He did not answer, but reached out and took her arm, turning her toward him. She hesitated, but then leaned into him, pressing her body against his chest. A feeling of warmth and safety permeated her whole being. She heard his breathing become more rapid, matching hers. They remained in a prolonged embrace, neither speaking. Finally she gently pushed herself away from him and quickly left the room.

She started to walk down the hall toward the room where the children were, but stopped. She knew she would not be able to sleep. She retraced a few steps and reached the top of the stairs. She would try to work on the remaining ledgers she had not mastered.

It was quiet when she reached the ground floor. Oona and the serving girl must have gone to bed too. She sat down. The candles on the table had been extinguished, and only one wall sconce still burned. For some time she remained sitting in the dark. She was relieved to be alone with her thoughts. She was not happy with her lot. It seemed as though she was being pressed and poked from every side, forced into a narrow path. Just short months ago she had been a contented mother with a father who looked after all of the important decisions in her life. Then at times since the dreadful arrival of the pestilence she had felt that she was directing her own future and the lives of the people in her village. Now did she have any choice but to marry Liebhard? She did not want to marry again. She felt that in the very marrow of her bones. Liebhard was a good man, and as Lord Franz said, very loyal and steady. He would be a good husband. If she were a man she would not have to marry.

All of these thoughts swirled around in her head. She shook herself. This was not useful rambling. She took a candle and lit it from the sconce fire, then lit another. She sat down and began to study the papers Lord Franz had been working on. It seemed as though he was trying to calculate the income he could make from wool, and how many sheep he would need, hay to feed them, land use, and lamb production. Since her Latin was so weak, she made many guesses about what all of his notes meant.

REINFORCEMENTS

Sir Reiner nudged Ajax a little to keep pace with Gebhard's charger. The other knight, Sir Heinrich, and the young squire rode slightly behind. No one talked. The silence of the landscape was foreboding. They had seen few people since they had left the count's castle. The crops were largely un-harvested. Those who were not dead from the pestilence were not showing themselves. At the castle they had lost one in four. He had seen plague before in Sicily, but not as bad as this. Perhaps this is how he would die. The image of Giorgio came into his mind. No, he would not think of him. He would be all right at the orphanage, under the care of the sisters.

Until late afternoon the previous day, he had known nothing about this travel. As a *ministeriale* of the count he did what he was bid. He wondered that he had been chosen, since he had only been with the count's retinue for a few months, after he had left Sicily with a recommendation from the count's cousin. Perhaps it was because he was an experienced fighter. Those he rode with were very young.

Lord Gebhard was an able swordsman, he knew well. He had watched the feud combat demanded by a young knight of the Rotfels family. Gebhard had drawn deep blood but received barely a scratch. The other knight had died. There was something about Gebhard's demeanor that suggested he had little interest in combat though. The count used him more for strategy and planning: he valued Gebhard's gifts. That was probably why he allowed him to take three of his own retinue to return to Gebhard's father's land. No doubt Lord Conrad's other son expected further retaliation from the Rotfels.

His mind wandered as he rode. Memories of Angela came. He thought about the first time he held Giorgio, the flood of love and anxiety that came over him. How could he care for this boy? He had spent many pleasant times with Angela.

She had been a needed respite for him during the horrors of years of sporadic fighting in Sicily, but there was no question of marriage. He was a knight and she was the daughter of a town merchant. Her father demanded that she give up the baby when he found a merchant willing to marry Angela. He was not surprised that she easily acquiesced: she would have other babies, legitimate ones. No, it had happened as it must.

It was already dusk when Gebhard said that they had entered Lord Conrad's fief. He picked up the pace. Even so, it was black night when they rode into the keep courtyard. There was an old acrid smell of burned wood. A young man ran out of the guard gate, asking who they were. When Gebhard gave his name the boy touched his forehead and held Gebhard's horse. As they dismounted, Reiner saw there was a dim light burning in the manor. Gebhard went to the door, tried it, then pounded loudly, giving his name again.

The bolt of the door was drawn back, the door opened, and a woman stood outlined in the candlelight. She stepped back, welcoming the young knight, giving her name as Lena when he asked. Gebhard called for the men to enter. As they began to take off their armor, Gebhard spoke with the woman. She was quite slender, but not unattractive. It crossed Reiner's mind that she must be some especially favored member of the household. She held herself very erect, almost like a person of authority.

Lena had been drawn out of her work by the sound of the horses entering the courtyard of the keep. Who could be here at this hour? It was now dark. She listened to the murmur of voices, then the sound of the Max's voice. Moments later, there was a loud knock at the manor door. The door was bolted. She sat where she was, frightened and not sure what she should do.

Just as Lena half stood, ready to run up to get Liebhard, Oona appeared from the pantry area, a blanket wrapped around her. She stared wide eyed at the door, then at Lena. She was frightened too. Was this the enemy knight returning again?

"Open up! It is Sir Gebhard, your master's son. Open up, I say."

Oona nodded to Lena, and mouthed, "That's Sir Gebhard!"

Both women rushed to pull the bolt back, and dragged the heavy door open. A tired, impatient young man stood before them. He was dressed in half armour: he wore his breastplate and arm protection. Behind him she could see three other men, all wearing breastplates. Sir Gebhard neither smiled nor gave the women greeting. He raised his hand, beckoning his men to follow him, and they entered the hall. The entry of four armored men into the hall made the space seem filled with noise and strange sights.

"Where is my brother? Who are you?" Gebhard asked brusquely. He sounded like Lord Franz had spoken when he first woke up at the mill. He looked a few years younger than Lord Franz, shorter and more solidly built.

"I am Lena, Miller's daughter from Millers Village. This is Oona, the widow of the village headman. Lord Franz is in his bedchamber asleep. He still suffers from a wound he received from the attack."

"But that was months ago. I thought from his letter that he was well." As he spoke he began removing his armor, as did the other men. He did not resemble Lord Franz, except for his eyes, Lena thought as she watched. One of the other men looked about Sir Gebhard's age, another looked as though he could not be more than fifteen. The third man was older, probably her age. Though at the end of a day's journey, his stance gave her the impression that he was ready and alert for any action needed. They were tall burly men except for Sir Gebhard. He was not much taller than her.

"Lena…he mentioned you in his letter. What is wrong with him?"

"One of his wounds festered. We cleaned it out today. It is very late, but I think he will want to know that you have arrived. I will light your way up to him," Lena said.

Sir Gebhard started up the stairs after her, calling down to Oona to feed his men and make them comfortable. She brought food out very quickly, along with some much-appreciated wine.

When Lena and Gebhard had reached the bedchamber, she quietly opened the door. Liebhard was up instantly and she wondered if he thought she had returned for another reason. She motioned for him to come out of the room.

"Liebhard, this is Lord Franz's brother, Sir Gebhard. Liebhard is the son of Karl the Older Plowman from Millers Village." Liebhard bowed his head and touched his forehead, towering over the shorter man. He stepped aside as Lena tiptoed into the room and lightly touched Lord Franz's forehead. He was still hot. He slowly woke.

"What is it Lena? Gebhard! You have come!"

Gebhard rushed forward and embraced his brother, kissing him. The brothers sobbed a little, then pulled back to look at each other, quickly trading information. Lena backed away and turned to leave.

"Wait, Lena," Lord Franz said. "Gebhard, I have had quite a set back from a wound, but I think I will get better soon. Let us talk tomorrow when we are both rested. What men have you brought? Three?" he said, when Gebhard held up three fingers. "The two back bedchambers are not in use, so plan to sleep there tonight. Has Oona been wakened? She will feed you. Lena, can you bring all of the papers from the table up here in the morning when you come, and Gebhard, please come up as soon as you wake. We have much to discuss. I am glad beyond telling that you have come."

The brothers embraced again. Lord Franz winced as he lay down, and Gebhard followed Lena out of the room.

When they reached the bottom of the stairs, Lena curtsied, intending to bid the young man goodnight, but he held up his hand, indicating he wanted her to stay. His three retainers sat at the table eating, so he motioned for her to follow him toward the back of the manor, and into one of the back bed chambers. Reiner watched. Who was she? Perhaps a mistress of Gebhard's brother? A short time later, she came back out into the hall with Gebhard and curtsied before she went upstairs—definitely not into servant's quarters.

. When they had entered the back chamber, Gebhard turned toward her.

"Sit, please. I left my father's house ten years ago, when I was eight. I have been home no more than once a year. I am trying to place you. I remember your father. He had two daughters, I think. Are you the younger one?"

Lena reddened. "I am the elder daughter. My sister Margit died of the pestilence, as did my mother, father and my son."

Gebhard drew in his breath as he processed this information. She saw that he did remember her, but differently.

"Tell me all, from the moment the great pestilence came."

Lena sat down, gathering her thoughts. So much had happened. "In mid-August, at the height of the harvest..." she started. She talked slowly, trying to leave nothing out that would be important for him to know. He listened attentively. It was a long narration. When she finished he had many questions.

"My brother praised you highly. He planned to have you act for him as his steward if he did not hear from me," he said, looking hard at Lena.

"Sir Gebhard, there are few people left to help him and no one besides me with any learning," she explained.

"He said you are like a tyrannical older sister."

Lena did not know what to say to this. Lord Franz had said that to her himself, but she had not expected him to say such a thing to anyone else.

"Now that you are here, you will be able to act for him instead," she finally replied.

Her answer caused a strange look to play over his face. She could not tell what he was thinking. "I think not. You must continue as he wishes. Do not overstep what is asked."

Lena bristled. She had not asked for all of the powers Franz had given her. She was on the verge of angrily retorting that she really had to go back to Millers Village, when she saw the mischievous twitch of Gebhard's mouth. She could not fathom what he was thinking, but knew he meant no insult. She bowed her head in agreement.

"Good night then, Lena," was all he said, and motioned to show her she was dismissed. She rose, left the room, and went up the stairs to the room she would share with the children. She lay down on the old lord's bed next to Greta. She finally went to sleep, still wondering what the morning meeting with the brothers would bring.

The next morning was very quiet. It was approaching dawn. Reiner lay dozing, waiting for the sounds of the morning. He was sleeping in the chamber with Gebhard, and heard when he woke. He sat up as the young man dressed.

"I am going up to talk with my brother. He was too exhausted from his wound last night. Apparently one of the wounds he received weeks ago festered, and Lena and another woman were able to treat it successfully yesterday. You may spend the morning as you wish. I think Oona will have food ready soon to break your fast."

Reiner nodded slightly. His interest was once again piqued about this woman Lena. Now it appeared she was some kind of a healer too. He got up as Gebhard left the room, dressed and entered the hall, just in time to see the same woman going toward the kitchen with a young boy and girl (members of Gebhard's extended family, he wondered?).

Not aware of Reiner's interest in her activities, Lena brought the children down to Oona so that they could break their fast. She was thinking she would have to bring them back home later in the morning after she spoke to the brothers.

Reiner was seated at the big hall table, listening to the voices from the kitchen and the sounds of the other knights getting up, when he saw Lena come out of the kitchen door with a large tray of mulled wine, cheese, bread and broth. For the briefest moment he thought she was going to bring it to the table, but she went up the stairs instead. She had not looked at him. Her mind was on other matters.

She came down a short time later, went to the kitchen, came out with a tray of odd items like wool, a jar and some linen. She stopped at the other end of the table and gathered up several ledgers, put them on the tray and hurried upstairs. She acknowledged his presence slightly as she did this. Now Reiner was highly curious. This might become quite a puzzle. She was prettier than he had first thought—though too slender by standards of beauty.

When Lena had brought up the food tray to the brothers, she opened Lord Franz's door quietly, but found there was no need for silence because the brothers were already together. They both nodded, and she saw the family resemblance more clearly.

Lena put down the tray on the table next to Lord Franz's bed. As soon as she had poured the wine, he reached over and took it. She noted that his eyes were clear and he looked rested. She began to reach out to touch his forehead, but suddenly thought that this might not be appropriate in Sir Gebhard's eyes.

"May I examine your wound Lord Franz?" she asked.

"Yes, yes. Don't mind Gebhard," he laughed. Sir Gebhard was watching her closely, his face inscrutable.

Feeling surer of herself, she felt his forehead. His fever seemed to have disappeared. She went around the bed, raised the back of his shirt, which he then began to pull over his head, finishing with her help. Carefully she unwound the bandage and lifted the linen patch. Sir Gebhard came around the bed and drew in his breath.

She quickly reassured Lord Franz, "The angry purple swelling is gone. The hard area below the wound is now much softer. The whole area is red, but it is a smaller area. It looks much improved. I think your fever is gone too." She stepped aside so that Sir Gebhard could see better, and so that she could gage his reaction. She knew that to him it looked like a terrible festering.

"I am going to treat it again as we did before. Sir Gebhard, have you broken your fast?" He shook his head. "I will go down to get everything I need to dress the wound, and arrange for more food to be brought up," she said and briskly left the room. Several steps down the stairs she heard the brothers murmuring and then laughing. If it was on her account, she did not care.

The rest of the morning raced by. Lena was unfamiliar with so much that was discussed, but tried to follow the conversation in case she would be asked to help in any way. The feud with the other knightly family was of long standing. Several generations earlier one of Franz's family was taken hostage in a battle. Ransom was demanded and paid, but the ancestor had died. The other family insisted it was an accident, but Franz's family attacked the other family in retaliation. Each attack since had brought on a reciprocal action. The most recent was a duel involving Gebhard. He had been challenged by a young man his own age from the other family. Both men had been wounded , although Gebhard only slightly, but the other man's wounds putrefied and he died. The knight who attacked Franz was the young man's uncle.

"I do not know if any of the attackers managed to get away. If so, they probably reported that I had been killed. At any rate, we cannot act now, but we must be vigilant and prepared. We also need to know something about what their family is doing and how it has been affected by the pestilence. This uncle, Roderick of Rotfels, is a vassal to the Archbishop of Trier, just as I am. This is one more reason that I urgently need to get to Trier. I must report to the archbishop and I must bring my wife Elena home. I have great confidence in my knights who I sent with her, but they may not have survived. Manfred especially is an exceptional knight."

"You will not be able to go for days. I will have to go for you."

"That just will not be enough, Gebhard. I think you can go tomorrow with messages from me, then send me a message as soon as you can. By then I will be able to ride."

"What about all of the problems here?" Gebhard asked. "I will need to take a man with me, and you will need a man. That leaves only one man here."

Franz looked at Lena. "With Liebhard and Lena, that will be enough. Which is the best fighter of your companions?"

Gebhard looked dubiously at Lena. "I am concerned that you overestimate the ability of Lena and Liebhard. But you will make the decision. Reiner of Oberland is new to the count's service, but he is a seasoned fighter, not easily rattled. I would leave him here if that is what you want."

"May I ask what you expect might happen Sir Gebhard?" Lena asked timorously.

"It is possible, even likely, that Roderick's family will come here with a challenge, if not a direct attack," he replied. "The attack Roderick made on the manor was a surprise, and really forceful, so I expect another attack."

Lena was silent a moment: she looked at Franz. "The pestilence has very likely hit this knight's family and fief just as it has yours, Lord Franz. Think what trouble you are having sending messages. If even so, an attack comes, we can be prepared. The villagers should be warned so they will be watchful and can act as a warning system."

"I am satisfied. I will write messages tonight. You should plan to leave early tomorrow," Lord Franz said. Gebhard nodded in acceptance.

This plan in place, the conversation turned to their father's fief. As Lord Franz had anticipated, the count expected Lord Franz to inherit the fief. Lena was asked to explain anticipated fees and dues. The brothers spent time trying to calculate how much money they would need to rebuild and to pay knights and squires plus other expenses. This was a somber conversation. It looked as though they would have to borrow at least a third of what they needed. But from where?

A silence fell among them. The coming months could be very difficult for Lord Franz. Lena tried to think of any other income sources, but her mind started to wander to other things. She started thinking about the recent slaughter of Klaus and Greta's pig. She could not remember if she had asked Mark to check the embers at the smoke house. She had never prepared meat for smoking before, and wondered if she had rubbed the salt into the meat thoroughly enough. SALT!

SALT

Lena jumped up from her bench. "Lord Franz, what about your father's salt mine?"

Both brothers looked at her quizzically. Was it possible they did not know?

"Millers village buys the use of the mine for salt some years. Lord Conrad did not like to have his villagers mine because sometimes they got sick. I have not been there myself, but my father used to bring several men to work the mine so that no one stayed too long. He once said it was easy to get the rock salt."

"Where is it?" Gebhard asked, leaning forward.

"That I do not know. But if our poor village would pay, perhaps there would be a market for the sale of salt in the towns. Matthew Headman surely knows where the mine is."

Lord Franz threw back his head and laughed. "It is expensive to buy and not always easily available! Perhaps we can see if we can find buyers when we are in Trier! Lena, find Matthew and ask him to come up."

Reiner had finished his breakfast with Heinrich and young squire Markus, and they had put on their breastplates in preparation to take a walk around the village, when Lena ran down again, and out the hall door. Curious, he followed in the direction she had gone, the others tagging along behind. She stopped at the village center to talk with a giant of a man, who took her hand as she spoke. He called out to another man who came up the hill and joined Lena as she started back up the manor. He nodded to her as she passed, while her companion touched his forehead. When he reached the giant, he gave his name and said he had come with Gebhard the previous night.

"Yes, I saw you. I am Liebhard from Millers Village, where Lena is miller. I have been guarding Lord Franz until you came."

"Lena is a miller? I thought she was a healer."

"Lena is our village leader now that her father is dead. She is the miller. She saved Lord Franz's life," he said, smiling down at Reiner. He had a clear open face, a very handsome face, and powerful physique. What knight would not like to have that muscular body! Reiner looked about and realized the men were rebuilding half burned houses.

"And you are a builder too?"

"I love to make things, and to work with wood. Here I am a builder and a guard. At home I am a farmer," he said.

Reiner was interested in construction as well, and told the other men he would stay here awhile. They walked on. Reiner asked if he might watch Liebhard's work.

Liebhard laughed. "Of course! And tell me if you see better ways." As the big man worked they continued a casual discussion, soon veering in many directions. Reiner guessed they might be close to the same age. Liebhard talked about the days of the pestilence, the fire that killed many villagers, and results of the attack on the castle. Liebhard spoke simply; very refreshing to Reiner.

A short time later the young boy and girl came down from the hall. They greeted Liebhard warmly and said they were going to see the young baker girl. He asked if Lena knew where they were. They were a little embarrassed but admitted they had not told her before they came down. After they had gone on, Liebhard told Reiner that he must go up to the hall.

"Lena will want to know where Klaus and Greta are," he said simply.

"They are her children?"

Liebhard laughed. "Now they are. They are orphans from our village, children of Lena's best friend. She lost her whole family and has taken them as hers." With that, he smiled and trotted up the hill. Reiner watched him for a while, and then walked on to find Heinrich and Markus.

Within a half hour, Matthew was in Lord Franz's bedroom. He had been to the mine many times and knew it well. He had also helped with the process of getting the salt out of the rock salt. He was cautious about how much salt could be produced with the reduced men in the village who could break up the rock salt and get it out of the mine. The brothers were too excited about the prospect of a revenue source to be concerned about the ability to produce the salt.

Lord Franz thanked Matthew and asked him to show Gebhard where the mine was, so that he could evaluate it before he rode to Trier. Gebhard said he would come down to the village a little later so they could ride out to the site. Matthew bowed and opened the door to leave.

Lena stood up and said, "Lord Franz, I think I should bring Greta and Klaus home this morning and arrange a few things. I may have to grind some grain too."

"Yes, all right. Bring them up to see me before you go," he said.

Lena walked down the stairs, excited about Franz's prospects, thinking about everything she had to do at the mill, and concerned about the dues collections. She looked up to see Liebhard at the bottom of the stairs. Last night's embrace sprang to her mind and she felt the flush of blood come to her face. He did not reach out to touch her, but she burned, nonetheless.

"I am looking for Greta and Klaus," she stammered. She felt silly.

He held her eyes for a long moment and then said, "They are down at the village with the baker's daughter. Shall I fetch them?"

"I will go myself," she said, but he turned and walked with her.

Not a word was said all the way down to the village. She hurried her steps when she saw them. They called to her and ran up to tell her all about baking. When she was able to get a word in, she told them that she was here to bring them back to Millers Village. This news was not happily received, and they wanted to know why they could not stay. Finally she and Liebhard were able to herd them back up to the manor, and to Lord Franz's room.

"Hello, you two," Franz said, just as Smoke rose to nuzzle them. They proceeded to tell Franz all about how they had helped baker's daughter bake some bread. He listened with interest.

"I know that you are going home now. If these times were not so difficult, and if I were well, I would have you stay longer. You will come again soon." He pulled Greta to him, and put his hand on Klaus' shoulder. "Now help Lena all that you can, because she has a heavy burden of things to do for me."

The children went to gather their things and Liebhard went to the stable for Pisces. When she walked out of the manor with the children, she saw that he had Pisces and the priest's horse.

"Can you be spared?" she asked, flustered.

"I will go with you. I want to see my family too."

"Have you leave from Lord Franz?"

His answer was puffed out cheeks. He was not going to be gainsaid. "We will be back before dinner," was his answer.

The ride back to Millers Village was filled with the children's chatter. Liebhard had insisted she ride the priest's horse, and he walked between the two animals. Lena hardly said a word. She could not think what Liebhard intended. She was not ready for any demands on her to make decisions about her future.

Liebhard went with them to the mill, but then continued on to his parents' house. Lena went in with Klaus and Greta, and they went over all that she expected them to do. She walked up to Hans' house, where he and Anna were working on their roof thatch. Hans said that the flour supply would be adequate for a week at least. He and Anna told her all of the local news. She told them about the idea of the salt production, which interested Hans.

When she got back to the mill, she changed into Margit's remade dress, sliding it over her best shift. She packed a few things, and when she opened the mill door she found Liebhard was waiting. He brought Pisces to her, and lifted her on before she could say a word. He mounted his horse and they turned toward the manor. By now she was becoming irritated. Why could she not go on without any change? She determined not to say a word.

They had barely started on their way when Liebhard said, "We should marry."

"Why? Why? Can I not continue as I am?" She realized she was close to tears.

"Lena, there is no other one for you to marry. You will have to marry sooner or later. I want to marry you. I want to care for you. I cannot remember a time I did not want you to choose me. And you yearn for me too. There is also Dieter. If he returns, only a husband can really protect you."

She started to cry. He spoke so simply. Every word was true. She wanted to run away.

"I cannot face this now," she said through clenched teeth. "Just two months ago I was a devoted mother, happy with my family…"

"You were not happy with Dieter," he observed.

"I had learned to hate him. But he is gone. I hope he is dead. I am free of him. I am now the miller. I have Klaus and Greta. This is my life now. It is enough for me. Everyone pushes me. Lord Franz says we should marry too. You know that you make me burn. Liebhard, sometime soon, you are the one I expect to marry. Not yet!" She kicked Pisces sides, and he jumped forward into a gallop, surprising her. By the time she had reined him in to a trot, Liebhard was beside her. He leaned forward and pulled Pisces' reins. The horses stopped.

"I do not want to make you unhappy. You know that. I am eager to marry you, to have you. I am able to wait until you say," he said.

Lena gulped back sob. He was so kind. Was she being selfish and cruel? She managed a nod. They walked on in complete silence the rest of the way to the manor. Her tears had long dried by the time they dismounted. She was able to manage a small smile for him before she went into the hall.

To her surprise, villagers were already there, waiting to settle their dues. Around noon, Oona interrupted her so that she could take some dinner and check on Franz. He looked rested and had no fever. His shoulder hurt a great deal, so she said she would send up birch tea and mulled wine. He was very pleased with the news that villagers had already started to come, but impatient to see Gebhard, who had not yet returned from his trip to the salt mine.

Lena continued to meet with villagers throughout the afternoon. Reiner returned with Heinrich and Markus. He was surprised to see several villagers in the hall, but soon saw it was dues payment time. Reiner saw too that it was Lena who was taking the dues. She had changed her dress, and now wore an attractive dark red one. And the woman could read!

Oona and Thirza took the food brought by the villagers as dues and put it in the larder. Some villagers had paid their dues in coin. Others had pledged a portion of their harvest, and she wrote this down with arrangements for when this should be delivered to the granary and to the mill.

Sir Gebhard returned in the middle of the afternoon, nodded to her and his men and went up to his brother. Reiner wondered where he had gone with the headman. The mysteries were intoxicating to him. For the first time in months, since he had left Giorgio at the convent, his mind was alive with interest about his surroundings.

Suppertime arrived. Lena went into the kitchen, ate a bit of food and then gathered food for Lord Franz and Sir Gebhard, relieved to not face Liebhard at this meal. The three knights, who had made themselves at home in the hall, were already eating at the table. Reiner, alert to her activities watched her.

While the brothers ate, she reported to them in detail the events of the afternoon. Lord Franz in turn told her about his brother's trip to the mine, with Sir Gebhard quickly interjecting more details. The mine was apparently entered through a cave entrance in a small cliff several miles east of the manor house. The entrance was very large, and the vein of rock salt began almost immediately. This explained why her father had said it was easy to mine. The problem was that the better, larger deposit was deeper and in a descending tunnel. He said that he felt his nose and throat burn after he had been in the deeper area only a few minutes.

In a lull in the conversation, Lena changed the subject to something that was preoccupying her. "Lord Franz, I thought while I am here, perhaps I should stay down at the mill," she volunteered.

"What? No, I will not allow that. Not alone." He sat silently a moment, and then said, "Gebhard, I wonder if I might speak to Lena alone for a moment. I think she does not want to say what is troubling her." Gebhard looked curiously at her, but rose and left the room.

"What is this about?"

"Your house is full now, Lord Franz," she started lamely.

"More likely something else has happened. Liebhard could go down with you to the mill, but then you would be bound to marry now," he said, chuckling until he saw her face start to crumble. "Well, all right. I did not mean to upset you. You would be safe with him there with you though. I will not allow you to be there alone. You must stay up here. Can you sleep with Oona? Do I need to speak to Liebhard?"

"No, please do not do that," she cried. "He is ever kind and careful of me. It is me. I feel so pressed."

"You must make the leap or continue with all of this difficulty, Lena."

"Lord Franz, we spoke of this on the way back from Miller Village this morning. I have told him that when I do marry I will marry him, and he said he will wait until I am ready."

Lord Franz smiled broadly, clearly indicating the direction he thought she should be taking. "Fret no more. I will say good night to you now. Go down and make your arrangements with Oona."

Lena gave him the best smile she could muster, and left the room. She bade Gebhard, who was waiting outside the door, good night. At the bottom of the stairs, Liebhard was sitting, sharpening some tools. The knights must have gone to the bedchambers at the back of the hall, because he was alone. He looked up questioningly.

"I think you can go up soon. The brothers are still talking now. I am to bed with Oona. Good night then," she said as she began to pass him. As quick as a cat, he was up and before her.

"Good night, Lena. Do not be troubled," he said softly, giving her a short gentle embrace, his lips brushing the top of her head. The delicious feeling of him against her was intoxicating. He opened his arms and let her go. Without looking back she hurried into the kitchen to find Oona.

When Gebhard retired to the bedchamber where Reiner was already in bed, he told the knight that he was leaving with his squire early in the morning, traveling to Trier to find Lord Franz's young wife. He told Reiner he would be in charge of any defense necessary, and told him more about the attack that had been made on the fief, and the incredible loss of life that had occurred in the manor village. Now Reiner understood the perilous condition of the brothers' father's estate. Many lives hung in the balance here.

Lena rose early, planning to take breakfast to the brothers, assuming that Gebhard would be with Franz. She found when she entered the room that Gebhard had already left, taking the young squire, Markus, with him. Franz was partially dressed, but having trouble with his shirt. She helped him, noting that his shoulder was much better than the day before. She poured the beer for him and sat back.

"Join me. Have you already eaten?" he asked, when she demurred. She poured herself a little beer. He continued, "I am going to come downstairs and join you at the table for a while. I should get to know my villagers better."

A short time later, they were seated together at the big worktable in the hall. When Reiner entered with Heinrich, he found Lena at the table meeting with villagers. Beside her was the man he had not yet met, Lord Franz. He did not look like Gebhard. He was a tall well-built young man in his early twenties, with a square discerning face, below luxurious brown hair. He went forward, bowed, and announced his name. Lord Franz greeted him warmly, asked if he had met Lena, and introduced her as his right hand. She reddened but smiled slightly as she raised her eyes to his. They were a light warm brown color, and there was some kind of a quizzical look about them which he did not understand.

One or two villagers were waiting by the door. The process was different from the previous day, since the villagers were honored that Lord Franz was there, and directed all their attention to him. He, on the other hand, was not comfortable with the fine points of the payments. The payments were generally a mix of produce, agreements to pay grain in the future, and coins. Very soon he whispered to Lena that he was going to sit in the alcove behind her.

Reiner and Heinrich had finished their breakfast. Heinrich had excused himself, probably to go down to tease one of the pretty village girls. Reiner remained in the hall, reading and half listening to the process of dues paying. When the door next opened, Liebhard entered. Lena noticed, and became somewhat rattled. She turned back to the next person in line. At first she did not recognize the woman. She led a big handsome goose by a cord and carried a small leather pouch. She stared at Lena. It was Etta.

"I am Etta, Gregor Plowman's wife. You do not recognize me. I am Dieter's mother."

At first Lena did not know what to say.

"Why are you here? Where is my son?""

"He ran away, stole my dead father's horse and money, and left me and his son to die." Lena choked the words out.

Suddenly Liebhard was there. That was why he had come in! "Your son is a thief and a murderer. I saw him leave the village with the money in his hand, on Miller's horse. Then I found Margit and Lena locked up. Margit was dead. He left his son Michael to die alone."

"He would not leave his son to die," his mother said, in disbelief. "You are his wife, and should not speak of him so!" she said to Lena.

"Dieter has committed grave crimes, Etta," Lord Franz said quietly, from behind Lena. "I intend to speak for Lena Miller in my court about the thefts, and name him outlaw here. He will lose all rights, be outside the law. For the murders I will speak for Lena in the royal court at the count's court. That is a capital crime. But that is another matter not to be discussed today. I accept you goose and coins as your dues."

She dropped the end of the cord and emptied the pouch onto the table. Liebhard placed his arms around the goose's wings and carried it out. Etta's face had disintegrated into lines of anger and shame. She hurried after Liebhard.

"You have no friend there," Lord Franz whispered, "but you will have me at your side."

Lena could not look up for some time. Lord Franz leaned forward and whispered, "Do you want me to take your place for a while, or can you go on?"

"I can go on," she said. She looked up to see only one villager remained, for which she was very relieved. Then she saw that the older knight, Reiner of Oberland was looking at her. He had heard everything. She flushed deeply. Reiner turned away. He had learned so much about her in these few moments, things she would not like a stranger to know. For Lena it was very embarrassing. But in her mind she was aware of how natural he acted in this setting. His tunic was so plain that if he had not had a sword at his waist, no one would have recognized him as a knight.

Several more villagers came during the day, and the few remaining ones came the following morning. She was able to tally up the dues, and with Lord Franz's help, total the coins before dinner at noon. He was well satisfied, because more hard money had come in than he had expected.

"After we eat dinner, I would like to try to ride out to look at the salt mine. Will you come with me? We can get some idea ourselves about the practicality of this venture. We will take Liebhard and Reiner with us. Sir Heinrich Weisskopf can watch here."

Lena did not disagree, though she was concerned about the length of the ride for the mending young man. "We must ride slowly." She ordered.

Sir Reiner received a request after dinner from Lord Franz to join him in the solar. He went up the stairs, curious. Lord Franz sat alone.

"Sir Reiner, you may have been wondering about some of the comings and goings during the past few days. My brother and I have been trying to establish the financial situation of our father's estate. Lena told us the day before yesterday something known by many, but not us. We have a disused salt mine at the eastern edge of the fief. Gebhard checked it with the village headman. Today, I propose to go out to see if we can work it. I wish you, Lena and Liebhard—do you know him?-to come with me."

"I would be honored to come. Is Sir Heinrich enough of a show of strength here though?"

"I think so. Lena suggested our adversary must have suffered from the pestilence as well as us, and will have trouble with communications too." Reiner bowed his head slightly in agreement.

About an hour later the four riders were on the way. Lena rode a rather splendid black charger, and Liebhard was on a serviceable riding horse. Lord Franz saw Reiner's close look at Pisces and laughed.

"Sir Reiner, this woman saved my life. Her horse was stolen by her snake of a husband, Dieter. I gave her my second mount. Liebhard's horse belongs to the dead priest from Miller Village," he explained. Reiner nodded slightly.

Little conversation passed among them. Liebhard seldom talked, so his silence was not unusual. Reiner listened to all that Lord Franz said to Lena, but he only spoke when spoken to. Lena wondered at his reticence. He seemed to be a modest alert person. He had some kind of a sadness or fatalistic air about him. Now in partial amour, he was very imposing as he rode slightly behind Lord Franz. She knew little about the knightly class, but wondered if the fact that he had no fief at his age was a sign of failure.

This side of the fief was not good farmland. The ground was rocky and more mounds of bedrock appeared as they rode. After about an hour they saw a brooding brown cliff to their left ahead. It was a strange outcropping. It looked as though it had come up out of the ground, alien in color to all around it. The whole area was nearly barren of vegetation and the ground was strewn with broken rock. A gaping entrance marked the cave. Reiner could see that this place had been mined for a very long time even though it may have been disused at the present time. He observed haze around the entrance.

After they had tethered the horses, they examined the entrance of the cave. Every section of the walls revealed hammer and cleavage marks. A torch lay near the entrance, which Liebhard lit with a practiced hand. He led the way and they slowly walked in. The air was not pleasant, even at the entrance. The air scorched the nose and lungs, and Reiner automatically covered his nose and mouth with his neck cloth. Lena felt the urge to take only shallow breaths, and seeing Reiner covering his face, she copied him, raising her cloak. Eventually all the others covered their faces as well. Along the side walls the rock gleamed like gray glass. As they walked deeper, whole large chunks were strewn on the ground. They descended a gentle decline. The tunnel was still very large, at least the height of two men, and more than thirty paces wide.

Liebhard stopped and turned back to Lord Franz. "The walls are different now. I see no cut marks."

Lord Franz went to a wall, rubbed it, and licked his hand. "Very salty. Good rock salt, but probably never mined this deep." He coughed as he finished speaking and put his cloak to his nose again. "Let's go back."

Once out of the tunnel, they all sat down on rocks, wheezing as they breathed better air.

"We will definitely have to learn some way to protect at least the noses and mouths of the workers. My eyes burn too."

Reiner volunteered, "I fought in lands along the Mediterranean where slaves worked salt mines. They succumbed quickly from this work, sometimes in a matter of months. There is often something associated with the salt that is in the air. The salt fumes alone are not harmful."

"I cannot afford to lose a single person, so the mining will be very slow work," Lord Franz acknowledged.

"It's not such heavy work though. Could women gather and carry out some of the smaller rocks?" Lena asked. "That would spread the labor among many."

Lord Franz leaned his head back, thinking. Sir Reiner looked at Lena curiously. "Will the women not object?"

"It depends upon how they are asked, I think. If they know it is a perilous time and their help is vital, and if they are paid, I think they would not object." Lord Franz nodded at her comment. Reiner looked from her to Franz, and then looked away. He was impressed how easily the young lord accepted her suggestion. Did she realize what sway she had over him? Lena noticed his reaction and wondered if he misunderstood Lord Franz's easy acceptance of her remark.

After they had rested, they mounted the horses and rode back to the manor. They talked about the salt process, but none of them understood it thoroughly. The distance from the village might prove to be a problem too, they decided. Lord Franz was far more sober about the project, but still hoped it might produce some income.

After they dismounted, Lena said she wanted to check with Matthew to see if milling needed to be done. She asked Lord Franz if she might return to her own village when she finished any necessary milling.

"You probably have much to do at home. I do not expect to hear from Gebhard for a few days. When I do, I will send Liebhard to fetch you. You will have to be in charge here while I am gone. Sir Reiner will be your military man, and Liebhard will be able to help you as you require," he said, somewhat formally, to establish the authority he gave her. "When you are ready to leave for your home, come in to see me." Reiner bowed in response to Lord Franz's remark, but Lena found his face inscrutable.

Liebhard accompanied her down to the village and they did find that several hours of milling were required. Liebhard was a joy to work with, she found. Each thing that he learned seemed to be burned into his memory, especially when she explained it in detail. His strength made the arduous part of the job easy, and he seemed to love the rhythm of the milling.

Having completed the cleanup of the hoppers and stones, they closed down the sluice and the mill, and walked back up toward the manor.

"I will miss you these days you are gone. Please greet my parents for me, and the children," he said, after a long silence.

"I will," she said. "Do you have any tasks for me to do?"

He shook his head, but took her hand for a moment and squeezed it lightly.

Lord Franz was sitting with Sir Reiner and Sir Heinrich at the table in the hall when they entered.

Lena made a curtsey for the benefit of the knights.

"I have finished the milling, Lord Franz. I will return to Millers Village now and wait for word from you."

"I thank you, Lena. Please greet Klaus and Greta and the other villagers for me. I will see you in a few days," he answered.

She gathered her few belongings from Oona's room. Once outside, she found Liebhard waiting beside her horse. He lifted her onto Pisces and kissed her hand.

Her next days at home were busy but at the same time empty. Her secure mill and life in Millers Village seemed humdrum after the intensity of planning and her duties at the manor. She scolded herself, thinking that her importance in Lord Franz's present situation was temporary. Her days were full, catching up on work, but her nights were restless. She missed both Liebhard and Lord Franz, and she worried that the latter would not be well enough for his trip to Trier. She worried that Etta now saw her as her enemy. She tried to imagine how the salt mining could be done.

At the manor, the time was also relatively quiet. Reiner and Heinrich exercised with Lord Franz, whose shoulder was better but quite stiff. They did a bit of mounted training with him as well. Liebhard was working hard on the houses in the village, and Reiner often spent hours each day with him, occasionally adding an extra pair of hands when heavy work was needed. Liebhard was expressively appreciative, laughed easily and made everyone happy to work with him. Reiner felt like he could ask him nearly anything, and often did find himself asking certain questions.

"I have been curious that you sleep upstairs at the manor, and I think Lena sometimes does too," he said.

"Oh that is because of me. I find it hard to sleep-impossible, really-when I am alone. Lena has only slept up in Lord Conrad's room when Klaus and Greta are visiting." He was not bothered by Reiner's question. He continued in a comical vein, "Of course Lena and Lord Franz shared a room for weeks on end when he was very sick and recovering. They had some cat fights over the silliest things too—like a pair of kids. She was really annoyed and she resisted the idea of marrying soon to protect her if Dieter came back. Now she has agreed."

Reiner did not know what to make of Liebhard's last sentences. He also felt his spirits plummet. Finally he said, "I don't understand."

"Oh, Lord Franz thought from the moment he started getting well that Lena and I were betrothed. That was not true. She wants time. She even became angry when I said something. Now she says she will marry me sometime when she is ready. I have known her since we were very small. We are almost the same age. I have loved her always."

Although he spent the rest of the afternoon with Liebhard, his heart was still heavy when they walked up to the manor. Liebhard was a very lucky man.

Reiner was sharpening his sword when Lord Franz found him the next morning. "Do you know where Liebhard is? I have had a message from Gebhard, and want to leave as soon as possible for Trier. I need Liebhard to go down and get Lena."

"Liebhard is out dressing wood, outside the village. I will ride down to fetch her if you like," he said. Lord Franz nodded.

Reiner ordered his horse, and rode down toward Miller Village with a light heart. He was curious to see this village where some of his favorite people lived. The fields were all bare or stubbled and frost had touched overnight. He was happy to be riding through this countryside on a sunny morning. The village came into view. A few cottages looked empty, but the stone mill stood strong and clean lined beside the track. He saw the curling smoke from the chimneys and roof holes of several houses. He rode up to the mill, dismounted, and knocked at the door. Lena herself opened it.

"Oh. Good morning, Sir Reiner," she said, and waited for him to speak. She noted the knight was dressed in a plain tunic, but his sword hung at his side. He was a handsome man, she decided. His long copper brown hair was clean and neatly cut, and his features, though strong, were pleasing. Reiner noticed her kerchief was slid back from her brow, revealing glistening brown hair, with just a touch of gold. She wore a patch over her right eye.

"Lord Franz has sent me to bring you to the manor. I was sent because Liebhard is not in the village at the moment." She nodded and said she must let her children and Hans know. He bowed slightly and said he would saddle her horse.

After she had grabbed her cloak and run down the road, Reiner went to the barn. It was clean and well kept. Pisces looked up alertly when he entered. He saddled the charger, and brought him outside, then waited.

Lena came running back and said she had to gather a few things together. He waited. When she came out, she still wore the patch.

"Are you going to wear your patch?" Sir Reiner asked.

"Oh," she said, flustered. She was so used to wearing it most of the day that she had forgotten she still had it on. She took it off and stuffed it into her bag without any explanation. She was not going to tell him her history.

"Do you have weakness in that eye?" he asked

"I will tell you about it sometime," she said noncommittally.

Her abruptness was unexpected. He bowed slightly and turned his eyes away as she mounted her horse. He was embarrassed. He had presumed too much familiarity. He set a quick pace. He could not tell if she was irritated, but she herself felt mean spirited. They did not speak at all, adding to her discomfort.

Lord Franz was eager and agitated when she arrived. He asked Lena to sit down with him at the table. First, he was bursting to tell her the news he had received. Elena was alive and well. One of his knights, Jergen, had died of the pestilence, and Elena's maid had died later. Sir Gebhard asked him to come as soon as he could. He had little to report about salt, except that there was none available to purchase in Trier! Lord Franz was worried because of his brother's urgency.

"You must hurry then. Do not overtire yourself. You are helpful to no one if you are sick. Is there anything more you would like to tell me about my duties before you leave?"

"Make the decisions you deem best if anything occurs that we have not discussed. I will try to send word if need be. I hope we will all be back within a week." Reiner, who was standing nearby, nodded that he understood. He thought they sounded more like family members than lord and miller.

Lena walked out with Lord Franz and Sir Reiner and stood with Liebhard, who had rushed up from the village, as Lord Franz and Sir Heinrich mounted their horses. They watched as the two riders disappeared into the distance. Lena sighed, "We are on our own." Something about those words pleased Reiner.

The rest of the day passed smoothly. Liebhard had left the manor immediately to rejoin the workers working on the rebuilding of the village houses. Lena went down to the village to find Matthew and learn the events of the past week. The villagers were in the midst of slaughtering several pigs and she made notes for Lord Franz. She checked the mill to see what work awaited her, and talked to the young baker, who reported what flour she would need in the next several days.

When she returned to the manor, it was not yet time for supper. Sir Reiner was seated at the table writing. She stood a moment, wondering if she should interrupt him. He had strong chiseled features, weathered from hard years of travel and war. His hands were beautiful, though scarred. He looked up and gestured for her to sit. He folded his paper and leaned back in his chair, apparently expecting her to speak.

"I do not know how I should work with you, Sir Reiner. I am only a miller, I am a widow, I am from a different village, and yet Lord Franz expects that I act in his place. I am certain that I can hardly command you to do something...." Her voice trailed off slightly as she looked at him.

Reiner looked up into her eyes, but did not answer immediately. Then he stood up. "Let us sit." When she did, he copied her. "It is an unusual situation for both of us. I do not understand why this is so. Yet I intend to support you as I would Lord Franz, because this is his wish. I will consider your decisions as his, but on any defensive matter, please allow me to advise you," he answered.

Lena sat a moment, wondering if this was a wholehearted commitment. She wanted more assurance that he understood her position. "I will tell you a little about the past few months so that you can see how I have arrived here," she said, thinking that it would be better that he know actual facts than hear what rumors might be about.

"My village was devastated by the pestilence," she began. She left out everything that was not pertinent, particularly her own intimate details, wherever she could, and finished at his arrival with Sir Gebhard. Reiner listened, combining this information with what he already knew. He also had a chance to look at her while she spoke.

"Your husband sounds like a scoundrel. You seem a woman of great understanding and I wonder that you married such a one."

"I will tell you so that you understand—you may know already." She told him about her shock when Lord Franz had named her "Dead eye Miller's daughter," and that only then had she known others thought her ugly. She had only known that before Dieter no one had shown an interest in her. Reiner was shocked. He had not imagined any of this. He could not even visualize her as other than she sat before him now.

"And Lord Franz suggested the patch?" he surmised.

"Yes. It was a great kindness that I could not accept at first."

Sir Reiner continued to look at her. To her surprise, he leaned forward and said, "Since you have told me about yourself, I will tell you a little about me." He told her the skeleton of his history, a second son of a vassal in the east of the empire. His father, a proud and intolerant man, wanted him to become a priest. He was educated at a monastery, but refused to take orders. His father cut him from the family. With some help from a cousin he was able to acquire a horse and equipment and became an itinerant knight, a ministerale, serving where he could. He was presently a member of the count's retinue, and sent by the count to assist Sir Gebhard. "At my age, I serve, but without great prospects," he finished.

"I am honored by your confidences, Sir Reiner. I will gladly accept your assistance," she said meekly. He held her eyes for a moment, a warm smile spreading over his face.

The following week proved uneventful. The three left in charge, Lena, Sir Reiner and Liebhard, found that they worked together very easily. At first, Lena's hardest problem was what to do at mealtimes. Ordinarily she and Liebhard would have eaten after the knight. When at the first noon dinner, Sir Reiner looked at her questioningly after she set food out on the table for him, she became flustered. What did he expect?

"Let us eat our meals together, so that we can discuss what we are doing," he said.

Lena put bowls and cups at two more places, had Liebhard sit across from Reiner and she sat next to Liebhard. They ate in near silence that first dinner. After that, Liebhard rattled on with the knight very naturally. She was surprised until she learned in the evening that not only had Liebhard moved down to sleep in Sir Reiner's room while Lord Franz was gone, but they had been working on the cottages together. Lena assumed that Lord Franz had explained to the knight that the young man found it difficult to sleep alone in a room. But of course this was not true: Liebhard had told Reiner himself. Lena trusted that Liebhard would not tell the knight personal information. Why this concerned her she could not explain to herself.

In fact the two men talked for some time each night after they went to bed. Reiner was curious about Miller Village and quickly learned a great deal about Liebhard's family and Lena's. Liebhard was full of information about the house construction, and discussed every detail with the knight. Reiner knew nearly as much about the subject as Liebhard.

Between Sir Reiner and Lena, there was far less direct conversation. She was pulled into their discussion by the knight's interest in their village. He was willing to listen to all of Liebhard's stories, which inevitably required participation by her. She could not fathom what he enjoyed about their bucolic homes. He would sigh occasionally after particular stories, and once or twice he even said they were lucky to have such happy memories. Reiner did see their lives as pleasant and almost idyllic compared to his own. He did not remember many pleasant times in his childhood.

REUNION

Lena was milling with Liebhard when Max, the bailiff's son came running down to find her. Lord Franz, his wife, brother, and the knights had returned. She stopped milling, left all the cleanup work for later, and rushed up to manor with Liebhard. When she arrived, everyone had already entered the manor except for Sir Reiner and young Markus.

"Lord Franz asked where you were, and sent for you," Sir Reiner said. He walked with her toward the door, speaking softly only for her ears, "Please remember he now has his family around him." Lena was not sure why this advice was given, but she knew it was well meant. He stood aside so that she could walk in ahead of him.

No one except Sir Heinrich and another knight was in the hall. She stood, not sure what she should do. Oona came in from the back of the manor a few minutes later.

"Oh, Lena, Lord Franz asked that you go up to the solar," she said.

Lena climbed the stairs. When she entered the room, Lord Franz was waiting for her. "We are back safely! I have much to tell you, but first, is all well here?"

"It has been very quiet. Sir Reiner has been a steady support," she replied.

"Good! Good!" He then launched into all of his news. Elena was resting, so Lena would be introduced later. She was still distraught over her experience, particularly the death of her waiting woman, a young woman from a knightly family. The archbishop's household had suffered many deaths from the plague, about one in three people. The archbishop did give Lord Franz's fief to his brother. About salt he had little to report. The city had been in turmoil and many merchants were dead, so little business could be transacted.

"I have asked my brother to consult with you about how to mine the salt. We need to use as many people from my village and Millers Village as possible. You will have to see what we must pay workers and how we can use men and women so that all stay healthy. I am sure you are eager to go home, so you must arrange with him how you will work together in the next days. He will have to leave soon to check on my, now his, fief. After he leaves, I hope you can oversee that mine work with Sir Reiner and Matthew. Can you do this?"

"I will do what I can. I thought you would want to oversee this," she said hesitantly. She was surprised by his brisk plans for her. She had expected she would now be going home.

Lord Franz looked at her for a moment. He sighed. "Something is troubling my wife. She was nearly hysterical when my brother arrived. She keeps saying she is relieved and happy now that she is with me, but she is not. I must see if I can calm her mind."

Suddenly he sat down, and motioned for her to do the same.

"Her waiting woman, Clara of Midlin, did not die of the pestilence. The terrible deaths had all but stopped. She fell downstairs and died. That is all that I have learned, but Clara's death is what troubles her. She does nothing but weep when I think she is on the verge of telling me more," he confided, tears causing his own eyes to glisten.

Sir Gebhard came in and greeted Lena. He sat down, launching in immediately about the salt mine. Lord Franz got up and left the room. Lena listened to Sir Gebhard's plans, volunteering information about the number of able-bodied men and women, and what pay incentive would be needed to get the largest number working. Some days could be automatically counted on from the manor's village, but many more days would be needed. Sir Gebhard wrote down information.

"Did my brother tell you that I am off to my new fief in just a few days?" Gebhard asked rather suddenly.

"Yes, congratulations, Sir Gebhard," she said, surprised that he should interject this.

"I am not looking forward to being a lord of an estate. I did not want a fief. I prefer to serve the count in his retinue, and have wanted to be a scribe for him," he said wistfully. "Or I would like to stay here and work with Franz to develop this mine and find markets for the salt."

Lena did not know where to look, or what to say. She sat mutely, looking past him. He had been brusque and commanding in his interactions with her. Yet she had sensed he was a gentle sensitive man. Now she thought how uncomfortable he was in a leadership position.

"I don't mean to trouble you with my problems. I will help with as much planning as I can. I have told Franz I will leave Sir Reiner here to help. He has seen salt mining, and I think he will be a great help. You will find him a dependable partner in this undertaking."

"He will be, I am sure. Sir Gebhard, you have been writing while we have been talking. You know that I can read very little, and only Latin…how shall I know what you are saying?"

He laughed impishly, and she saw that bit of a tease she had noticed before in his demeanor. He leaned over, passing his paper to her. He had written a few words, several simple pictures and many numbers. She studied it and realized she knew almost everything he had put on the paper. It was wonderful. She could not smother a chuckle.

"Thank you, Sir Gebhard!"

The young man laughed, but he had turned quite red. She sensed that the sharp abrupt man she had thought him to be was a complete facade. He did not enjoy the role of a man of action, a man in charge. She thought about his future with his own fief. He would not be happy.

Putting that thought aside, she asked him several questions about his notes. They went over detail after detail, hammering out plans. She asked Sir Gebhard if they should not bring Sir Reiner into their discussion, and he agreed. She went down to the hall, but found that Sir Reiner was not at the table with the other knights: he was standing before the fireplace at the end of the hall. Sir Heinrich sat with Lord Franz's knight, Sir Manfred, who eyed her and made some remark to Heinrich that she could not catch. Sir Reiner turned abruptly, a face suffused with irritation, but when he saw her he came forward to her immediately.

"Yes, Lena?"

"Sir Gebhard has asked if you can come up to the solar," she said, for the first time seeing this new knight, Sir Manfred, close at hand. He was a stunning young man: his long copper gold hair glinted each time he moved. He had turned and stared at her, making her feel very uncomfortable. Did he wonder why a peasant seemed to have a position of intimacy here? He looked about Lord Franz's age. His clothing was superior in every way to all the other knights and lords she had seen in her life. She would have judged him handsome except for his unpleasant demeanor just now. He was about the height of Reiner and Franz, but slightly more heavily made.

When they arrived at the solar, Sir Gebhard launched into their plans. Sir Reiner laughed at the younger knight's page of information, but he had many questions. His germane questions sobered the other two. His approach helped them to concentrate on how they were going to proceed. It was late in the afternoon by the time they had finished and decided on plans for the next day.

As their meeting broke up and they stood up, Lord Franz looked in at the door.

"Finished planning?" he asked. "Lena, please stay a moment. Lady Elena will be coming in soon."

Sir Reiner, bowed and would have left, but Lord Franz motioned for him to stay. They began to tell Lord Franz some of their plans, but stopped as the young lady appeared next to Lord Franz.

"Elena, you have met Sir Reiner. This is Lena, our miller, from Millers Village."

Lena curtsied. The woman nodded slightly to her, as Lord Franz described in a few sentences how Lena had helped him in these last months. Lena was able to study the young lady, glancing up at her once or twice. She was young, probably only seventeen or eighteen. She was fair haired, elegant, and probably quite pretty. Her eyes were swollen from the many tears she had shed. There was a shadow of dread or fear about her.

"My husband would be dead today, but for you. I thank you from the bottom of my heart. Now you continue to aid him for which I know he is appreciative."

Lena felt herself blush, but she replied, "I have been honored to help Lord Franz, and hope to assist you also in any way that I can." To her surprise, Lady Elena gulped back a sob, tried to smile, and turned and left the room. Lena as well as Reiner was stunned. Lena looked sharply at Lord Franz, wondering what she had done. He raised his hand slightly and shook his head. He then quickly entered into light discussion and a short time later their group broke up.

Lena took this moment to ask Lord Franz if she might go back to Millers village overnight. He readily agreed that she should, that she must have many things to do. Lena left the solar a few moments after Sir Reiner, but found that he had waited for her at the top of the stairs. He leaned back to let her pass, then followed her down. When they were halfway down the stairs, she half turned and asked, "What is it?"

After a pause he said, "I was thinking we should ride out to the mine tomorrow with Matthew, and maybe Liebhard, and see how we will set up our rock grinding and brining." She was sure that he had changed his mind about what he was originally going to say. She continued down the stairs.

"When I come back tomorrow, we should go. Will you talk to Sir Gebhard and Matthew and arrange for us all to go?" He nodded slightly. He followed close behind her down the stairs.

When they reached the hall, they saw Sir Manfred still seated at the table. Once again she sensed a boldness about him toward her. Perhaps he just wanted her to know her place. He seemed to be a pompous person. She was happy to have Sir Reiner near her. Reiner, who had already taken a dislike toward Manfred, walked with her to the back of the hall and waited while she went to get her things, then walked with her out of the manor. He was not about to let this quite special woman be pestered by the likes of Manfred. It was apparent to Lena that Reiner was showing her special care: he had noticed the young knight's unpleasantness.

Lena asked Max to get Pisces ready, bade Sir Reiner goodbye, and went down to find Liebhard. He was sitting with several men, looking at the house that they had just finished roofing. It was the final damaged house they were repairing before

89

they started new construction on six houses. He got up and came to her when he saw her. She told him she was going home for the night, and he immediately said he would go too. They walked back up to the courtyard and she waited while he went in to get his things.

When Liebhard came out, Sir Reiner followed him. They were joking about missing their roommates. Max brought the horses up and they mounted. Reiner raised his hand in goodbye. They waved and turned toward home. Lena was so happy to be heading toward Millers Village. She had felt overtaxed by the responsibilities she had shouldered, and had trepidations about what the next few weeks would bring. She was escaping to security for at least one night.

Mirroring her thoughts, Liebhard exclaimed, "I am happy to be on the way home!" Lena laughed and nodded. They urged their horses into a brisk trot, enjoying the invigorating early December wind gusts. They were in the village in no time. Liebhard jumped off his horse, grabbed Lena from Pisces and twirled her in the air. He put her down and hugged her tightly, still exhilarated by their happiness. He let her go, to her surprise, and took the reins of the horses. She followed him with her eyes as he led them into the barn. She had not wanted their intimate moment to end, yet he had ended it. She followed him into the barn, and unsaddled Pisces herself.

"Christmas is only three weeks away. I have not had a moment to think about it," she said, taking off the horse's bridle as she spoke. "I hope we can spend the twelve days of Christmas here, and not working at the mine."

"You must tell Lord Franz that these days are always days of celebration," Liebhard answered.

He did not speak often, except to Sir Reiner, she thought, but he always spoke to the point, and honestly. The thought came to her that there was really no reason to put off marrying. Perhaps they had to wait until Dieter was declared an outlaw. She would have to ask Lord Franz. Why not marry as soon as all seemed settled? She felt almost a jolt come over her when she realized what a turnabout in her thinking this was.

"Liebhard, I am thinking we should marry as soon as Lord Franz tells us it is acceptable, you know, that Dieter is no longer my husband," she said hesitantly. He turned toward her and looked over her horse's back into her eyes. His eyes were not filled with unbridled excitement, but rather happiness mixed with a frown of concern.

"Lena, we do not have to hurry. I just want to know we will marry, and I want to be sure that I can protect you from Dieter if he returns."

"I know," she said meekly. "I will talk to Lord Franz about it." She reached her hand up above the horse's back, and Liebhard leaned forward, kissing it and taking it into his own hand.

They returned companionably to the work of settling the horses for the night, and then left the barn together. They embraced and she kissed him on the cheek. He went with her into the mill to greet Klaus and Greta, but left a few minutes later to go to his family.

The evening was filled with many tasks that she had not been able to do because she had been away. Klaus seemed very restless but she was not able to discover why. Greta had missed her very much, and wanted to sit close beside her as they worked. This business of being away so much was not good for the children. They had lost their parents and now she was gone for long periods. She would have to work something out with Lord Franz so that she could be home most or all nights, and only go up to the manor on those days she was really needed.

She spent a restless night, worried about what she would say to Lord Franz, about what she was expected to do in the salt mine work, about how much more Lord Franz would need her at the manor, and about what her future with Liebhard would be. The next morning she woke with a heavy heart. She did not want to go back up to the manor. It was different now, with the knights, Gebhard and Elena there. She no longer had the close relationship with her once almost brother. She sighed. Of course everything had to change, had to come back to normal. She was silly to expect otherwise.

She had finished breakfast with Klaus and Greta by the time Liebhard opened the door and gave them a jovial good morning. He had been happy to be with his family: that was plain to see. He had a new dark blue tunic under his cloak, she noticed. It brought out the blue in his eyes. He sat down to take some small beer while she finished getting ready. Just before they left, Lena untied the patch from her eye and put it in her pocket. Liebhard went ahead to prepare the horses while she made her goodbyes to the children. She told them she would be home in the evening. She hoped it would be so.

When they reached the manor courtyard, all was still quiet. Lena mused to herself that villagers rose earlier to do their many chores before knights and lords stirred. They handed their reins to the waiting Max and entered the manor. At odds with her previous thought, Sir Reiner was waiting for them. His greeting was particularly warm to both of them, and she had the impression that he had missed their company. They had been a very successful trio. Reiner and Liebhard fell into a lively conversation about Liebhard's family. Lena listened with interest, both because Liebhard shared all of his news so freely, and because Sir Reiner was evidently interested.

At a pause in their conversation, Sir Reiner turned to her and said, "Sir Gebhard will be down shortly. He went up to see if his brother might want to come along after all." He seemed to expect her to respond, but she had nothing to say, and only nodded.

A few minutes later, both brothers came down. They greeted everyone, Lord Franz giving Lena a warm smile. "I would have liked to come along, but I am sure my brother will be able to report to me all that I need to know. While you are there, please try to plan how we are going to prepare the rock to get the salt out. Besides getting it out of the mine, it's is our biggest challenge." He came out with them as they prepared to saddle up. Matthew was waiting for them on one of the village draft horses. In moments they were off.

They rode together in a companionable group, and during most of the ride Sir Gebhard rode beside Lena with Reiner on her other side. Sir Gebhard and Lena had fixed upon a simple plan of moving the rock out of the cave by using as many people as they could muster, possibly as many as three dozen men and women, constantly rotating them so that no one was in the cave overlong. This was about half of all the people in the two villages, a huge challenge. Lena and Matthew were expected to find these workers, and Lena was to try to feel out what pay they would need to offer to get the workers. They discussed how many hours it was reasonable to expect the workers to spend at the mine. The winter days were short and the travel to and fro cut into possible working hours and they worried over the unhealthy air in the mine. It was settled that the hours would be no more than five each day.

As the mine came into view, Lena noticed how different the area looked around it. She had observed this when she saw it for the first time a few days before. There were no bushes, no plants, but it was a field of broken rock. She unconsciously pulled up on the reins, and her horse stopped. Sir Gebhard stopped his horse too, and looked at her quizzically. Everyone turned to look in the direction she was looking. Off to her left Sir Reiner suddenly whooped, spooking the horses.

"What's going on?" Sir Gebhard asked. Lena guessed that Sir Reiner had seen something different than she had.

"I was noticing how all the rocks are strewn around in small, crushed pieces, and there is hardly any plant growing here. I thought it showed that the earlier miners broke up the stone right here, after taking it out of the mine. All of these little pieces are full of salt, and now nothing grows here."

Sir Reiner laughed and said exultantly, "You are right. But there is something far more exciting, I think, if we ride around to the left, just beyond the edge of the cliff!" He turned his horse and edged it into a gallop. Everyone copied him. About five minutes later they stopped their horses. They were at the edge of a very large marsh. The harsh grass growing there, now brown in the winter cold, was unfamiliar to Lena. Sir Reiner jumped off his horse, with the energy and excitement of a young boy. He walked along the edge of the marsh his arms held wide. In his simple dark green tunic and leggings, with no sword on his wide leather belt, he looked more like a wealthy peasant than a knight. His hair, ruffled by a light breeze looked almost bronze. His excitement was contagious and they all waited for him to speak.

"We are looking out over a salt marsh! Water must be seeping out from the cliff. I noticed this raised ground next to the cliff. It is not natural. Someone built this long ago, making brining pools to reduce the salty water to a very thick brine, so that it can be cooked down much more quickly. I have seen this, or something like it, in Venetia."

"How does it work? Explain it to us," Sir Gebhard said.

"I am not sure how it was done here, but this is what I guess. The marsh just next to the cliff has a salt spring, water seeping out of the salt in this cliff. That area was probably dug out to make a deeper pool. There might even be a pool, just covered with this grass now. Briny water is carried to the top of this raised ground and dumped into a manmade pool. A sluice gate could be opened after some of the water has evaporated, to let this water into a lower pool, and then a third pool. This final water would be very thick and briny."

With that explanation he trotted to the top of the raised area. Everyone dismounted and followed him. At the top of the hill he stopped and rubbed his foot back and forth several times. As the others reached him, he threw back his head and shouted. He knelt down, Sir Gebhard copying him, and ran his hand along the ground.

"Do you feel that? It feels like pottery, doesn't it? The surface has been tamped down hard and finished to be nearly waterproof." Lena and the others followed his lead, investigating the deep wide depression. Liebhard had gone to the far side, carefully feeling along the edge with his foot. He stopped, knelt down, and ran his had along the far edge of the depression.

"Sir Reiner, come to see this spot," Liebhard shouted. They all got up as one, and hurried to the other side. After pulling away the sedge grass, Sir Reiner, dug loose soil away to reveal the remnants of finished wood. He looked up beaming. He and Liebhard fell into excited ideas about how to rebuild the sluice. Now everyone was in a fever to check the lower areas, and able to discern, as Sir Reiner had, the terraced structure of the hill, with its three pooled depressions.

"I can hardly believe our good fortune," Sir Gebhard whooped. "Do you realize how much labor this will save?" he laughed and grabbed Lena unthinkingly by her shoulders. She did not mind, she was as excited as the rest. Everyone talked at once, like the story of the tower of Babel. Finally, Sir Gebhard raised his hand to quiet the group.

"We will have to rethink all of our plans. We should need far fewer workers. We will need to dig out the spring pond, which will take, what ten workers to do it quickly? After that, and cleaning out these standing pools, building sluice gates and filling the first pool, we will need only a few to watch the water and release it, then more to refill the upper pond. But how do we cook down the thick brine from the third pool?"

Matthew leaned forward. "That I know. We have a giant caldron we have used in the past. It is in the manor stable, I think. We cart it here, which we have not done for a few years. Reducing the brine takes quite a pile of wood, because the fire is kept going day and night. There is a whole process to do this. I am not sure I know those steps."

Sir Reiner, who had been silent, listening, more like the quiet man Lena had learned to expect, then said, "I think I understand it. You have to add blood at first when it boils, to pull away non salt parts. When the water has become a thick sludge you add beer to clean it again. During all of this time you have to stir and stir. Then you let this very thick white sludge cool slightly and salt begins to form crystals on the bottom, which you take out. You heat and cool, heat and cool, removing salt each time."

"So this stage would require just a few people? One who watches and stirs, someone to feed and tend the fire, and a wood gatherer?" Sir Gebhard asked.

"Maybe one or two more, because you have to do this day and night," Sir Reiner answered.

During all of this discussion, the group had been standing in the depression of the final pool. They turned back toward the horses and talked as they walked about the changes their discoveries would make on labor needed and time. It was clear that Lena's charge to find enough workers was greatly reduced, and her oversight of labor was much less. As the other continued their conversation, she smiled inwardly because she would not be expected to be at the mine very much at all. She could spend most of her time at home at the mill.

When they arrived at the manor, Sir Gebhard was off his horse almost before the horse stopped. By the time the others had entered the hall, the brothers could be heard running down the stairs. The excited cacophony of voices was hard to follow for Lord Franz. He laughed, threw up his hands and pleaded for one description of what they found. Sir Gebhard turned to Sir Reiner and beckoned for him to speak.

"As we arrived within view of the cave, Lena noticed something and stopped her horse. It was then that I noticed something quite different," he began. Everyone listened with rapped attention while he explained what they had found to Lord Franz, even though they knew the discovery. When he finished, all clapped and cheered, including the knights sitting at the table. After several questions about the discovery had been answered, the conversation subsided. Matthew and Liebhard bowed and left.

Sir Gebhard asked Lena and Sir Reiner to come up to the salon to discuss with him and Lord Franz how the discovery would change their plans. When they entered, the Lady Elena looked up from her needlework. Her face was drawn and sad, though she managed a warm welcome. They all sat down and Sir Gebhard asked them to please suggest how they should now proceed. After a pause, Sir Reiner, looking at Lena, said he thought their workers could probably be reduced to a dozen. He looked at her questioningly.

"I agree. This should be manageable, just more complicated in the scheduling. The way you described the work, the gate preparations will require great skill, and then for the brine reduction we need about a half dozen very steady and careful workers. For the other parts of the job, we could need a dozen altogether at the beginning. Does that sound right to you?" She realized she had directed her question to him, and not Sir Gebhard. No one questioned this.

Sir Gebhard nodded and said, "I think it is pretty clear that Sir Reiner must be in charge of the whole process. Lena, you may think your task is reduced, and in some ways it may be easier just because fewer will be needed. In fact, now, who you suggest for each job will be far more important."

Lord Franz, who had sat down by Elena, had listened closely to this conversation. He interjected a pertinent question at this point.

"When shall we start?"

Lena held her breath. She could not be the one to suggest they wait until after Christmas. Sir Gebhard would not have thought of this, since he was leaving the next morning. Sir Reiner glanced at her, but she could not read what he thought. He was thinking that he would like to start immediately. He was eager. They would make a good team, Lena and him.

"Can we not wait until after the twelve days of Christmas?" Elena asked. She had looked at Lord Franz, but then her gaze fell on Lena. Lena knew that she had flushed and smiled at the lady's question. Elena rewarded her with glad eyes and a slight smile.

Lord Franz stretched his legs out in front of him, smiled at Elena and responded, "That is an excellent idea! We will start in the new year."

In the following conversation, Sir Gebhard bemoaned the fact that he could not be part of their exciting project. He said many kind words of thanks to Lena and Sir Reiner. Lena caught Lord Franz's eye and mouthed her own question, "wedding." He grinned and said, "Stay a moment, Lena, so that we can talk about a few things." The knights left the salon together.

"Lena, would you be embarrassed if Elena stayed?"

"Franz, of course she might be," Elena said, getting up.

"Please stay, Lady Elena," Lena said, although she was not sure why she said it.

"Lord Franz, Liebhard and I have decided to marry, as I told you. But what about Dieter?" Her eyes flicked toward Elena, and she saw that the young lady was apprised of this information. "Can we marry before he is brought before the court and judged?"

"This is an apt question. I can declare a court date here this week on the question of the thefts. He will be declared outlaw for that. For the murder accusation, I can write the count to bring that before his court to have him charged. This can all be done before Christmas. Murder, as a capital offense, must be judged in a royal court. The count will let me know when that can be arranged. I will ask in my letter to the count if the murder charge itself would free you to marry."

Lena felt the tears come into her eyes even though she laughed happily.

"I suppose you are eager to make plans for Christmas with the children?" he asked, smiling. "Elena, I think Lena should bring Klaus and Greta up to meet you tomorrow. You have heard a lot about them already. They entertained me through some trying times."

"Yes, do bring them," she agreed. "Can you come in the morning and have dinner with us?"

Lena nodded happily, curtsied, smiled at Lord Franz's wink, and left the room.

Downstairs again, she found Sir Gebhard in conversation with his knights and Sir Manfred. She nodded and would have gone out quietly, but Sir Gebhard turned with her and followed her out the door.

"I am sorry to leave and go to my fief. You know it is not my wish. I want to thank you for your help while I have been here. I think I owe you an apology for how brusque I was at first."

"No. You were worried about your brother and your family. You have been fair and kind to me," she replied.

He smiled, called Max to get her horse. He waited with her, telling her a little about the fief he was acquiring. They both turned when the manor door opened and Sir Reiner came out.

"Shall we see you again before Christmas?" he asked. The manor would not be interesting to him without Lena and Liebhard. Lena, oblivious of his thoughts, explained that she would be bringing her adopted children up to meet Elena in the morning.

"And Liebhard, will he be riding home with you now?" he asked.

Just then Max returned with Pisces.

"Sir Reiner, will you do me the kindness of informing Liebhard that I have gone home to Millers Village? He must speak to Lord Franz to see if he may come to spend the holidays at home."

Sir Gebhard interjected, "Yes, he must spend the holidays at home. I will tell Franz I have said it will be so." In a surprise gesture, he took Lena's hand in his. "I leave at sunrise, so I bid you goodbye," and he bowed slightly.

Max held her horse while she mounted. She looked down at these two very kind knights, smiled and thanked them.

Klaus and Greta were thrilled to hear that they would go to see Franz and his wife the next morning. Together with Lena they checked their clothes, sponged and brushed them. Lena practiced with them how to bow and curtsey, and how to address the lady. They were so excited it was hard to get them to go to bed. Lena waited restlessly for some time, expecting Liebhard to come by. Finally she decided he must be staying at the manor for the night and she went to bed too.

The next morning after all the chores were done, Lena sent Klaus to tell Hans and Anna that they were going up to the manor for the day. Then they all cleaned up and dressed in their best clothes. Klaus had already saddled Pisces, so Lena lifted Greta up into the saddle, and Klaus climbed up behind her. Lena tucked up the skirt of her remade red dress so that it would not get dirt on the hem, and she walked along beside the horse to the manor.

As they entered the courtyard Max ran out to meet them. Sir Reiner was waiting near the manor door. He came forward somewhat shyly, and greeted Lena. He helped the children off the horse as she introduced them to him. They knew each other, but only by sight. After he had complimented the children, he turned to Lena. "Liebhard asked me to let him know when you arrive. I will go down to find him now—he has started on the first new house, and is very caught up in his work," he said with a chuckle. Lena had been startled to find him there waiting for them, but learning that he had a message from Liebhard, she relaxed.

They entered the manor hall. The only person there was Sir Manfred. The other knights had left with Sir Gebhard, of course, she thought. He came boldly toward her. She could feel her hair stand up on the back of her neck. She felt like she was in danger. He stopped suddenly when he saw the children behind her. To her relief, Lord Franz came running down the stairs, shouting to the children. Sir Manfred backed discreetly away. Lord Franz noticed nothing of this. Smoke came bounding behind Franz, barking in excitement. The children were smothered in greetings by man and dog. Lena's heart was full of happiness for them. They had been very lucky to be befriended by the lord of the fief.

With some pomp he ushered the children upstairs and led them to the salon. Lady Elena came forward to greet them. Klaus and Greta, suddenly very shy, remembered to bow and curtsey, causing Lady Elena to laugh happily and take their hands. She sat them down by her and asked them many questions. The morning sped by, and soon they were called down to dinner.

The whole visit was a great success. As they prepared to leave, Lady Elena came down the stairs with them, and gave each child a little package, telling them to open them at their Christmas celebration. She leaned down and hugged Greta, and Lena saw tears in her eyes. This had been a visit that had for a short time overcome the shadow of grief that engulfed her. Lord Franz bade them all a happy Christmas, and took Lena's hand in his two hands, thanking her again for all of her kindnesses. She laughed happily and felt her face flush red. When she was outside she opened her hand to see what he had put there. It was a gold coin!

Once home, she went down to visit Anna and Hans. They gave her a warm greeting and invited her in for a hot cider. After exchanging all their news, Lena asked them about village Christmas traditions.

"This is going to be a hard Christmas for us. So many have died yet we have much to be thankful for. Father Johan always kept the holiday traditions for us. Since he died we have hardly used the church. I thought we might think about all of the things we do at Christmas and when. We should try to plan for the twelve days of Christmas, and you two are the ones who can best remember all the details."

The next hours were spent trying to organize their ideas and plans. When they finished, Lena leaned forward and suggested, "I thought I might invite everyone down to the mill tomorrow so that we can include everyone."

"Yes, Lena! That is just what your father would have suggested," Hans beamed. "Why not send Klaus and Greta to ask everyone to meet at the mill after dinner tomorrow."

And so it happened that the villagers all came together, cleaned the church, practiced hymns, and made decorations for Christmas. Liebhard and Mark found a large fir tree for the church, and the women and children trimmed it with the decorations. Without their priest, their services were a little muddled, with more singing than prayers, but their sense of wellbeing soared.

Lord Franz rode over two days before Christmas with small presents. He also had a surprise for Lena. His court had named Dieter an outlaw for his thefts, only redeemable if he paid the value of what he stole. In answer to his letter to the count, he had been informed that a royal court was to be held before Lent. While she was not yet pronounced free, the wheels were turning.

Liebhard spent every afternoon during the whole holiday season with Lena and the children. Klaus greatly admired Liebhard and liked to have him there. Lena found Liebhard was a calming influence for her as well. He was capable of great stillness. He did not press Lena though the tingling excitement that each engendered in the other could not be missed. Simple kisses and embraces were the tokens of their feelings for each other. Sometimes when he left in the late afternoon, she had trouble controlling her loneliness.

A surprise visitor on the third day after Christmas was Sir Reiner. He came bearing sweetbreads and some excellent wine. He entertained them with many stories about his experiences in foreign places. Toward the end of his visit, he confessed that although he had missed Liebhard and Lena very much, he also wanted to be away from the manor because Sir Manfred had come back from his visit to friends. He said it in such a way that his audience was greatly amused, although Lena remembered her inexplicable fear of Manfred.

All that Reiner had said was true. But Reiner was quite sure that neither of these two could imagine how much he had missed them. The few short days they had been responsible for the estate had been some of the best days he had experienced in his life. There was also no doubt how much he disliked and did not trust Sir Manfred. The young Knight was insufferable. He never stopped talking about women as if all were women of easy virtue, and had certainly put fear into the hearts of some of the pretty girls in the village, and in their fathers. From other remarks the young knight had made, Reiner deduced that he skirted loyalty and truth whenever he could.

"I beg you to let me come each afternoon until the end of the holidays. It will be a kindness to me." As he said this Lena saw the request was directed toward her. He knew that Liebhard would agree gladly. He was not quite sure about her feelings.

"We will be honored to have you here," she responded. She noticed limpid warmth in his eyes, which for a moment overcame his habitual melancholy. He bowed slightly. A short time later he bade them goodbye.

Sir Reiner's visits continued each day. He was introduced to all of the villagers and was well received. He was happy to learn that Lena had arranged to have Mark, Lars and Karl join Liebhard in working at the mine. When Klaus wondered if he could work also, Sir Reiner said he was big enough that he might help. Lena was at first shocked. She mentally shook herself. Klaus was nearly twelve. He was a big twelve-year-old. Now she thought she had been tardy in thinking about his future. He should be learning his father's blacksmith trade as well.

Finally the holidays came to an end. Sir Reiner had asked on the last day that Lena and Liebhard plan to come to the manor early the next morning, along with the other villagers who planned to work. He asked that they bring wooden clogs, shovels and other specific tools. Liebhard laughed and thanked Sir Reiner for their marching orders. This was so typical of the boisterous relationship between the two men. There was no class distinction between them. Sir Reiner's reaction to Liebhard's remark was to slap him on the back and laugh. For his part, Reiner saw Liebhard as the kind of brother he wished he had.

When they arrived at the manor village the next morning nine villagers and Sir Reiner were waiting for them. They had harnessed horses to two carts. Most of the workers climbed into the carts, while Liebhard, Lena and Sir Reiner rode their horses. Lord Franz came down just before they left and saw them off. He said he hoped to come out later in the morning.

Sir Reiner had plotted out in his mind how they would proceed. He rode beside Lena, explaining to her what he thought they should plan to do. They had barely arrived before he had the men organized at the side of the manmade hill, carefully checking the marsh at the edge of the cliff wall. They used long poles and hoes to pull at the dead grass laying on the surface of the pool. In no time they had begun to open the center next to the wall. The pool seemed very deep, and there was a slight current visible in the water. Sir Reiner himself waded carefully along the edge into the cold whirling water. He reached down along the wall, laughed and came back out of the water.

"What luck! There is a salt spring just where I reached my hand. We have no digging to do here! So head up this hill everyone and I will show you what to do." He got everyone started carefully digging out the first shallow pond. A fire had been started near the edge of the first pool, and Reiner sat down, removing his boots. He had heavy socks over his leggings, which he removed and began to wring them out. Lena took them from him without ceremony, wrung them out and used sticks to hang them nearer the fire. Reiner smothered a chuckle. She was definitely a take charge person.

"Put your feet nearer the fire or you will get frostbite," she ordered.

With so many workers they had the first pond clean before noon. Two of the manor village carpenters had begun building a gate to Sir Reiner's specifications for the pond. Meanwhile the rest of the crew began clearing the second pond. When the gate was ready, they stopped to eat a packed meal that Sir Reiner had in one of the carts.

"What do you think, Lena? I think we will need fewer workers tomorrow. We have had thirteen today, plus Klaus. In fact, with eight men tomorrow we can make a good start on cutting wood. We should finish clearing the third pond tomorrow and cut wood all day. Then only one or two will be needed to check the evaporation of the water in the first pond and some wood cutting for at least a week or two."

"So few! It will be weeks before we are ready to cook the brine then?"

"I am thinking we will not be cooking before February. The evaporation is a slow process, especially if we get wet weather. We should think of a way to cover the ponds during rain or snow. Do you think we could stitch together cow hides or weave this marsh grass? What can we use?"

Lena looked at the grass. It was very tall, well above her head, and very coarse. She took a sickle and walked out to the edge of the marsh. She cut an armful and sat down to try to do a rough weave. She was not a good weaver. The grass edges were sharp and she soon had several cuts on her hands. But the grass was very tough. She was hopeful that this might work. Reiner came over, squatted and watched her work.

"Don't watch too closely. I am not very good at weaving," she laughed.

Reiner picked up one of the long marsh grass blades. It was extremely tough but not brittle. There were small sharp teeth along the sides of the blade. He saw Lena's hands already had many small cuts in just these few minutes. He thought her hands were well shaped with straight fingers and well-made nails. They were a little chafed. This was not pleasant work to be doing outside in the cold.

"We know these will weave well, we just have to decide how to do it. Are there women yet alive in either village who might be able to choose a good method? Stop, Lena, you are hurting your hands."

Lena stopped immediately. His tone had been abrupt. "Yes, I know of one in my village, and at least one well known weaver in Lord Franz's village."

They both stood up, each holding some of the marsh grass. Reiner took her hand and turned it over, looking at the scratches. He did not immediately drop her hand. He called to two of the workers, and asked them to bring sickles over.

Lena picked up her sickle, and with the workers was able to fill one cart before the other workers had filled the first pond. Liebhard had picked up a sickle and cut enough to start a pile in the second cart.

Everyone had worked very hard and willingly. Sometime before sunset, Sir Reiner called it a day, praising all the workers. Having talked to Lena earlier, he named the workers he wanted on the following day, and picked three men he wanted to work each day for the following week. They packed up their tools and headed back to the manor village, tired but content that they had done a good day's work.

Riding behind the carts, Sir Reiner and Lena planned forward for the next several weeks what workers they would need. Lena was to manage the pay each worker should receive, based upon her discussions with Lord Franz and with these men. She was to organize the weaving of the marsh grass into mats during the next week. Liebhard rode on Lena's other side, listening. Sir Reiner had asked him to oversee the work when the knight was not at the mine.

"These will be very large mats. I will ask Lord Franz if we can work in the keep," Lena said.

"Better to ask him to use the manor hall. These mats will have to be twelve feet across, and circular, if that is possible." Reiner suggested.

"Twelve feet!" I have not had very much experience weaving, and certainly nothing of any size like that. Let us hope Anna and some of the older women will have some good ideas," she said thoughtfully.

Back at the manor village, she walked down quickly to find the woman she knew as a good weaver. She explained what she wanted to do, and asked her if she could get together at least a half dozen women to start weaving early in the morning.

The Miller Village people travelled home together, Klaus riding behind Lena. He had had a very big day, and nearly fell asleep on the way home. When they reached their village and said their good nights, Liebhard lifted Klaus off the horse, and Lena walked with him into the mill. When Liebhard had put Pisces away, he came in too.

Greta had managed to keep the pottage warm, and the pig shank gave the stew a delicious aroma. Lena busily got the food on the table, and they ate the bread and stew ravenously. They talked and laughed as they told Greta about their day. Lena praised the young girl for how well she had managed while they were gone. Soon it was bedtime for the young ones, and Klaus drowsily said good night as he and Greta went up to bed.

Lena and Liebhard sat comfortably at the table. Liebhard stretched out his legs, arched his back and yawned. "It was a big day, but a very good day. Reiner is a good leader, isn't he?"

"Yes. It is too bad he did not have the support of his family, because I think he could have become a great lord," she answered.

Liebhard said nothing for a moment. "He is satisfied. He has been happy in these days he has been in Lord Franz's service."

"I think he was not a happy man when he first came," she countered.

"We two have made him happy," he answered. Lena stared at him, but knew he spoke the simple truth. She wondered what he thought about Reiner's obvious attraction to her. He looked up and she felt the magnetic pull of his eyes. She got up and stood before him. He reached out and pulled her down into his lap, drawing her close against his chest. She found her breath coming fast, as was his. She wanted to stay there, pressed into him. After a tantalizing moment, he sat up straight, kissed her face and mouth, sighed, almost shrugging himself, and lifted her back onto her feet.

"I love you, Lena. Now I will go to my parents." He hugged her and they kissed several times affectionately. The moment had passed.

The next morning was the coldest of the year. The sky was grey and menacing, the worst weather possible for their drying ponds short of actual rain. Lena fussed with the children, telling them to take care while they did their chores outside. Liebhard and Mark travelled with Anna and Lena to the manor. Seven village men were waiting with Sir Reiner. He saw them off under Liebhard's direction, planning to follow shortly.

Lena found eight women waiting for her from the manor village. Ten women to weave would be enough she hoped. Lord Franz came out to meet them.

"Good morning, Lena. Sir Reiner spoke with me last night about this weaving. I agree that we should do this work in the hall," he said. He could not resist asking teasingly, "And you know how to weave too?"

It was a nice note upon which to start their arduous work. The women gathered up armloads of the marsh grass from the cart and carried them inside. A fire roared in the fireplace, warming the huge room slightly. While most of the women continued to bring in the grass, Anna, Oona and the other village woman, all experienced weavers, proceeded to plan how they could make a large mat. They settled upon an ingenious plan, based upon a basket weave often used. After a few false starts they found a way to work in teams of two in different positions around the big table always interweaving with the next team in.

As soon as Sir Reiner saw they were off to a good start he left. Lord Franz was very interested in the process, and walked around their circle watching. He even took Lena's position to see how the work was done. In moments he had several cuts.

"This grass is coarse! You will not be able to work long without protection. Oona, we need rags from the kitchen to wrap on fingers and palms."

When the rags were brought, he insisted upon devising makeshift coverings. Everyone had ideas about how to do this, and in the end they all had rag coverings on both hands, their fingertips free to weave better. There was much merriment about the way they all looked, and soon they were singing as they worked. Lord Franz stayed on awhile, but left with Sir Manfred when that knight came in. They had put on their breast plates, no doubt they were going out to do weapons practice.

The women laughed and sang, and the time passed smoothly. Lena's turn came to bring more grass to refill their various piles, and as she turned she saw Lady Elena watching from the stair. She smiled, and the lady came forward hesitantly.

"You sing so happily, I wanted to come," she said shyly. "Can I help?"

"Thank you, Lady Elena, you are so kind," Lena said, as the other women murmured welcome and curtsied. "This work would rip your hands. But we would love a story or a song while we work," she suggested. She did not want to discourage her.

Lady Elena brightened. "I can play my lute?" she suggested. She smiled and hurried up the stairs. The women all talked softly together, admiring the pretty young lady. In moments she was back with her instrument. She pulled a stool closer to the table and bent over the lute, concentrating on tuning it. All of the women were extremely curious and honored that she took an interest in them and their work.

In moments, a hush fell, as the beautiful sounds of a melody floated from her fingers. For some time they wove quietly. She then played a ditty they all knew, and she began to sing. One after another the women joined their voices with hers. This song had many verses and a rousing chorus which made their work seem light. Lady Elena knew others similar songs and soon the women had mastered those as well.

By noon they had finished all of the grass they had. The mat was about half finished. Some of the women rose to go home to eat, but the lady asked them to stay, and that Oona and her kitchen helper would bring food. The workers rolled up the mat, and all sat down to a meal of porridge, bread and cheese with small beer. Lady Elena joined them. Lena saw that her constant veil of sadness had been pushed away by their company.

When they finished, Lena said, "thank you all for your work. I did not think we could go through that huge pile of grass so quickly. I must ride out to tell Sir Reiner we need at least three times as much tomorrow. I will see you all in the morning."

They all bade each other goodbye, curtsying to Lady Elena. When the others had gone out, just as Lena began to thank the lady once again, Lady Elena took her hand.

"May I come tomorrow? I have been happy with you here today."

"Of course. We will be honored and happy to have your company." She curtsied and they bade each other goodbye.

Lena rode quickly out to the mine. Although it was only early afternoon, all work on the ponds was complete and all of the men were cutting and carting wood. Reiner came forward as soon as he saw her, at first anxious that there might be a problem. She described Lord Franz's ingenious rag gloves, which made him laugh. With Lena's news that they had already worked through the first load of grass, Sir Reiner turned all of their efforts to cutting marsh grass. They filled both carts high and turned homeward. Another successful day had been completed.

When they returned to the manor, Reiner looked at the mat work they had completed, and asked for three additional workers to cut grass to fill four carts the next day to make sure they cut enough grass to finish all three mats. Meanwhile the women continued their weaving, joined by Lady Elena. Sir Reiner came to check their progress the next two days before he went to the mine or out to weapons practice with Lord Franz and Sir Manfred. In just a matter of days work at the salt ponds had reached a wait and evaporation period, with only Liebhard or Sir Reiner overseeing one or two workers.

Before the beginning of Lent, all that could be done at the mine was done. The cold quiet of winter and of waiting settled in. Lena fretted. When could they cook the brine? Where would the salt find a buyer? When would the royal court meet to discuss Dieter's crimes? The short days were filled with sewing, milling, carving, woodworking and animal chores. Lena saw too little of Liebhard, who was either at the mine or building the village houses. In his place, Mark helped Lena with milling in both villages. She enjoyed working with him, but missed conversation more than she expected. Mark was very quick and precise with the milling and he seemed to enjoy the work.

Lena saw Sir Reiner hardly at all. Liebhard told her things were progressing with the evaporation. The first salt pool had gone down a couple of inches, and the wood was stacked and ready for the cooking process. Occasionally Reiner sent a message about the workers through Liebhard.

Reiner and Liebhard were rooming together on the nights Liebhard did not come home. There had been no question that Reiner would sleep in the same room as Manfred. They were barely on speaking terms. Reiner did not hold back when he talked to Liebhard, who himself had not found Sir Manfred a friendly person.

Reiner also ate his meals with Liebhard, which irked Sir Manfred, who was angered by this mixing with peasants. He sat disdainfully at the other end of the table, and was further chagrined when Lord Franz occasionally sat down with the other two. When Liebhard told Lena about this, he wondered at Sir Manfred's behavior. Liebhard wished to see the best in people and supposed that Manfred was just surly. Lena thought otherwise.

For Lena, it would have been a very lonely time if the children had not kept her busy. Since the day Reiner had said Klaus was old enough to help at the salt mine, she had thought about how he could learn his father's trade. The blacksmith at the manor village was very young, only fifteen, because his father had died in the pestilence. Even so, he was experienced compared to Klaus. She checked with Lord Franz, who was amenable to Klaus taking an apprenticeship in the manor black smithy. She organized a simple apprenticeship for Klaus that would last until after Easter. He started immediately, and roomed down with the young blacksmith. Now she was down to one child. Concerned about how Klaus got along, she went with Greta to see the young man at work in the blacksmith shop almost every day.

SHOCK AND ACTION

Greta loved to stop and visit the young baker as well. On one of their visits, after they visited with Klaus, Lena left Greta with the baker, and went up to find Matthew to ask about milling. She learned he was not in the village, so she stopped in the mill to check that all was ready if they needed to grind. She cleaned up a little, scraping the stones. She thought she heard the door open. Matthew must have heard she was looking for him.

As she came down from the milling floor, she saw Manfred standing inside the door of the mill. He had not come from weapons practice, since he was dressed in a tunic. He had closed the door behind him, and he leaned against it looking at her. Once again fear overtook her.

"What is it, Sir Manfred? Has Lord Franz sent for me?" she asked, aware that her voice shook slightly.

"Hardly. I am not an errand boy," he said. He stood as quiet as a cat. Her skin prickled.

"Excuse me. I am waiting for Matthew. We plan to mill now," she said boldly, picking up her milling apron and starting to put it on. She could see that he was surprised by her remark, uncertain now that he had caught her in a defenseless position.

"Perhaps you would like to open the sluice gate for me?" she asked. That was enough to convince him. He smirked, but turned and went out the door.

She ran to the door and silently bolted it. She turned and leaned against the door, her heart pounding. She remembered her short knife she used to clean the millstones. She pulled it out of her apron pocket as she wondered what she should do. There was no doubt in her mind what he intended. And what could she have done? He was a knight. There would have been no witnesses. Who could she tell? Not Liebhard. What would he do? The image of the two dead drunkards popped into her mind. Liebhard would want to attack Manfred, and then he would be hung as a murderer. There was only one person she felt she could tell.

She unbolted the door, opened it slightly. Instantly she was knocked backward and would have fallen had she not been grabbed by the wrist. Without thinking, she yanked out her knife and struck at the hand that held her wrist. The knife struck at an angle, but she had put the full force of anger behind it and it slid up Manfred's arm. He was so surprised that he jumped back, and she used that moment to slip by him and run up toward the manor.

She was breathless by the time she reached the courtyard, relieved to see the knight had not followed her. She called Max, and asked him to come into the hall for a moment—she wanted to be absolutely sure Manfred had not somehow got there ahead of her. They entered, and to her relief only Reiner was there. She thanked Max, all the while holding her damaged arm against her chest.

Reiner came forward, looking from her damaged arm to her nearly loose kerchief. Some of her hair had come lose. What on earth had happened? He was now fully alert, wondering what kind of attack to be ready for.

""What has happened, Lena? Are you injured?"

To her chagrin she burst out crying. Reiner took in this new and strange image of Lena, someone who needed protection. He managed to refrain from putting his arms around her, holding her close.

"Something happened just now. I cannot tell Liebhard. He will protect me with his life, without any thought about what it could mean," she said in a rush.

"Speak," Sir Reiner said, stepping toward her, gently taking her injured arm into his two hands.

Now she felt tongue tied. How could she tell him? It touched so closely on her mixed feelings for him. She also suspected his feelings for her were strong. She closed her eyes and began speaking as though she was talking aloud to herself. She described what had happened in detail. When she opened her eyes, she saw intense anger, but also a fleeting moment of gratification that she had trusted him with this information.

"I will kill him!" he swore.

"Reiner, that is not what I expected to hear from you!" she said, forgetting to address him properly. Even though he was hot with anger, he noticed.

"I do not mean I will go and kill him this moment. I will not kill him in cold blood. But his days are numbered in my mind. Will it shock you when I say I am not surprised that he has attacked someone, even you? I have listened to him, lived with him these days, and he sees unprotected women as his game. He is not a person to be trusted. He has no honor or loyalty. How Lord Franz has not seen this I cannot understand. Thank you for telling me. I will help you in every way within my power. But I think you do need to tell Liebhard. Why can you not tell him? Can we both speak to him?

"Reiner, something happened during the height of the pestilence. I will not tell you what, but the result is that I think he does not understand how dangerous force can be."

"Lena, I can help you by being on my guard when I know you are here. But when you are any other place, you will be safest if Liebhard knows. And you must try not to be alone. Plan to lock the mill when you are there alone. Try to be with Liebhard, Mark or me as much as you can. I cannot bring this to Lord Franz's attention without witnesses. This is a very dangerous time for you until we can find a way to act against him legally, because he is a knight and you are an assarted free peasant. Now, let's check this wrist."

He lightly felt the hand, wrist and upper arm, turning the arm as well. "No break, but a bone could be cracked. It could also be just a serious sprain." She had a lovely arm. He took the scarf from around his neck, and looped it, putting it over her head, and carefully sliding her arm into the makeshift sling.

At that moment Manfred entered the hall, his arm dripping blood through the cloth Manfred had covered it with. Reiner looked at him menacingly. "Do not speak unless you are going to say you accidently slit your arm."

"What?"

"I mean it. If you say anything else, I will lay before Lord Franz your dealings with Otto Plowman's daughter, your remarks, and the injury you have done to Lena, Millers daughter."

Manfred gave Reiner a withering stare and stamped to his room, slamming the door.

"He will surely try to make us pay for this," Reiner said, taking her good hand into his. He called Max, asking him to saddle both of their horses.

They rode down to get Greta, and he accompanied them home.

"I will come back with Liebhard as soon as I find him," he said as he turned his horse for the ride back to the manor.

In less than an hour, Liebhard and Reiner were back. While she was waiting, she tried to fend off Greta's questions about her arm, saying she had been injured and she would tell her more later.

Reiner had only told Liebhard that he and Lena needed to talk to him about an injury she had suffered. Liebhard's face was a picture of anxiety when he came into the kitchen.

He took her shoulders, touched her injured arm lightly, and stroked her hair.

"What happened?"

After a quick look at Reiner, and a nod from him, she slowly told him what happened, leaving out no details. She told him she had told Reiner first because she was afraid what Liebhard would do if she told him.

Liebhard was livid with anger, and he looked like he would have liked to run straight to the manor and confront Sir Manfred. There was no doubt in Reiner's mind that Liebhard was capable of killing Manfred with his bare hands.

Reiner put his hand on the giant's shoulder. He clearly and simply laid out the dangers and pitfalls, particularly because of the character of Sir Manfred. He also spelled out the legal dangers any attack on a knight might cause. Liebhard calmed down, listening carefully to Reiner.

"What can we do then?"

"We must be very vigilant. Sir Manfred has a healthy respect for me, I know. He will remember that Lena has the ear of both Lord Franz and Lady Elena. But he will undoubtedly try to waylay Lena and pay her back."

After more somber discussion Sir Reiner left. Lena leaned into Liebhard, who sat down, taking her into his lap. They sat quietly together for some time.

Lena slept poorly that night, and was on guard, aware of every unusual sound, careful to be with someone when she went about, and to lock her doors throughout the days after the attack. Liebhard spent every night in Miller Village, and stayed at the mill until late at night.

On the third night after the attack, Lena was awakened in the middle of the night by a strange muted thud. She lay motionless, listening. The sluice gate had opened! How was that possible? Then the sounds of the water and the cogs stopped. None of this was right, she knew. She slipped out of bed and moved soundlessly to the door and opened it. There was someone down in the kitchen, and from the tentative movements, it was someone who was not familiar with the mill. Lena ran up to the hopper floor as quietly as she could, and waked Klaus, who had come home for the night.

"Someone has broken into the mill, Klaus! Be very quiet! Have you got a staff or a club? I will wake Greta. Then you and I will confront this person while Greta runs to the church to ring the bell." Before she finished, he was up with a heavy club in hand.

Lena went to Greta's bed, and woke her, whispering instructions, urging her to stop at nothing, that all depended upon her getting to the church to sound the hue and cry.

Lena, followed by Klaus, slipped down the stairs, Greta several steps behind. The mill stone floor where Lena slept was empty. She heard noises at the bottom of the stairs. Motioning to Klaus, she flung herself down the stairs.

Even without any light, she knew it was Manfred. As she hurled herself at him, striking out with the iron bar she used to clean the mill stones, he seemed three times her size. Klaus was already past her, his club catching the knight's upper arm. Because Manfred had not expected the attack, their first blows hit home. Lena had managed to knock him hard on his hip or stomach, and she thought she had knocked the wind out of him.

Before she could raise her arm and hit him again, he had his arms around her, pinching her arms against her body. She kicked and kicked at his legs, but without shoes on she could hurt him very little. Klaus continued to pound on his back and tried to hit him on the head, hurting the big man enough that he let Lena go. He picked up Klaus and threw him against the wall. The awful shriek from Klaus filled her ears as she hit Manfred in the face with her iron bar. The blow was not enough to bring him down, but the sound of the church bell stopped the assailant momentarily.

When he grabbed Lena again she feared more for her life than she had during the plague. He was not trying to control her now, he was trying to squeeze life from her. She struggled and kicked but she felt so lightheaded.

At that moment, the door was broken down with a mighty crash, and Liebhard threw himself on the knight. Manfred was at first completely overcome, but managed to pull his sword out of its shield. Liebhard jumped away, but wrapped his tunic over his hand, and as Manfred slashed at him again, Liebhard held on to the blade. The knight's strength was no match for Liebhard's, and before he could be stopped he hurtled past Liebhard and out the door, leaving his sword in Liebhard's hands.

Moments later, as Lena lit a candle, Mark and Liebhard came back into the mill.

"He got away. His horse was just around the corner," Liebhard said, and then saw Klaus. "God help us! Klaus!"

He joined Lena as they leaned over the boy. There was some blood seeping out of his nose and mouth. He lay in a crumpled heap. Lena put her head against his chest, and felt the erratic thump of his heart.

"He is alive. Pick him up very carefully and put him on the bed here. Mark, can you go and get Anna?" she asked, not thinking about how a mute might run this errand.

She felt all of Klaus' bones, and checked as best she could for any injuries. If he was knocked senseless, he should wake. She felt Liebhard's arm around her, and leaned into him. Now tears came.

They sat together quietly for a short time as more and more villagers arrived, responding to the alarm Greta had raised. Anna came, checked Klaus, but had no more knowledge about what they could do. She saw what Lena had missed though. Liebhard had a deep gash in his right hand and a smaller one in his left hand, where Manfred's sword had cut through the layers of tunic cloth. The women worked together to bandage his hands.

It was almost dawn. Lena determined that they had to go up to the manor and lay this attack before Lord Franz, no matter what the consequences were. Liebhard would not let her go alone, so with Mark's help he saddled Pieces and the priest's horse.

110

Just after dawn they rode into the courtyard in front of the keep. Max came out to greet them. From him they learned he had had a busy morning already. Sir Manfred had left in the middle of the night, after he had received an urgent message that his father was dying. Lord Franz had left just a short time ago with Max, riding to the count's royal court.

As they dismounted, Sir Reiner came out of the hall, surprised to see them and stunned by their news. They went inside, pondering what to do next, when Lady Elena came down the stairs. As Sir Reiner and Liebhard listened, Lena told the lady about the attack.

Suddenly, Lady Elena slumped down on a bench, covered her face with her hands and cried. "This is all my fault! I cannot go on like this! I should have told Lord Franz but I was afraid."

Lena stared at her. What could be wrong? She cautiously sat down next to the young woman, and put her good arm around her shoulder. "Lady Elena, tell me what troubles you if you can."

The lady raised her tear-streaked face. She whispered, "I am going to tell you my awful secret. I am going to show you something." She reached into her sleeve and pulled out a small folded letter, holding it tightly in both hands. "My waiting lady was murdered. She was raped repeatedly, and she was murdered." Her voice had dropped to a low moaning growl. Her chest heaved and she could not go on immediately.

After a few minutes she continued, "Clara was my childhood friend. Her family is a proud knightly family, but quite without good lands or any wealth. Her father is now old, perhaps infirm, and her brothers are dead. She had no marriage prospects, so to stay with me was a happy arrangement for both of us. "

"When Franz sent us to safety in Trier, I anticipated no danger except from the deadly plague. Many died, but we were lucky. We lost Franz's loyal knight, good Sir Jergen, to the pestilence. Then the deaths stopped. Something far more sinister began for little Clara. I had not known that Sir Manfred had already begun pestering her. He was very secretive, and she was highly embarrassed and ashamed. I learned only two weeks after it had begun. He forced himself on her at every turn. She reached a point where she hardly talked. I thought the plague had changed her somehow. Then one night, she left this on my table after I had retired." She held out the letter to Lena. "The next morning she was dead. Manfred said he found her at the bottom of a flight of stone stairs. He said she must have tripped and fallen downstairs. I then found the letter, and the whole rotten truth lay before me. I was afraid. I know he saw my fear, and he suspected I knew what happened."

Lena took the letter, hugged the lady closely, and handed it to Sir Reiner. He looked it over before reading it aloud.

Dearest Elena,

I go now to meet Manfred, the most despicable creature I know. I am so ashamed. He has forced me again and again, and menaced me by saying he would report to Lord Franz that I was a lewd woman, not fit to serve you. Tonight I will tell him this stops or I will tell Lord Franz about his actions.

I love you,
Clara

"Tell me why you have not told Lord Franz," Lena asked quietly.

"I was afraid. Manfred will declare he is not guilty. He will demand a duel. If he wins…"

"Lord Franz was in danger because you did not tell him. He innocently trusted this man who has reason to do you harm. He is blind to this threat. Lord Franz will know what to do when he knows. He will know how to act."

"How can I tell him? And he will be angry I did not tell him earlier."

"Elena, he will be angry. Angry that you kept the weight of this terrible thing to yourself. It will seem to him that you did not have faith in him. He will be irate. He will bluster. But, Elena, he will be so glad to know what has been troubling you all of these weeks. Don't you know he has been sick with worry? He is a naturally cheerful energetic young man, but these weeks he has curled inward around you. He has wanted to protect you and calm you, and has not known how. Knowing this, he will act. The future will be dangerous, but it will be visible and understood."

Lady Elena continued in silence for a long time, eyes lowered. She had stopped crying, but Lena could not tell what her reaction was.

"Lady Elena, I am going to tell you something that I first told only Sir Reiner because I was afraid of Liebhard's reaction. Sir Reiner insisted Liebhard must know." Then she told Lady Elena in detail about her experience with Manfred, and all of the ensuing events. She explained what steps Sir Reiner and Liebhard had put into effect. Lady Elena listened wide-eyed to this story, looking first at Sir Reiner and then at Liebhard.

Finally, she raised her shoulders, took a deep breath, and said, "I will tell him if you will help me, if you will be there with me."

"I will. But we must think carefully about this. Sir Reiner, what do you advise? I know that he thinks Sir Manfred is an excellent knight. Perhaps in arms he is. Lord Franz might be in danger at this very moment. What is Manfred doing now? Lady Elena, when do you expect them back from the royal courts?"

Sir Reiner, who had been listening silently, said "I plan to ride now to try to warn Lord Franz. We should get him back now. He will want to put off his business with the count." He bowed to the lady, and hurried away with Liebhard on his heels.

The two women continued to discuss this perilous situation, trying to imagine all eventualities. Lady Elena told her more about their time in Trier, about Clara's family, and about Manfred. The young knight was from a new *ministeriale* family and very protective of his rights. He was easily angered by imagined slights, and this made his prospects for advancement less likely. He considered his position with Lord Franz as below what he should have had. Lady Elena thought it likely that he had had no other choices and that was the only reason he had pledged to Lord Franz. The women talked about the similar pattern Manfred had used toward Clara and Lena, dominating someone weaker or in an inferior position. Lena told the lady about Klaus's fearful injury.

A short time later Liebhard returned. Lena promised Lady Elena that she would come back in the afternoon after she checked on Klaus and surely before Reiner and Franz returned.

Once home, she found there had been no change in the boy's condition. Anna was sitting with him. He no longer bled from his mouth or nose. He lay very still. Anna anticipated he would develop a fever and might then recover. Lena sat down and cried, her hand on Klaus' face, which was beginning to turn black and blue from the tremendous force with which he had hit the wall.

"I hate to leave him, but I must go back up to the manor. Sir Reiner will be returning with Lord Franz."

Anna patted her hand. "Go, then. There is no use having two hanging over the boy. I will send word if there is a change."

Lena nodded and wiped her eyes. She went out to the waiting Pisces and rode back to the manor. She had barely rejoined the lady when they heard the clatter of hooves. Lord Franz was in the hall before they were down the stairs.

"May God be thanked that you are alive, Lena! Curse that man! How could I not see this coming?"

Sir Reiner, who came in just behind him, stepped forward. "I have told Lord Franz about the attack, but you must tell the rest, Lady Elena." Lord Franz wheeled around and stared at Sir Reiner, then looked at his wife, his brow knitted.

"Please forgive me for not telling you. This is all my fault!" she answered tremulously.

"What is it? Speak!" he demanded curtly, but then took her hand, which immediately brought forth tears. Through occasional sobs she told Franz everything that she had told Lena. She gave him Clara's letter. He read it, his face turning a blotched red.

He jumped up, and strode across the room. His anger welled up, making him seem larger and more formidable. He turned around. "Why did you not tell me?" he whispered harshly. Lena had never seen him so angry. She was glad that she had told Lady Elena that he would be furious. He ranted for several minutes. Finally he calmed himself, ran his fingers through his tangled hair and looked down at his wife. He came to the lady, knelt before her, held her face gently between his hands.

"It is not your fault. But you should have had faith in me from the first." That was the last unkind thing he said.

"There is even more," Lady Elena said, and turned to Lena, who then told him of her experience with the knight.

Franz listened with amazement, shaking his head. "Lena, I am so sorry. So that is what happened to him. He said he had had a careless accident....Everything Sir Reiner suggested was right. Thank God he is your close friend and you could tell him this."

Franz said it was clear to him that Sir Manfred should be accused at once of the killing of Clara, a gentle woman, the daughter of a knight. Lady Elena was horrified at the thought.

"He will try to kill you, Franz!"

"No, not likely. He will deny all of this, but he cannot dare to attack me as I am his liege lord. That would mean immediate death for him.

"Will he be tried like Dieter?" Lena asked.

"Knowing him he will demand trial by combat. For the attack on you, where we have many witnesses, he will no doubt pay the war geld due. But for Clara's death, he will be found guilty and possibly be put to death unless he wins in trial by combat. Clara's family must be given this news. This is their feud, they are the aggrieved family. Who can champion Clara? Does her family have any strong family members, Elena? I do not know them."

Elena told him all that she had told Lena, but also mentioned that her mother's brother was the abbot of a monastery in Frankfurt.

"He might be able to help," Lord Franz mused.

Lord Franz immediately planned action. He called together his villagers in the hall.

"Listen, everyone. He looked around at all the villagers, Sir Reiner, Liebhard, Lena, Lady Elena and the household staff. He then spelled out in full detail what had happened to Lady Clara, and that he had intended to try to take the knight into custody and bring him to the count for trial. There were excited cries and mumbling at all of this shocking news.

"He has grabbed time by running. Now we must act quickly. I must get a message to the count, and also ride immediately to Lady Clara's father to give him the evidence against Sir Manfred. Sir Reiner, can you ride out now, as soon as possible to the count? Matthew, I ask you to go with Sir Reiner. I will prepare a message and a copy of Clara's letter. I also have a letter I planned to give to him regarding the trial of Dieter in the royal court for murder which I will want you to deliver. Liebhard, I need you to ride with me this afternoon to the Midlin lands to meet with Clara's father."

Lena felt Liebhard's breath stop. She leaned up to his ear and whispered, "You must go, you must! Steel yourself!" He let out his breath loudly. Reiner had edged over and stood on Liebhard's other side. "You will be fine, Liebhard. You will be with Lord Franz."

Lord Franz continued. "Lena, can you go back to the village and get Mark? Have him come up to stay with you and Lady Elena tonight. Sir Reiner should be back by noon tomorrow with hard riding."

This call to action sent everyone scurrying to follow their orders. Lena had mounted Pisces and nudged him into a gallop in no time. In the cold air he responded friskily and she was at the mill in minutes. She raised the hue and cry by ringing the bell at the church. When everyone had come running, she quickly told them what had happened, also telling them about Lady Clara's death. The villagers were stunned.

"Lord Franz has asked that Mark come back with me to stay with Lady Elena until tomorrow when Sir Reiner should be back. Everyone, be on your guard. We do not know where Sir Manfred is, but Lord Franz thinks he is riding to his father's estates east of the Rhine."

Everyone rushed to help Mark and Lena get ready. Lena checked in on Klaus again, but there had been no change. Lars said he would bring his family up to the mill to stay with Greta and Anna. Mark bridled his father's work horse and jumped on bareback. The two riders rode off amidst the sound of the horses' thundering hooves.

By the time they reached the manor, Sir Reiner and Matthew were just ready to leave the keep yard. Lena rushed to the knight's side to wish him safe journey, and pressed his hand. He gave her one of his rare warm smiles and mounted. In a few minutes Liebhard and Franz came out from the manor to their waiting horses.

"Lord Franz, do you have special orders for us?"

"Just be on your guard, Lena. It would not be beyond his cunning to be following our actions, and to attack the house when all of the knights are gone. Mark, what weapons can you handle?" Mark stared at him, and Liebhard came forward. "He is good with a blade and a staff. He has no experience with a sword." Lord Franz nodded, remembering that Mark did not speak.

Lady Elena came out with a small velvet pouch, which she handed to her husband. "These are Clara's jewels. Please ask her father if we should send her belongings to him or which of her female cousins will inherit them."

He nodded, and stuck the pouch inside his tunic. He quickly embraced her before he mounted. Liebhard hugged Lena tightly. She whispered encouragement in his ear and kissed him. They mounted and galloped out of the gate. The lady, Lena and Mark stood for some time until the riders were out of sight. Lena took Lady Elena's arm and they walked back into the hall. The lady asked them to sit at the table to plan for the night. As they spoke Oona brought out a platter of food, and they all ate ravenously as they talked. It was determined that Mark should plan to sleep here in the hall after the door was bolted. Lena would sleep in one of the back rooms so she would be near at hand.

The warmth of the fire, the food and the excitement of the day caused all of them to feel sleepy, and Lady Elena bade them good night. Lena sat for a while, finishing her mulled wine.

"Will you be all right here, Mark, here on your own? I can bring out a straw mattress and sleep in the hall too." She looked up to see what he wanted her to do. To her shock, he spoke.

"I will be well on my own."

Lena jumped to her feet, pressing her hand against her chest. She was frightened and awe struck to her core. It was like a nightmare, a dream that had cut into the reality of the horrible day. Mark looked at her, but she almost thought he could not be real, that this could not be happening. "But I don't understand...."

"Liebhard will say," was all the answer he gave. He looked at her hard, willing her to ask no more. She stared at him mutely. She backed away a few steps, not daring to take her eyes of him. She must be in some kind of night dream. Finally she whispered good night as she left the hall. She prepared for bed, lay down and closed her eyes. She was very weary, but could not sleep. She dozed and woke many times, always remembering Mark's strange secret. Or was it a dream?' What did it mean? If it was real, how had he and Liebhard kept this to themselves?

When first light came, Lena got up. It was useless to lie in bed: she could not relax. All she could think about was Klaus, the danger posed on all those she loved, and this strange revelation by Mark. She hesitantly entered the hall. Mark was already up and out of the building. Lena went into the kitchen, where Oona and Thirza were busy preparing food for the day. Lena volunteered to bring breakfast up to Lady Elena. In a few moments she was on her way up the stairs to her bedroom. She tapped lightly at the door, and Elena called to her to enter.

"Oh, thank you, Lena. I hope you rested well."

"I couldn't sleep. I worried all night. I am so worried about Klaus."

"I did not sleep well either."

Lena put the tray down on the table. Elena sat down and motioned for Lena to do likewise.

"Mark is not downstairs. It is his habit to wake very early and be out checking everything and anything."

"How early do you think Sir Reiner can be back?" Lady Elena asked as she cut cheese and laid it on her bread.

"Lord Franz said possibly by noon. But any number of problems could delay him. I hope he will be back today, though. I will go downstairs now and wait for Mark to return. When he comes, I will go home to check on Klaus."

"Will you wait for me to dress before you go? I would like to go with you."

Lena nodded, honored by the request. She went down to wait for Mark. Sometime later Lady Elena came down. They waited for a few minutes and then Mark entered. "Is everything well, Mark?" she asked tremulously, half fearing he would answer. Mark nodded and smiled.

"Lady Elena and I are riding to the Miller village to see Klaus. We will be back before dinner." If Lady Elena had noticed anything different in her demeanor toward Mark, she said nothing. Lena told herself that Mark's revelation should not frighten her, and that Liebhard would explain all. She took a deep breath and tried to close her mind to the trepidation she felt. They set a quick pace to Miller Village, and tied their horses outside the broken mill door. Lady Elena had never seen such a place and was awed by the huge cogs of the mill. Lena determined that she would give the lady a quick tour of the mill after they checked on Klaus. There was still no change, and Lena saw that Anna was now troubled that he had remained unconscious for so many hours. They sat quietly and talked for some time.

Just before noon they returned to the hall. Mark was walking in the courtyard and nodded to them. Lena asked if all was well, and he nodded again. When Oona heard them enter, she came into the hall to see if the lady wanted to dine there, and Lady Elena said she would eat with Lena and Mark in the hall. A short time later, food was laid on the table and Lena called Mark in. They had a subdued dinner, half listening for the hoped for sound of hoof beats.

It was not until late afternoon that they heard the thunder of hooves. Lena and Mark ran out. Sir Reiner nearly slid off his horse, he was so tired. Matthew sat on his horse as though he was asleep. Mark manhandled him down, and they all entered the hall, urging the tired men to sit by the roaring fire in the fireplace. Oona brought food and drink. After Sir Reiner had taken a deep draft of beer, he started to tell them of their trip.

They had made good time to the count's estates, arriving just after dark. Unfortunately, the count was away at one of his villages, and they had to ride on to find him. He received their news and Lord Franz's letter with consternation. He immediately rode back with them to his castle and gave many orders. He sent a message to the royal court to raise the cry against Sir Manfred. He knew Clara's uncle, the Abbot of a Dominican Abbey, and sent a rider with a message explaining the situation, as well as a copy of Clara's letter. He also read Lord Franz's letter about Dieter and the royal court, and said that the court would name Dieter an outlaw, and the count's priest said his marriage to Lena would be null and void. He urged the men to rest, but Sir Reiner explained Lord Franz's concern that the accused knight might strike. He lent them fresh mounts, saying he would send their horses back the next day. Without resting the two men had returned.

Many exclamations of thanks and concern followed his words. Sir Reiner looked at all of them as he spoke, his eyes bloodshot and tired. He had tried to take off his breast plate and other armor as he spoke, but his fingers were stiff. Lena brushed his hands away and unbuckled the pieces for him. He bowed slightly, caught her eye and tried to smile.

By this time Matthew had slumped back and fallen asleep. Oona got a quilt and covered him. Lena pushed Reiner down too, leaning over him. "You must sleep now. You have done all that you could." He did not resist, and Oona covered him too. His last words were about Klaus before he fell asleep.

Leaving the sleeping men by the fire, Mark, Lena and Lady Elena went to the far end of the table. Lady Elena expressed her thankfulness that they had returned safely.

"Lord Franz has a much greater distance to go. They are probably halfway there by now. I think they might be expected to stay with Clara's father for a day or two to plan the next steps to be taken. He will want to decide how to communicate all of this to his brother-in-law, the abbot. I met the abbot once when I was visiting Clara. I was probably about eight. He is a large, bony man, very ascetic. His eyes are piercing. I remember being quite frightened of him. His whole bearing is forceful, and his voice...I thought that must be what God sounds like when he is angry."

Mark, Lena and Elena waited patiently for Sir Reiner to wake, doing their chores and the women talked quietly. It was not until dark that the sleepers woke. Matthew got up and said he must go home, so Mark got up, left the hall and walked with him down to the village. Lady Elena asked Sir Reiner if he would like a late supper. He got up stiffly and limped to the table.

"What is wrong, Sir Reiner?" Lady Elena asked. Lena had just been ready to ask the same question.

"Just an old war wound. I was hit in the hip by a dagger, and it acts up when I ride too hard," he laughed quietly. Even with this impediment, Lena saw him as a hero, their protector during this dreadful time. He sat down opposite Lena, next to the lady, who sat at the head of the table. Oona brought in some thick meat stew and bread, and Thirza brought wine. Sir Reiner ate ravenously. After he had eaten his fill, he pushed his plate away.

"I am glad to be back. I have had a fear that Manfred would attack you here. He has an over weaning arrogance and belief that he is not treated as he deserves. A knight serving the count told us that he had lost his position at the court of a great magnate in the eastern provinces because he had killed several peasants in cold blood. I think now he will be smoldering with hatred. It pains me to say it, Lady Elena, but he will hate you most, and you Lena for coming to the lady's support. He thinks of women as lesser beings, and peasant women no more than cattle."

"I know he has thought he could take advantage of my position," Lena said. "I felt his disdain each time I was near him, but I thought it was just a difference of our class—that I was above my station."

Reiner cocked his head, all the time looking into her eyes. "You are above your station. But it is a natural situation for you, Lena. You may be from a peasant village, but you stand on the shoulders of your father, the miller and leader of an assarted village. Add to that your knowledge and leadership in a catastrophic time, and you would inspire a great desire in Manfred to overpower you."

Lena sat without words. She saw out of the corner of her eye that the lady was nodding her head in agreement. Lena wondered if this was why she felt like an outsider sometimes. Where did she fit? Of course, she was of the peasant class, but she was a free villager. Yet the knightly class, to which she did not belong, had taken her as a support and trusted aid. She was drawn out of her thoughts by Reiner, who scraped his chair back and got up wearily. He still looked at her. No shield hid his feelings for her at that moment. He dropped his eyes, his face slightly flushed, and began to say good night to them. Suddenly he dropped back to his chair.

TEAM

"I forgot a very important piece of news! How could I have forgotten! Did you know that Lord Franz had told the count about our salt project? He has two merchants who are coming to make purchases and see our site. Of course, the count will tax the sales!" he chuckled.

Lady Elena clapped her hands and laughed. Lena leaned forward excitedly. "How soon are they coming? Will we have salt in time?"

Reiner laughed. "We will have to start boiling brine now, rather than waiting for any more evaporation. I think we will see these buyers in the next week or two." With that he got up again, raised his hand in good night and left the hall. Lena watched him walk out. He still limped. Such a life he must have had. She wondered if he was even thirty years old.

"What wonderful news, Lena! This solves Franz's worries for the running of the estate, for the repairs and recovery, for the costs that have been mounting up. He will be able to take on one or two retainers, and maybe find new workers with crafts to move to the village."

Lena, ever taking the realist side, said, "We may well be out of the woods for this year. I am cautiously optimistic."

Elena drew in her breath in surprise at Lena's words and asked her to explain how she expected the rest of the winter to develop. She listened with rapped attention as Lena explained all that had to be done before spring, how Lena wondered if the spring field work could be done with a very limited number of people, Franz's plans to put his hopes on sheep and wool, the possibility of more pestilence, and especially this worry about Sir Manfred causing them more trouble.

When Sir Reiner left the hall, he was scolding himself. What had allowed him to let his guard down? It must be that he was so tired. The last thing he wanted was for Lena to know his feelings for her. He loved Liebhard like a brother. He had not had such a close friendship in his life. He knew Liebhard felt the same. Lena had committed herself to Liebhard. Reiner was not of her class. He could not offer her a life good enough for her. Even if they received permission to wed, any children would be of her class, tied to her village. She would not gain from a union. She would never agree to anything less. "Stop this," he said to himself, cursing his wandering mind.

It was very late by the time the women got up from the table and said good night. Lady Elena went upstairs while Lena put out the candles. She put out the wall sconce as well, and made sure the glowing coals in the hearth was well banked. Then she took the remaining candle and entered the passage leading to the bedrooms. She paused for a moment, trying to decide which room Reiner had entered. Surely he had gone into the room where his belongings were stored, that he shared with Liebhard. She had slept the previous night in the room that had been Manfred's. She passed Reiner's room and went on to Manfred's. She opened the door and in the dim candlelight saw it was empty. She denied to herself that she felt a little let down.

She poured some water in the wash basin, washed her face and hands, and took her birch twig to brush her teeth. She pulled her grey wool dress over her head, and as she started to remove her shift, she heard shuffling feet. She stood motionless. He was pacing the floor. She quickly put out her candle and climbed under the quilts. He continued walking up and down, sometimes stopping for several moments. Then she heard the sound of the door opening. For long moments, no sound came. Then the door closed. Had he come out into the passage? Moments later she heard his steps back into the room and the soft sounds as he lay down. She pressed her head into the pillow, waiting for sleep.

Reiner had not been able to sleep. He heard the murmur of the women's voices. After they said good night, Lena came into the back hall. He heard her pause by his door. He caught his breath. After a moment she walked on to the other chamber. Now he was wide awake, aching and tormented at the thought of her there just beyond the wall. He got up slowly, walked to the door, turned back, walked to and fro several times. When he came to the door again, he opened it. He stood for several moments. He dropped his head forward, leaning against the edge of the door. He straightened up, closed the door and returned to his bed.

It was late dawn, almost sunrise, when she woke. She lay in bed, letting her mind roam. It was the first week of Lent. In just a little over a month, she and Liebhard could marry, if Lord Franz had success with the royal court. She was sure she would feel more settled then. She loved and trusted Liebhard: he was honest, brave, fair and kind. He stirred her body in a way she had not known possible. She loved Reiner too, she knew that. They must be only friends. She was already betrothed, and they were of different classes. She sighed, threw back the quilts and got up. After she had pulled on her shift and dress, she used the little looking glass on the wall to re-arrange her hair before she put on her scarf.

Reiner was at the table writing when she came out of the passage. He turned, stood up and bade her good morning. He was his gentle self again, and she relaxed.

"Do you have your eye patch with you?" She was surprised, but pulled it out of her pocket. When he motioned with his hand, she put it on. "Your left eye is tired, I think. Perhaps you did not sleep well." It was not a question.

"I don't wear it while I am here. Usually I put it on first thing in the morning and wear it at least until dinner," she explained. It seemed so normal and necessary to tell him everything.

"Just tell Lady Elena the truth when she asks what it is for, and she will not be bothered, I am sure." It seemed so acceptable when he directed her. If Lord Franz had said the same, she probably would have argued.

He continued talking, unaware of her thoughts. "I have been planning what we will need to do, starting today for the drying out of the salt. Do you want to breakfast with me while we go over my notes? I need to know who you think we should use for round-the-clock boiling."

Lena nodded to both his questions and went to see if she could get them some bread or porridge from the kitchen. Oona had porridge ready, so Lena filled two bowls, put them on a tray with bread and beer, and carried them out to the table. Reiner pushed his paper aside and she set the tray in the center of the table. She walked around to the other side and sat down opposite him. As with Lord Franz, she felt quite at home eating with him. She smiled to herself, wondering what her father would have thought of his daughter eating with knights and lords.

Between spoonful's of porridge, Reiner suggested they use three shifts for three people to bring wood, stoke the fire and stir the brine. Stirring had to be continual. As brine started to settle, the fire was let go very low, and the salt that was settling at the bottom had to be scooped out. Then the fire would be rebuilt and the process repeated, adding more brine as needed. From now until they decided to stop, or thick brine was gone, this would be a 24 hour a day job. They thought about their workers and decided upon which to use. They also chose back up workers, and planned for more wood cutting as well.

Reiner decided to take Matthew and two of the local villagers for this first shift, Mark to direct the second with Lars while Matthew stayed for a while to help. Reiner would return and later two manor villagers would join him for the third shift. After that, until Liebhard returned, Matthew, Mark and Reiner would lead shifts. Lena should plan how to bag and measure the salt for the sales. They hoped Lord Franz had an idea of what to charge.

Thirza came out of the kitchen with a tray for Lady Elena. Lena got up quickly. "May I take her tray to her?" she asked. Thirza bobbed her head and handed Lena the tray.

Reiner rose also and said, "I will go down to find Mark and Matthew and give them my plans. Mark will go to Miller village to tell Lars, check on Klaus for you, then come back here and stay until I return near the end of the first shift. I will see you again after dinner."

After Lena came down from seeing lady Elena and bringing her the breakfast tray, she sat for a moment wondering how she would find cloth for the bags. There was the old clothing of the eleven lost families. Some of that would undoubtedly include useful linen. Older cloth would be too weak against the weight of the salt. The bags could not be too big, or they would be too heavy to carry and would burst more easily. She found the trunk with the clothes in the back passageway. She sat down and slowly went through all of the articles. With the quilts there was a good quantity that could be cut apart and used. After she had finished this project, she went into the kitchen to see what Oona had in salt supplies. The bag she found was nearly full and she estimated it weighed less than twenty pounds. She did a rough measurement of the bag, deciding that this was possibly a typical salt bag size.

After she had finished this project, she walked down to the village and found Gudrun, the village woman who had seemed the most experienced weaver. She told her of the new project, and asked her who among the women there would be good at sewing up salt bags. After having arranged for the five women, plus Gudrun, to begin the sewing project the next morning in the manor hall, she got Pisces and rode home.

All was in hand, and Greta was praised for her bravery, for the work she did at the mill and at her own house. Klaus had developed a bit of fever, which seemed to soothe Anna's worries. She continually plied cold cloths to his forehead, and said they would know soon his fate. Lena could not decide if she felt relieved or more worried.

The flour was running fairly low, and they would need to mill in three or four days. This reminded Lena that she had not checked in at the manor mill. Either Mark or Liebhard would have to be spared a half day to help her grind flour. When she got back to the manor, she asked Oona for dinner for them, and helped Thirza bring out food to the hall. Lady Elena came down and joined them.

Shortly after they had finished eating, Reiner returned. His arms were white with salt dust from stirring the brine. Lena shooed him out of the hall and got a small brush to brush him off. He laughed but agreed with her that the caustic salt was hard on him, his clothes, and the hall. He said he would remind everyone to try to clean themselves after each shift.

"You are a tyrant, just as Lord Franz said," he murmured. At her look of astonishment he relented, "Lord Franz did not say that to me, but Liebhard told me of it." Even this did not sit well with Lena. She did not like to hear that she was spoken of by these two men. Reiner read the dissatisfaction in her demeanor. He looked down and shook his head slightly. He and Liebhard did talk about her sometimes, mostly because Reiner was thirsty for every morsel of information about her. He did not want her to be upset or blame Liebhard. It was not his fault. "Don't fret. Do not be angry at Liebhard." She remained mute but took in what he said. He followed her into the hall, asking after Klaus.

As Reiner ate, Lena told him about the bags and the work she had set for the next day. He listened closely. He agreed that twenty pounds was a good size for handling. He also told her he would need one or two large finished cowhides onto which they would lay the finished salt for final drying for bagging. Once the salt was on the hides, she was expected to take over the salt process. He estimated they would have the first salt for the hides the next morning, and bagging to start the following day if the weather was dry.

"This is a project full of surprises and scrambling to figure out how to overcome them, isn't it?" she remarked raising her eyebrows in mock shock.

Reiner laughed. "I think we are doing pretty well as novices to this business!"

"I am off to find those hides. When will you go back down? Without Mark back before you go we will have no one here at the hall."

"You are right, I did not think of that. I will send Mark back as soon as I can."

It was a busy afternoon. Lena found hides and brought them to Matthew to bring for his shift. Lena watched as Reiner left. Less than an hour later Mark was back.

Just as she rose the next morning, she heard someone come into the hall. She rushed out. It was Reiner, and he was visibly exhausted, once again white with salt dust. He went to pick up the brush, but she was there first, and followed him out of the hall. As she brushed him, he told her that they would have first salt this morning and thanked her for sending the hides with Matthew.

"Do you want to eat or sleep now?" she asked somewhat teasingly. Reiner smiled happily.

"Eat!" he exclaimed. Even in his weariness he was incredibly happy, living in a special bubble with her, working on this project.

Within a few minutes Lena had porridge from the kitchen, and Mark was back from a look around the village. Reiner had laid his head on his arms and had actually nodded off, but was awakened by the voices. Lena watched Reiner finish his second bowl of porridge. His face was lined with weariness.

"Sir Reiner, you have pushed yourself too hard. We cannot afford to have you exhaust yourself. You must sleep until you go back down tonight. Matthew will have the processing well in hand, and Mark will do all right running his shift."

He was able to muster a chuckle. "Yes, Mother. I will sleep now. But I will go down about midday. The salting out of the brine is a little tricky for Mark to master so fast."

"You are your own master," she answered pertly, but softened her answer with a small smile.

He rose, smiled in return, and went to lie down.

A short time later the women arrived and they began to work on the salt bags. Lena welcomed the lady who came down to join them. She insisted upon helping them with the sewing, drawing smiles all around when she said she could sew even if she could not weave. They made quick progress once they had cut out the pieces from the old clothing and quilts. By the end of the afternoon, when Reiner came out of his room, they had nearly finished all of the bags for which they had cloth. He was eager to see what they had accomplished.

Oona brought out food for him and he ate heartily, watching the sewing work. He gathered his cloak and opened the door to go out.

"Oh, God help us! It is sleeting rain!"

"Oh no," exclaimed Lena, realizing immediately that the salt could not be moistened now that is had been salted out to crystals. "I will ride out with you now. Is there a cart out there? We must bring the hides filled with salt back here. Maybe we can dry it in the keep?"

"Yes! Hurry! We must ride out now!" he answered, and ran out calling Max. Lena ran to her room, grabbed her cloak and gloves, and was on Pisces in minutes. They rode at a wild pace to the salt mine. They both leaped off their horses and rushed to fold the hides over the salt, which was already a little wet. Mark ran over and helped them carry the hides to the cart.

"Mark, I will take your place. You drive the cart back to the keep. Lena, can you sit in the cart to keep the hides in place, covering the salt?" Mark and Lena responded immediately while Reiner tied Pisces to the cart. They started off quickly and travelled as fast as they dared drive the cart. The sleet was sheeting by the time they reached the keep. Max helped them unload the cart and carry the hides into the keep. Lena used a broom to spread the salt out on the hides as much as she could. She asked Mark to build a fire in the fireplace, hoping she could dry the salt faster. As she sat back on her heels, she realized she would need to get two more hides to send out with the villagers who would be working with Reiner on the late shift. "Just one surprise after another," she thought.

The sleet stopped later that night, and the next morning was cold and clear. The day progressed on the regular schedule. Lena rode back and sat with Klaus several hours. He had a fever but had not wakened. He no longer lay still, but thrashed around in an erratic way. Anna was as perplexed as Lena by his condition. When she returned to the manor, she checked the salt. It was too moist to bag. Lena found Lady Elena in the Solar and asked if she could help her with her sewing project. They exchanged stories and talked about themselves. In a lull in conversation, Lady Elena leaned forward and touched Lena's arm.

"Lena, I was wondering…I mean…well, would you allow Greta to stay here with me for a few months after Easter? She would be company for me, and I can teach her some fine sewing, or reading, or whatever you think might be good."

Lena smiled. The lady might well want Greta with her, but she was also thinking that Lena and Liebhard would be newlyweds. She thought this would be a very good experience for Greta too. "You are very kind and considerate, Lady Elena. This would be a wonderful experience for Greta. And a present to me," she said impishly. Lady Elena colored but laughed.

Late in the afternoon, they heard horses in the yard. They went to the windows and saw below that Lord Franz and Liebhard had returned. They hurried down the stairs. Lord Franz entered the hall followed by Liebhard. Lord Franz hugged Lady Elena tightly, and lifted her into the air. Liebhard gathered Lena into his arms, kissing her face and temples, impatiently asking after Klaus. The men shrugged off their partial armour and cloaks, all the while telling the women about their trip.

Thirza and Oona came out with wine, and later brought hot stew and bread. Franz and Liebhard were famished, not having eaten since morning, and they hardly spoke as they ate. While they were eating Reiner, who slept through the day after his night shift, came out of the back chamber. He exclaimed when he saw them.

"I am so glad to see you back," he said, as he gave Liebhard a bear hug and then took Franz by the fore arms. Oona brought out more food for Reiner.

Finally, Lord Franz leaned back and began to tell them about their journey. The trip to Midlin lands had been fast but shocking. There were so many areas that were completely without people. House after house empty, animals roaming freely, crops rotting in the fields. There were people on the road, but fearful and wary. The second day they reached Clara's homelands.

Her father's little village had been nearly spared, with only two deaths from the pestilence. Her father, Lord Frederick, was quite old, in his sixth decade, but hearty for his age. His shock at the murder of his daughter overpowered him. She had been his only living child. For some hours he withdrew to grieve, leaving his visitors to the care of his family servants. Late in the evening, just as they prepared for sleep, he came down to speak to them.

He had thought over what could be done. He wanted revenge, but he had no near family to carry his feud to Manfred's family. He did not even have anyone to stand for the family if Manfred demanded trial by combat. His brother, on the other hand, Abbot Wenzel of Midlin, was the Abbot of the Dominican Monastery of Mainz. He had position and power. It would be his brother who would carry this fight forward.

Lord Franz told him that the count had already sent his brother news of the murder of Clara, with a copy of her letter. Lord Frederick determined he would also send a messenger to his brother immediately, asking him to decide on a plan.

The next day was filled with discussion about how to proceed. The messenger had already been sent. Lord Frederick wanted to ride back with them to meet with the count. He had only a young retainer whom he could bring with him, leaving his bailiff as steward of the fief while he was gone. Franz agreed that they would ride with him to the count's castle before coming home. The count was most gracious and very concerned by all of Lord Franz's troubles. He also gave him some good news. Dieter had been found guilty of murder, named an outlaw in the empire, and even the priest stated Lena's marriage was null and void. Lena thanked Lord Franz profusely. It was a ray of sunshine amidst her worries.

"I think Lord Frederick counts on his brother-in-law to come to the count's lands, or maybe go to the Archbishop of Mainz to place an interdict of some kind on Manfred and his family until Manfred gives himself up. I do not know what the church can do, but we all know it has great power, even in matters of criminal law like this." After a pause, he reached into his tunic and pulled out the pouch with Clara's jewels. "Her father says that these should go to you, as well as all of her other belongings. He said he knows that you loved her like a sister."

Reiner, who had been listening closely volunteered, "The Archbishop of Mainz will throw his whole weight behind the abbot. The idea that a knight has ravished and ruthlessly killed a lady, the daughter of a vassal of another archbishop, will stir him to harsh action."

There was silence for a moment while each thought about the situation. Then Franz looked at Lena. "What has happened here since we left? No trouble? What about the salting?"

The ladies laughed excitedly." We have so much news!" Lady Elena exclaimed. "Lena, you explain." Lena looked and Reiner, who nodded.

Lena eagerly told the men all that had happened, all the surprises and the scrambling to make things work. She explained how they had set up the salting shifts, with Reiner leading the third shift. She explained where the salt was drying, and that merchants were expected any day to purchase salt.

"We have managed so far, but neither Sir Reiner nor I have any idea what price to put on the salt. We hope you know this, Lord Franz."

"All good news! Music to my ears after these days of worry and sorrow. I do have a good idea of the price we could expect from Gebhard's visit to Trier. I don't know how all the devastation of the land will affect prices though. Is any of the salt bagged?"

Lena explained that it seemed too moist as of noon, but suggested they go over to look at their drying process in the keep. It was very cold, so everyone pulled on their cloaks before they walked over. Liebhard walked between Reiner and Lena, with arms around both. He leaned down toward Lena and whispered, "I have been so worried about you. I missed you. I dreamt about you." She stood on tiptoe and kissed his cheek.

Once in the keep, Lord Franz knelt down and felt the salt. "Too moist yet. Tomorrow I want to sweep it off these hides and put it on cloth. I think if we can suspend the cloth off the ground it will dry fast." Lena saw immediately that he had a good idea, and was sorry she had not thought of it. She looked at Reiner who smiled and shook his head. They had figured out almost everything except this.

Back at the manor, Lord Franz suggested Liebhard get some rest, because he would be expected to take Sir Reiner's shift the next day. Since it was already getting dark, he said Lena should stay the night, and go home in the morning.

"I do have to get back to the village. I must check on Klaus. The flour must be all but gone. Can Liebhard come with me in the morning? Reiner's shift starts after dark. We have to mill here too."

"You are the miller," Lord Franz laughed.

A short time later, Lord Franz and Lady Elena retired. Liebhard was visibly tired, like Franz, but he was very excited too. Lena and Reiner sat with him as he told them of his experiences. The trip had been to him like a vision of a different world. In short staccato sentences he told Lena what he had seen and how he had felt about this avalanche of sights and experiences. "Even the way people talk just two days ride from here is different. How big this world is! But we met with trust and kindness from almost everyone." He stared down at the table, his thoughts far away remembering moments of his trip.

Reiner leaned toward him, touched his hand and said, "Now you know that you can travel the world over. It is not too different from experiences you have at home. But now I must be off to my shift. Sleep well. Tomorrow I will go with you for the third shift so you can see what we do." With that, he stood up, threw on his cloak, and went out to get his horse.

Lena had been enthralled by Liebhard's story and his ease with the experiences he had had. Maybe what he had really lacked in his life was breadth. She had hoped though to speak to him about Mark, a topic that troubled her greatly. Now was not the time. She pulled him out of his reverie by saying it was late.

Liebhard walked her to her door and held her for a long time. The interlude with Reiner while Liebhard was gone had shaken her understanding about her feelings. Now she thought she should lead Liebhard into her room. She wanted him to come. When she took his hand, he brought her hand to his lips, kissed it and whispered good night. She entered her room, closed the door and leaned against it, catching her breath. He had gone immediately to the other room. He had not hesitated.

Liebhard woke and was in the hall before Lena. They breakfasted on porridge and were soon riding home. Greta rushed out to meet them, followed by Margit. There was so much news for each to tell the other. Klaus had opened his eyes! He seemed not to know anyone, but he was awake for short periods. Margit asked if she would now be home nights, and Lena thought it would be so. There was much work to be done here too. After she looked in on Klaus, who was not awake, Lena put on her big apron, and went up to check the mill works. Liebhard walked around the village to tell everyone they were ready to mill.

Hours later they finally finished, cleaned up the stones and hopper and closed the sluice. Liebhard and Anna went home, and Greta and Lena sat down to dinner. Lena spent a quiet hour with Greta by Klaus' bedside. He was very restless, but did not wake. She took the occasion to talk to the young girl about staying with Lady Elena. Greta was very shy about the idea at first. After they talked about other things, Greta began to ask questions about staying with the lady, and Lena saw that it would be agreeable to her.

Liebhard looked in the door to say he had the horses ready. On the way back to the manor, Lena walked Pisces slowly, and finally stopped. "Liebhard, something strange happened while you were gone, and only you can tell me what it means." Liebhard looked at her quizzically, a little anxiety on his face. "The first night you were gone, Mark spoke to me."

"You say! I cannot believe it!"

"Liebhard, tell me about this!" she pleaded impatiently.

Liebhard walked his horse around in a circle, a frown on his face. "Oh, this is a long story. My family is very different than it appears. You think my father has no mind of his own, don't you? You think we always do what Mother asks. That is not really so. My father says nothing against her in the house, but has his own plans and thoughts when he closes the door and is outside.

We did not have a good childhood. Mother demanded we be one way, her way. I let it roll off my back, saying yes to everything, and doing what I thought I should. If she was angry when I did not do something, I pretended to not understand.

Mark talked all the time. He asked why about everything. Mother slapped him when he talked. She tied him outside for hours when he would not stop. He was stubborn. Then one day he stopped. He has not talked since, except to me. It is a puzzle to Mother. She has not beaten him or me since. She does not know he speaks to me. He says he will talk when she dies. But now, he has talked to you. I will talk to him, but I think he wants this to remain a secret."

Lena was dumbfounded at this story. Liebhard was not finished.

"I want to tell you something else. You wondered why I had not shown you how I felt. Did you know that I was engaged when I was seventeen? My mother arranged for me to marry a distant cousin who lives in a village north of here. She was three years younger, and her parents wanted her to marry when she was eighteen. I never met her. She died less than a year before we were to marry. The next year you started to walk out with Dieter."

"So many secrets, Liebhard. I am glad you told me, but why not tell me earlier about your engagement and the girl's death? Maybe we would have come together then and I would not have married Dieter."

"Maybe. I don't think so, Lena. You did not see me then."

129

Lena, bowed her head. It was true, she knew. "Yes, you speak truly." There had been so many occasions when he had singled her out, treated her as someone special, but she had barely acknowledged it at the time. She had been a thoughtless fool. She smiled at him and turned her horse toward the manor. They rode in quiet ease to the village mill and worked companionably through the afternoon.

Back at the hall, Reiner greeted them warmly. The two men caught up with each other's news, Lena a willing listener. She marveled at Reiner's ability to draw Liebhard out, making him like a different man. Glancing outside, she saw the afternoon sun was waning. She needed to ride home.

"I am going up to greet Lady Elena before I ride home," she told the friends. She ran up the stairs. Lady Elena was alone in the solar. Lena thought that she must often spend lonely hours. Greta would be good for her until she could get a waiting woman. The women greeted each other and Lena sat with her a half hour. As it happened, Lord Franz had ridden out to see the saltworks. Lady Elena said that Sir Reiner and Franz had also found a way to suspend the salt on an open cloth in the keep. Lena laughed and said she was not surprised at Lord Franz's ingenuity.

Back down in the hall, she said she must take her leave. Liebhard took her arms and kissed her on both cheeks. Sir Reiner took her hand and thanked her for all her help in the last few days. He quickly leaned forward and kissed her cheek. She reddened and did not know where to look.

"I'll be up in the morning, maybe to bag salt!" she said hurriedly.

Liebhard followed her out of the hall and waited while Max saddled Pisces. He lifted her on the horse, as he liked to do. She smiled down at him, and rode off toward Miller Village.

The following week was quiet and methodical. Brine was cooked, salted out, brought to the keep, dried and bagged. Lena spent most of her time at home watching over Klaus, working with Greta and catching up on many chores. Klaus continued to sleep most of the time. He could not remember anything about Manfred's attack. He needed help standing and walking. Lena worried, but made herself see that he improved very slowly.

She was at home when the first salt merchant came, and missed the excitement of a large sale, paid for in coin. When she went up the next day, Lord Franz was impatient to settle the debts he owed to all of his salt workers and all the milling and other debts he owed. She sat down with her ledgers and between Lord Franz and her they were able to cause much joy among the villagers.

When they had finished and the last worker debt was paid, Lord Franz leaned back and laughed. "Now we can make some improvements! I want to first get a waiting woman for Lady Elena. I have also arranged to have the count—when I had income—to send two of the young men from his retinue—older than pages but not quite old enough to be squires. I must teach them weapons and pay their keep."

"So where do we stand on the salting? Will we continue like this? And for how long?" Lena asked.

"The salt is always there. Reiner suggested we produce about fifty more bags now. We have another merchant coming, and I think he will take at least half of those. Reiner thinks we will cook brine for about two more weeks, till a few days before Palm Sunday. It will be time to think about spring field work by then anyway."

Lena nodded. It would be time for her and Liebhard to prepare for their wedding too. She had hardly prepared anything. "May I go up to see Lady Elena before I go home?" she asked.

Lord Franz rolled his eyes in mock surprise. "Do you have to ask?" he quipped.

Lady Elena was once again in the solar alone. Lena gave a little curtsey and sat down next to Elena, who greeted her warmly. After they had talked about Klaus for some minutes, Lena turned the conversation to Greta.

"I talked to Greta. She was a little timid at first about the idea, but now is quite excited about the adventure. But I wonder when would be best to send her down?"

"You arrange what is best for you, Lena. I would have her tomorrow, if you will allow it," she said somewhat shyly. "I was also thinking about a wedding dress for you. Would you allow me to give you one of Clara's dresses? You are similar in size," she stammered. Lena wanted to kiss her at that moment. She was an excellent young woman. She took the lady's hand and kissed it, then bade her goodbye.

THE WEDDING AND THE ABBOT

Lena rode home across the fields, her mind far away. She had about five weeks to prepare for her wedding. She would see if Greta would like to go to Lady Elena the coming week. She would have more time to spend with Klaus, helping him to get his strength and balance back. A year ago she could not have imagined all that had happened. She could hardly remember how she was then. The pestilence seemed far away. She thought of her family often, almost every day, but her memories were usually happy ones. Then suddenly an image of her mother lying dead, or Margit dead in a pool of vomit, or the horrible stench of death would flood into her mind. She drove those images away with thoughts of Liebhard and her future life. Riding home quietly, she was not sure if she was happy. She was not sure she was satisfied. A thought floated through her mind that if she were Lady Elena's waiting woman, if her father had been a knight or a landowner, she would be expecting to marry a knight. She heaved a sigh and kicked Pisces lightly. He leaped into a canter.

The following Monday Lena brought Greta up to begin her stay with Lady Elena. She sat several hours with them to assure herself that the young girl would be comfortable in this new setting. Late in the morning she left them, hoping as she went down the stairs to find that Liebhard was up. She had not seen him for a few days. She did not find him in the hall, but Reiner was there reading. He looked up, saw her and stood up smiling.

"Lena, good morning. Are you up to check the salt?"

"Good morning. I will check it, but I came up to bring Greta to the lady." She explained the planned visit to him, about which he had not previously heard. When she said that Greta would be staying until early summer, he nodded. His next comment betrayed the direction of his thoughts.

"So now you will be preparing for your wedding."

"Yes. I think having Greta here has been planned as a kindness by Lady Elena," she said, her cheeks reddening as she looked down. "And I will have more time to spend with Klaus."

"It is thoughtful of her. You will be busy with your wedding plans and will want some time together."

Lena could tell nothing of his feelings by the tone of his voice. When she looked up he was looking away from her, so she could only see his profile.

"Yes," she answered. "I must be off to check the salt, and then I will head home. I will walk with you," he said, but then added, "May I?"

"Of course, Sir Reiner," she said, trying to get back to a more casual footing.

They put on their cloaks and went over to the keep. The fire was blazing in the fireplace. The salt was cradled a foot off the floor on a large cloth sheeting. The sheeting was tied to benches which had been weighted down with bagged salt. It was quite ingenious. Lena felt the salt in several places, raking some from the center toward her. It was all ready for bagging. She threw off her cloak to begin the process, and Reiner did the same.

"This is not a job for you. You do so much already," she insisted.

"I want to do this. I wish to help you." He said this in such a way as to raise the point that it was his right to do as he wished, and hers to allow it. She felt both annoyed and happy, giving him a bag and a scoop.

During the next hour they bagged up all the salt. They had untied the sheeting to get the last of the salt, and worked together to retie it.

"We have another week of salting to go, so I estimate we will make another eight to ten bags," Reiner said, as they wiped their hands with damp clothes.

"You have had a great success with this process, Sir Reiner. Lord Franz is very lucky you had the knowledge and fortitude to see this project through."

"I have enjoyed it. I could not have done it without you." He held out her cloak, put his on, and opened the door, waiting for her to walk out ahead of him. Without any conversation they walked back toward the keep. She searched for some subject that would not be personal, but he broke the silence for her.

"You and Liebhard are the best of people. I have met so few since I left home that I would call friends, and here I have found two. I wish you great happiness, and only hope that you will find a little room in your hearts for friendship to me."

Lena's eyes filled with tears.

"We treasure you, both of us," she said, in a trembling voice. "Now I must be off home. Tell Liebhard I am sorry I missed him. Tell him to look in on Greta to see that she is well," she said in a rush. They stood together in silence until her horse was brought and she mounted. She looked down at Reiner and nodded slightly before she turned Pisces toward home. She turned around and waved. Reiner held up his hand in salute.

The next weeks were filled with remaking Clara's dress, working to help Klaus, milling and giving the mill a thorough cleaning top to bottom. Klaus was over-eager to start blacksmithing, but he had hand and leg tremors if he exerted himself too much, so Lena forbade anything more than walking about the village. Mark was her helper in the milling. She told him Liebhard had told her all. She did not expect an answer, but spoke her mind about his silence. She rattled on, saying he should forgive his mother, begin to speak, but make his own decisions. In the back of her mind, she could just about hear Lord Franz saying she was a tyrant and a busy body. She told Mark that she wondered that he did not think about his future, that what woman would take him if he did not speak. Finally she stopped, and was surprised by Mark's laughter. He did not say anything though.

On Holy Thursday Liebhard came home. Reiner had finished the last salting, and now the last crystallized salt was drying in the keep. Lena hugged Liebhard tightly at the wonderful news. She bustled him into the mill, gave him dinner and bombarded him with questions. She had not seen Greta for half of a week, but Liebhard said she was well and happy.

"Lena, Lady Elena has asked if you would allow Greta to stay with her over the Easter holiday. She wants Klaus to be brought up to the manor on Holy Saturday and Easter Sunday too. What do you say?"

"I will miss having them here. Do you think I am being selfish? They both like being with the lord and lady and with Sir Reiner."

"Let them stay there. We can bring Klaus up tomorrow morning. Maybe we can see them on Easter Sunday too." He pulled her down onto his lap, pulled her head down against his shoulder, slid off her kerchief and stroked her hair. She felt as though she was melding into his body. The stroking stopped; he sighed, kissed her cheek, and lifted her off his lap. He got up.

"Now I go home to see my parents and Mark. In two weeks it will be different." Before he closed the door, he said, "I will be down after breakfast and we will ride up to the manor."

The next morning when they arrived at the manor, Thirza said that Lady Elena invited them up to the solar. The lady sat with Greta by the fireplace, and the latter jumped up and ran to Lena. They all greeted each other, making much of getting Klaus settled. Lena found that Lady Elena was impatient to give them incredible news.

"Lord Franz and Sir Reiner are on their way to meet Carla's father and uncle, the abbot. They will be our guests over Easter. Abbot Wenzel wishes to gather information about Sir Manfred and all people here. He also plans to visit Trier after he leaves us. He has begun proceedings to bring an interdict against Manfred, and even his family if they shelter him. He thinks that this is how he will make the accused come forward to face the charges."

"But Lady Elena, you will be very busy. Should Greta and Klaus come home after all?"

"No, not at all! In fact, you must stay and meet the Abbot and Lord Frederick. They will want to speak to you," Lady Elena answered. After a short conversation, Liebhard said he would go down to the village to see how progress was going on the last new house. This had been an exhilarating project for him, and he was glad he had been able to see it through to completion before planting started.

Just before noon a village boy came to the manor with a message that Lord Franz and his guests were just within sight of the village. Lady Elena said they must greet the abbot and Carla's father out in the courtyard, so they all hurriedly put on cloaks and rushed out. They could hear the horses approaching. They came in, Lord Franz riding with the abbot, followed by Sir Reiner and Lord Frederick. Following them were two knights with the emblem of the abbot, Lord Frederick's squire and a very young monk.

Lena, Greta and Klaus stood behind Lady Elena, and curtsied and bowed when she did, as the abbot dismounted and turned to them. Lord Franz took Lady Elena's hand and brought her to the abbot.

"Abbot Wenzel of Midlin, Lady Elena, my wife."

The abbot bowed his head slightly. He was tall and very gaunt, brows jutting out over his clear hazel eyes. His brother-in-law, Lord Frederick, came forward and greeted the lady warmly, raising her hand to his lips. Everyone was invited into the manor, and Lady Elena led the guests upstairs, followed by Lord Franz. Sir Reiner welcomed the other knights, the young squire and the monk into the hall.

A moment later, Lord Franz came back down and beckoned to Lena.

"Lena, please come up into the solar. It will help Lady Elena."

He also beckoned the young monk to follow him up the stairs.

Lena looked around, but could not see Liebhard. He must not have come back up from the village. She did not want to leave Greta and Klaus alone with all of these people they did not know. Then her eyes met Reiner's. She motioned toward the children. He immediately came over to her.

"Greta and Klaus, I must go upstairs to be with Lady Elena. Here is Sir Reiner. He will keep you company until Liebhard returns." Sir Reiner held out his hand to Greta and smiled at her, and the young girl took his hand trustingly. Lena thanked him with her eyes and went up the stairs to join Lady Elena.

The abbot was wasting no time in his interviews. He was asking Lady Elena about Clara and her interactions with Sir Manfred before they travelled to Trier. Lena walked around the edge of the group, and sat down immediately behind the lady. She put her hand on her back. Lady Elena turned around and patted the place on the bench beside her. Lena quietly came around and sat next to her. Lady Elena took her hand. The lady's hand was trembling. Lena squeezed her fingers lightly in encouragement.

For over an hour the abbot questioned her closely, pulling out even small incidents and facts that might make a difference. It was a very hard time for Elena, whose tears slowly trickled down her cheeks. As time went on, she became less anxious, and her trembling stopped. At last he was finished with this initial interview.

"I will interview all that knew Sir Manfred here. No doubt I will need to speak with you again about what you have told me."

Lord Franz spoke up. "My lord Abbot, might we break now for dinner? And perhaps you will want to rest before beginning again this afternoon."

"You are kind and thoughtful. We will dine as you wish. However, immediately when we finish, I would like to interview you." This was said not as a request, but as a plan of action. Lord Franz bowed in agreement.

Lena leaned toward the lady and asked if she should run downstairs to see if the dinner was organized. Lady Elena nodded. She got up quietly and went downstairs. She found that the tables were all set up and ready for the family and all of their guests. Lena saw Liebhard and Reiner with the children, and went over to them.

"Thank you, Sir Reiner. The abbot has interviewed Lady Elena during this whole time. They are coming down to dine now with the knights."

He bowed and smiled. Just then Lord Franz came down with the abbot, followed by Lady Elena and Lord Frederick. The monk, who had functioned as a scribe followed. As everyone began to sit, Oona came over.

"Lord Franz says that you are to eat with the group. Please come and sit here." They went to the foot of the lower table, but still felt honored to be included. Lena looked up to Franz, and he smiled.

The abbot interviewed several people, all the knights and squires involved, and villagers who had had interactions with Sir Manfred. Finally, late on Holy Saturday Lena was called. She went up to the solar, and found the abbot, the scribe, Lord Franz and Lord Frederick. She sat down on the proffered bench.

"And you are Lena Miller? Please explain your relationship with Lord Franz and Lady Elena."

"My lord Abbot, I am a member of the assarted village west of here," she began. She explained how she had first seen Lord Franz after the pestilence had subsided. She asked him once or twice how much detail he needed, and he told her to speak on and he would say what she did not have to explain further. She described the lord's nearly fatal wounds, his recovery, the work to salvage his village, his brother's arrival, the salt project, Lady Elena's secret, the emergency planning after Sir Manfred left up until this moment. The abbot interrupted once or twice for more details.

"Did you have any conversation with Sir Manfred?"

"Yes. I had seen him in the hall a few times. Then one day he found me alone in the village mill," she said. She went on to describe what happened.

"So he tried to attack you?" he asked.

"I was certain that he wanted to impose his will upon me. He wanted me to know he was superior to me, or maybe did not approve of me," she answered.

The abbot looked at her for a long moment. It was hard to tell if he was scowling or meditating on what she said.

"And how did you escape? Please explain in detail."

Lena tried to remember everything that had happened, including running up to the manor, telling Sir Reiner, and his responses.

"So you attacked Sir Manfred with a knife?" he asked.

"I did strike him with my free hand after he had grabbed my other arm. He is very strong. It was my only defense." She looked directly into his eyes. Was he implying that she, a mere villager had acted improperly by defending herself?

"Now describe his attack upon you and your son in your home," he said.

Lena told him about the whole event, trying to leave out no details.

"I see. And is your son recovered?"

"He improves slowly. He was unconscious for several days. Then he woke. Now he can walk again, but tires easily."

"That is all. You are excused," he said tersely.

On Easter Sunday, the abbot broke off his interviews and celebrated mass in the manor church, which was packed with everyone from both villages. It was a joyous occasion, regardless of the stern sermon that he gave.

On Monday morning, interviews began again. He called Liebhard and several more villagers. He called several people back. He called Lena back too. He surprised her when she sat down.

"I have no more questions for you. You are to be thanked for listening to Lady Elena and urging her to come forward. I begin to see why, even though from a lowly background, you have been asked to advise and help. I counsel you to be careful of your position, which rests on no status. You recognize this I think."

"I have learned too, that you and the young man Liebhard plan to marry in a short time. Your situation with the outlawry of your first husband is very irregular. I have reviewed all of the facts, and support the idea that you are free to marry. There is no priest here, I understand. Do you expect to make your vows to each other in your church with witnesses?"

"Yes, my lord Abbot."

"That is enough. My scribe will give you wording for your vows. If I am back at that time from my trip to Trier, I will bless your union." He offered this in such a commanding tone that it took Lena a moment to understand this great gift.

"We thank you, my lord Abbot, for your kindness," she answered.

"That is all," he said, and turned away slightly. The interview was ended. She got up quietly and left the room, her heart beating wildly. What an honor!

Early the next morning, the abbot, his brother-in law, and their retinue left for Trier. It had been a trying and exhausting time for everyone. It was a relief too, because it seemed as though justice was coming for the murderer.

The next ten days were an odd combination of restlessness, sadness and excitement for Lena. Almost all of the preparations for their wedding and marriage had been made. She had finished refitting the dark blue wool dress that Lady Elena had given her. Liebhard was back in the village now, working with the men to get ready for spring plowing and planting, which would start in just a few weeks. He came to see her and Klaus every day in the late afternoon and stayed to supp with them. Their companionship had become stilted in anticipation of the great change that would occur between them. Liebhard was far calmer than she was.

They had determined that they would make the mill their home rather than move to one of the abandoned cottages. For Lena this had not even been a consideration, but Liebhard smarted somewhat that he was moving to her home. He resolved to enlarge the barn so that he could buy more livestock. He had earned a large amount of coins through the salting work and cottage building.

They decided to make their room out of one of the two rooms on the mill stone floor, and move Klaus up to the hopper floor. Greta would stay on the mill stone floor in the second room. Liebhard reminded Lena that Klaus might well want to move to his parent's house when he turned fourteen. She was shocked when he mentioned this, but realized he was right.

Reiner rode over twice to visit, joining them for supper. He was lonely for them, she could see. She and Liebhard also went twice during this time to see Greta, and to do the milling for the manor village. Lena visited with Lady Elena as long as she could each time. Lady Elena was glad to see her, full of praise for Greta, and obviously contented with her life. She was working on a new dress for Greta, saying that it was a good way to teach sewing, and Lena was grateful and pleased. Lady Elena also had news from her mother that a waiting woman had been found for her. The young lady, only fourteen, was a distant cousin whose parents had died in the pestilence. She was now a ward of Elena's mother and had a small inheritance, so she would stay with Elena until she married. Elena expected her arrival in late May.

The morning of the day before the wedding, Sir Reiner came to the mill. Lena was cooking in the kitchen, and was surprised when he knocked and opened the door. He stood a moment looking at her, his face inscrutable. She was very aware at that moment that she was wearing her oldest dress, and had thrown off her kerchief while she worked.

"Sir Reiner, welcome. Please come in," she said as she hastily placed her scarf back over her hair, which she had not tied back this morning.

"Please don't trouble yourself, Lena. Lord Franz has sent me. Did you know that late last night the abbot and Lord Frederick returned from Trier? They were both over-taxed from the strenuous travel and interviewing they had done. Even so, this morning Abbot Wenzel has called a few people back for interviews, including Lady Elena. He wants to make sure the facts are in agreement. Lord Franz wishes you to be present while she is being interviewed."

"Of course. But I must change my dress. Please sit down. Let me get you some cider," she said, and filled him a cup from the keg. He watched her in silence. She did not meet his eyes.

She hurried up to the millstone floor to her newly prepared bedroom and quickly changed to her red dress. She took off her eye patch and combed her hair, which had been hanging in loose locks around her shoulders. She quickly tied it back before putting on her kerchief. In just moments she was back down to the kitchen. Reiner was not there, but she heard the horses outside. He had already saddled Pisces for her. He held the horse while she mounted, mounted himself, and they were off. Instead of setting a fast pace, he put his charger into a slow trot. Lena rode beside him, happy to be there, but she could not think of anything to say. He smiled slightly when she caught his eye, but remained silent. It was an unsettling time for both of them, this day before her marriage.

The interview was once again conducted in the solar. Lady Elena was far calmer, but smiled and beckoned for Lena to sit beside her. From the questions asked it was clear that others in Trier had known something about Sir Manfred's imposition upon Clara. He had apparently implied to a young squire that a young lady with no prospects was defenseless and easy game. He wanted to verify the days that a couple of events had occurred, and Lady Elena, who kept a daybook, was able to respond to these questions.

The interview was short. When the abbot excused them, he held up his hand. "I have said I will bless your union, Lena. What time tomorrow do you wed?"

Lena thanked him again for his thoughtfulness, gave him the time and shyly asked if he would join in their celebration after the wedding. He nodded slightly.

Lady Elena walked down to the hall with Lena. Greta had been waiting there with Sir Reiner and the other knights. Lena hugged the young girl and then bade her and Lady Elena goodbye before she left the hall. Reiner followed her out.

Pisces was still saddled and waiting. Reiner's charger was there too.

"Sir Reiner, thank you. I can ride home alone."

"I will accompany you," he said. Lena bowed slightly. It was his will to do as he wished, she knew.

They mounted and once again rode at a slow pace.

"I do not mean to impose my will on you, Lena. It is just that....I do not want to explain all to you. It is a hard day for me. Please be patient with a friend."

"Yes," she said softly.

When they got back to the mill, he took Pisces into the barn to unsaddle him. She stood at the door and watched him. Her heart ached. When he finished he came toward the door. For a brief moment she hesitated, but turned and walked out ahead of him. She went to his horse and put her hand on the horse's neck. Sir Reiner took her hand in his own, kissed it, and mounted. He rode off. He did not look back.

In the late afternoon, Liebhard came. She rushed to him just as he entered the door. She wanted to push her body into his, to stop her ache and sadness.

"What is this? What, Lena?" he asked, as he held her and quieted her.

"I went to the manor today. Lady Elena was interviewed again. Reiner came to get me and he brought me back after the interview." She could not bring herself to say any more.

Liebhard kissed her hair several times, holding her close. "He loves you too. I know. He cannot help it," he said. She laid her cheek against his shoulder. How could she have ever thought he was unable to understand things, things that mattered. And he had such great love for Reiner that he was not jealous of Reiner's love for Lena. He would love her and be a good husband, and she loved him. And the other ache would go away someday.

The wedding day dawned clear, with just a few puffs of clouds in the sky. It was warm enough now, in late April, so that cloaks were not needed. The church was crowded for the wedding, decorated with green branches and a few early flowers. Many people came from the manor village as well, and Lord Franz, Lady Elena, Greta, Klaus and Reiner arrived together. The abbot, Lord Frederick and the young scribe followed a few moments later. The scribe came and stood in front of the altar, between Liebhard and Lena and read their vows, which they repeated. He said a few words after they exchanged their vows. Next, the abbot came forward and pronounced his blessing over them. With a respectful murmur of approval the attendees waited as the abbot walked out of the church followed by the newlywed couple.

Food and drink was laid out on long tables along the track in front of the mill. Lord Franz had also brought wine and food. The abbot and his retinue stayed only a short time, as they planned to leave for the count's estate very early the next morning. Hans had put together four musicians from the two villages, and everyone else danced and ate, celebrating until late in the afternoon. Finally it was time to bring Liebhard and Lena to their door. Amid wild cheers, hugs and kisses, everyone wished them well. Lord Franz gave Lena a resounding kiss to the hoots of his villagers. Reiner followed his example, though to him and to her it was a farewell kiss.

Liebhard waved and closed the door. He turned to Lena. "At last," he murmured as he picked her up and carried her up the stairs to their bedroom.

Lena experienced a bliss she had not imagined. Dieter had not been adept she now learned. Liebhard was so very gentle, but he was also passionate beyond anything she had dreamt possible. She completely lost herself in their lovemaking. They rested in each other's arms, saying very little. Later, when he had fallen asleep, still holding her comfortably in his arms, she felt herself to be enveloped in a cloud of bliss, safety and comfort.

When she woke the next morning, Liebhard was just climbing back into their bed. She was reminded again of his habit of waking before dawn. He kissed her good morning, a long and loving kiss that quickly became passionate. Once again they made love. He pushed himself up, still astride her, and looked down at her laughing.

"I promise not to wear us out! But you know, I have been waiting for you for years!"

She laughed too, and they kissed lightly and lay together for a few more minutes before they got up. His eyes followed her as she dressed.

"I will never tire of looking at you," he said.

"I hope you will say you will never tire of me!" she responded archly. When he laughed and grabbed her, they tumbled back on the bed and kissed a few more times affectionately.

Liebhard went out to do the chores while Lena prepared breakfast. They had a companionable meal, Liebhard taking her hand twice and squeezing it lightly.

"I love you, Lena," he said.

"And I you," she answered.

"And today I will get much teasing," he chuckled. She laughed, knowing that Anna and others would come down to see her and make some ribald remarks. It was the custom, and she knew she would enjoy it today.

SOFT SPRING

April flowed into May, sweet weeks of love, everyday activities and the welcome smells and sounds of spring. Klaus had resumed his apprenticeship with Lord Franz's blacksmith in late April, staying there until the end of May. When he came home, he settled in and began to try to work his father's blacksmith shop. Liebhard helped him as much as he could, providing the brawn. Klaus had learned several basic skills, and these would help in the planting preparation. He still had the slender body of a boy, but he was growing taller very fast. He was now taller than Lena, which pleased him.

Three days after the wedding, Mark arrived at their doorstep after supper. Lena opened the door, and welcomed him.

"Thank you, Lena!" he responded as he entered.

"So Mark, now you will talk to me?"

"Yes. Now you are with Liebhard."

"Did nothing I said to you matter?" She asked querulously, though she smiled.

"I am still thinking about it," he returned, as he sat down at the table opposite Liebhard. The two greeted each other as any brothers would, and Lena knew this had been their secret pattern all of these years.

"Think about it, Mark. This grudge against Mother is now very long. And you do not need to speak to her at first. Maybe if you speak to others and not her, it will give her pause. It will be obvious it is a grievance against her."

Lena spoke up then. "Why not speak to her. Tell her why this happened."

"Maybe soon I will speak to others. I am not ready yet."

Following that first visit, Mark came by almost every night, often managing to come right before supper so that he could join them. From the first visit, Lena understood Liebhard's remark about Mark's talking. He wondered why about everything. Lena liked this about Mark, but thought that for their commanding mother it must have seemed unendurable.

About a week after his first visit, Mark looked at Lena and smiled ruefully. "I am going to take your advice now about talking because I have reason now to speak."

"Why?" they both asked at once.

"Do you know Astrid down in the manor village?"

Liebhard did not answer, but Lena said she knew her. She was newly widowed from the pestilence, and had two children.

"I have decided I will ask her to marry me, and so I need to speak.

"What? How can you ask her now if you have never spoken to her, if you do not know her?"

Mark laughed a little. "There is knowing someone by speaking, and knowing someone in the complete sense."

Lena sat down abruptly on her chair and covered her mouth. Liebhard shouted.

"Mark, you are a rascal," he said, though he had trouble smothering a chuckle.

"Are you serious?" Lena asked aghast. "How on earth did you manage this? But don't tell me, I don't really want the details. Don't you think she will be angry now when you speak to her?"

"Well, Lena, that is why I am here. I need help. Is it possible that you can go down to speak to her, and explain?"

"Oh no, hardly. Mark you have dug yourself into a hole over the years, and now it is you who must dig out." He was surprised at her answer. She relented. "I will go with you when you try to explain this to her."

Liebhard, who had been listening now said, "Mark, once you speak to Astrid your secret will be out. You must think now about Mother."

A long discussion ensued between the brothers. From their conversation, Lena learned how deep and painful the wounds were that Mark had suffered. She wondered again if this was why Liebhard had seemed slow: was it from his mother's treatment?

Finally it was decided that Lena would go with Mark the next day, after he helped her with the milling in the manor village. Before he left, Mark took her hand and thanked her.

The next day, after they had cleaned up at the mill, Lena asked Mark if he was ready to see Astrid.

"I am worried, I have to admit. And I am not used to speaking much, except to Liebhard."

"Let's go then," she said, and they walked down to the end of the village, to Astrid's little house. Lena knew Astrid, as she had helped with the mat weaving.

When Astrid opened the door, Lena could see the familiarity in her look toward Mark. He had not been lying. She invited them in, and asked them to sit down. Lena sat down, but Mark remained standing.

"Astrid," he began, but stopped when the woman jumped up and grabbed her throat, frightened.

"Astrid, please do not be afraid." He launched into a messy explanation of why he had not spoken before, but Astrid only turned red with anger.

"You brute! How could you have deceived me so?" she ranted and walked about the room.

Lena decided to intervene, because Mark had made a dreadful start of an explanation. She stood up and went to Astrid, putting her arm on her back.

"Astrid, I felt the same way when Mark first spoke to me only weeks ago. Until then in all the years since he was six, he never spoke." She described Mark's childhood, and the hard punishments by his mother. She explained that in all that time he had spoken only to Liebhard, vowing not to speak until his mother died.

Astrid's first words were not unexpected. "If you could do this to your mother, you could do it to anyone! When you got angry enough you could do this again."

"Astrid, it has been painful for me many times over the years, and I regret that I have made this vow. It was stubborn of me, and I see from Lena's counsel that it has been cruel to my mother and everyone else."

"Well, why tell me all of this now?" she asked. At this question, Lena jumped up.

"Mark and Astrid, now this is between the two of you." She leaned over and pinched Mark's cheek very hard, hard enough so he yelped, and left.

As she walked up the road, smiling as she thought about the two she had just left, she heard her name called from behind her. It was Reiner. She turned around. He was coming up the road on his charger, dressed in full armor. The metal glinted under the sun's rays, making the knight seem larger than life. She felt uncluttered joy seeing him. He was a wonderful man, a wonderful friend.

"Sir Reiner! How good to see you! We have missed your company!" She realized her anxiety about him had been washed away by her new deeper relationship with Liebhard.

Reiner, dismounted, and came to her. "I have missed you and Liebhard these days. You do not come down as often."

"But you must come up to us! Come tonight. Come for supper."

He bowed slightly and smiled. Her remarks had pleased him.

"What are you doing in the village today?"

"I came with Mark on an errand, and to mill, of course. You will know the reason I had an errand when you come to us tonight," she said mischievously.

Reiner raised his eyebrows and laughed at her spritely remark. She was an enchanting woman. "I can hardly wait. I must hurry on now. I have the two young retainers on a practice mission, and I must see how they are doing." With that he mounted his horse and was off, his spirits raised.

Late in the afternoon Reiner arrived. Now in his best simple tunic, without his sword, he was dressed exactly like Liebhard. He smiled somewhat shyly as he came in, and gave her some spring flowers he had picked on the way. Liebhard gave him a slap on the shoulder and pushed him down on a bench. The two were both talking at once. Lena wondered how they heard what the other said. She continued to prepare supper, interjecting a remark here or there when she had a chance. She was on the lookout for Mark's arrival, and saw him before he came to the door. She hurried to the door and opened it.

"Well Mark, how did your interview go?"

"Oh, it took a long time before she was civil," he said as he entered.

Reiner had stood up abruptly, transfixed.

"Lena, you scamp!" Mark said, and gave her a pinch on the arm.

Everyone laughed and talked at once, explaining to Reiner all that had happened. Reiner in return had a surprise for them.

"Mark, I have known you could speak ever since we started the salt project. Once when you are out cutting down some trees, I happened to come past, some distance from you. I heard you singing."

"So, you knew he could speak, but that he chose not to," Lena said. "I did not know until you all rode in different directions after Manfred fled."

Mark spoke up then. He had been thinking about his own actions over the years, and digressed, remembering many incidents of his childhood. Finally Liebhard, rolling his eyes, whistled.

"Mark. Mark. Admit it, sometimes you just don't stop!" He was smiling, but he was also chiding his brother.

"Fairly said, brother. But it will be hard to talk to her."

"You needn't hurry, Mark. I would not be surprised if she came to you, once she has heard you are speaking," Lena interjected.

The brothers thought about that, nodded and spoke no more that evening about their mother.

The supper was long and lively. Klaus, who had come in just after Mark, sat down with them. Reiner had many stories about the two young retainers. He and Lord Franz were sharing the training of the boys, who were about fourteen. Reiner called them rascals, but he was enjoying their company and the training. He had other news as well. The last of the bagged salt had been purchased: their first buyer had come back to buy all that he could. He also told them that Lady Elena's new waiting woman was to arrive in a matter of days.

During a short silence after he had spoken, Lena asked, "Is there any news about the charges against Sir Manfred?"

"Yes. We heard that Abbot Wenzel, based on his interviews, has requested an interdict against the knight and his family. As it happens, Sir Manfred has a checkered history. His father had to pay a vast sum to Manfred's previous lord over the murders of several peasants. He also started a frivolous feud with another knight who was in service with him, and the other knight's family attacked Manfred's brother, who was maimed. His brother has blamed Manfred and has shunned him. The abbot expects a judgment within weeks. He thinks his family will force Manfred to give himself up to the count."

Klaus started to yawn as the conversation turned to the legal problems ahead. Liebhard laughed, and said, "Off you go to bed! You will have to work more on that plow tomorrow." Everyone said good night to the twelve-year-old as he climbed the stairs.

It was late when Mark and Reiner left. Liebhard and Lena walked out of the mill with them. It was a warm night, and they enjoyed the night sky together for a few moments. Mark gave Lena a kiss on the cheek and waved good night before he trotted toward home. Reiner brought his horse out of the barn, also gave Lena a kiss, Liebhard a sock on the arm, and mounted. He called good night as he trotted off. Lena leaned into Liebhard, and the two embraced. Very quickly, their passion reached such a height that Lena feared they would have each other right there in front of the mill, but Liebhard scooped her up, carried her into the mill and laid her down on the bed mat in the kitchen.

"Let's hope Klaus is sleeping soundly," he murmured against her ear before he sucked her ear lobe.

At the end of May, Clara's cousin Emerlind arrived. She was a big girl for her fourteen years, and she was an unhappy girl. Like Lena, she had lost her entire family. She was also a person of substance, since she had inherited land and goods at the death of her family. A young woman in her position would be an attractive wife, and her father's lord would be eager to find a powerful knight for her to wed.

Lena received a message from Elena, asking her to come up to the manor. She wondered as she rode along if Lady Elena thought it was now time for Greta to come home. She had been with Elena for nearly a month and a half.

Lady Elena was sewing with Greta and Emerlind when Lena entered the solar. She had not been up to the manor for five days. She thought Lady Elena looked flushed. She wondered anxiously if she had been called because the lady did not feel well.

"Lena, Welcome. It is so good to see you!" She introduced her cousin to Lena, and it was apparent by Emerlind's reaction that the girl knew who she was. The teenager was at an awkward age, and she looked very sad. She was already taller than Lena, and she would probably be a stately, handsome woman if she gained confidence. Lady Elena was unusually talkative. Lena thought she was trying to make her cousin feel more comfortable. After about half an hour, Lady Elena asked the girls to go down to Oona and ask her how to properly prepare the table in the hall for dinner.

After they left, Lady Elena leaned over and hugged Lena.

"I am so happy! I am bursting to tell you," she breathed.

"What? Tell me," Lena said excitedly

"I am pretty sure I am with child!"

"Oh Lady Elena!" Lena exclaimed. They laughed together, and after they had calmed down, Lena asked her what her symptoms were. She said she had missed her time a few weeks ago, and that most mornings she felt nauseous. She had vomited a few times, but that seemed to have stopped.

Lena felt Lady Elena's forehead. She had no fever. Lena said, "You look flushed, and I thought you might have a fever:"

Lady Elena smiled and said, I have felt very hot sometimes. Is that normal?"

Lena smiled back. "That I do not know. I am wondering if perhaps having both Greta and Emerlind here might be too much for you? Should Greta come home?"

"Oh, no, not yet! Emerlind does not feel comfortable yet. I think Greta is the only person that she has found reassuring. Can she stay for a couple more weeks?"

"I will let her stay if she would like. I will talk to her."

The girls came back and the four spent an hour sewing and talking. Lady Elena slipped in the fact that not only Greta was an orphan, but so was Lena. Emerlind's eyes widened as she listened. They also glistened because of the tears standing there. Lena switched the conversation slightly and talked about how difficult she had found it at first to be the last one in her family alive. She was surprised when Greta piped in.

"I had Klaus, but we were so frightened and alone when Mama and Papa died. Then you came, Lena. You and Liebhard and Mark. You hugged us, and Liebhard and Mark put their arms around all of us. I knew I was going to be safe then."

Lena looked at the girl. How amazing she was, and only nine!

Late in the morning Lena said she must go home, but said she would come back the next morning for a while. She had to encourage Pisces into a canter, because she had little time to prepare dinner. It was already late in the planting season, and she like the other women in Millers Village always took the noon meal to the field workers. She determined that instead of walking to the field, she would ride Pisces to save time. Leaving her horse tethered outside, she hurried into the kitchen and pulled together the food she had prepared early in the morning.

When she arrived at the field where Liebhard was, she sat on her horse, enjoying the beauty, strength and fluidity Liebhard exhibited as he seeded the field. When he saw her, he waved. Hans, Lars and Mark were already just coming off the adjoining fields, to take their meal baskets from the other village women. Lena dismounted, opened her cloth, set out the food and cider, and waited for him. He walked up, squatted down behind her, and put his arms around her, quickly cupping her breasts, kissing her hair, then sitting down next to her.

"Someone will see you do that," she remonstrated, smothering an excited giggle.

"I would not be embarrassed. They know I love you to the heights," he laughed.

She was embarrassed though. It was a thing he loved to do, early in the morning while she dressed, as she made breakfast, or when she came to the field with the dinner. She reminded herself that other women might yearn for such constant fondling. She nodded, pouring cider into their cups. They had a companionable meal together. Liebhard kissed her, got up, pulled her to her feet, lightly rubbed his lips several times along her cheek, and said, "I will see you at sunset."

The early summer was gentle and idyllic. The cycle of milling, spending time with Klaus and Greta (who came home in mid-June), working in her little vegetable garden, and her time with Liebhard was joyful. Even though she wondered if most young couples made love almost every night, she could not imagine how she could feel more loved and wanted than she did. Time seemed to stand still for her, a kind of sweet bubble.

The day before summer solstice, a strange cart came down the village path. She stood up from her garden weeding, rubbed her back and watched the approaching wagon. Then she froze. Tied to the back of the cart was Jake, her father's horse. She dropped her trowel and ran up to the cart. The driver stopped. It was not Dieter.

"Why do you have that horse?" she blurted out.

"I was given a coin by the master of the fief up by the Mosel River. His bailiff knew the horse belonged here."

"How?" she asked, walking around to Jake. He looked careworn.

"He found the horse standing beside the road during the winter. The saddle and bridle had the name Jan Miller at Millers Village. Not many travelers these days, but I was bringing this wool to the wool market, and the master asked me to deliver the horse. Is the miller here?"

"He died during the pestilence. I am his daughter. I am the miller now. This is Jake. He was stolen by my outlawed husband, who tried to kill me. He killed my sister and son," she gulped as tears started in her eyes. "Was no one found with the horse?"

The man shook his head. "I don't know."

Lena invited the trader into the mill, gave him cider and sat with him, learning about the lands to the north. He said about an hour later that he had to be on his way.

Lena waved to him as he left, took Jake into the barn, fed him, brushed him, examined him closely, and pondered what had happened. Was Dieter dead? But the horse was not found until months after Dieter left. Maybe the horse was wandering after Dieter died, and someone else took him?

When Liebhard came home, she silently led him to the barn, and pointed to the horse. He put out his arms and blew out loudly.

"What does this mean?" he asked.

Lena told him all that she had learned during the afternoon. They did not know what to think, but Liebhard calmed her worries. "He is most likely dead. If he is not, he cannot harm you, you know that." He hugged her, gently sliding his hand over her back. They walked back into the mill, and throughout the evening occasionally wondered again about the strange arrival of Jake.

Reiner came down the next evening, as he did regularly, and joined them for supper. They told him about the strange arrival of the horse. He was impressed that the master of the northern fief had made the effort to return the horse. His next thought was that Dieter's reputation had impressed upon Reiner that he was a very selfish person. That being the case, he was sure that Dieter would not have left the horse. The conclusion had to be that the horse had either been sold or Dieter had died. Lena and Liebhard agreed with his logic. Lena remained anxious, nonetheless: she could not forget how he had treated her family in the time of the pestilence.

They also talked late into the evening about Mark and Astrid. Mark had won Astrid's agreement to wed. An obstacle Mark had not considered then popped up. Astrid was from Lord Franz's village. Her children belonged to the village, to their father's land allotment. Lord Franz seemed to want to work with Mark, but he insisted that the ten- and twelve-year-old boys remain residents of his village. He was working out with Mark that Astrid could move to Millers Village and become a resident there, although Mark would have to pay a large fee for this to happen. Since he had earned a fair amount of coin during the salting and guarding of the manor, he did not quarrel with this demand from Lord Franz. Because the boys would be part of the manor village, they would be responsible for working their allotment, and paying those dues. This Mark would have to take on somehow. Mark had asked Lena to help but she explained that she was loath to discuss these negotiations with Lord Franz. She knew from her friendship with him that he held the lord and tenant customs as legally binding. Liebhard said nothing, but Reiner agreed with her.

Finally Mark and Lord Franz agreed that Astrid and her sons would move to Millers Village. The boys would retain their house in the manor village and be responsible for working the land. When they each turned fourteen, they would be expected to return to the manor village. They would each have a house and a land allotment. The wedding was set for early in July, and not a moment too soon, since Astrid was expecting to deliver her baby about frost time.

Dizzily hurried work began on preparation of a house in Miller Village. Mark had asked Lena if they could rent her Aunt's house, now hers. At first this troubled Lena. It was like finally having to let go of her family. Until then, when she looked at her aunt's house, standing empty, it seemed as though a connection with the family was still there. She talked to Liebhard about her feelings and he did not say anything to change her mind, but she knew he wanted Mark to be there, near him. In the end, she agreed.

The house had already been thoroughly cleaned and whitewashed. It was a good-sized cottage, and the furniture was good. Lena took a few cherished items of furniture and brought them to the mill, and sold the rest to Mark and Astrid. Because Astrid's eldest boy would inherit her house in the manor village, she brought very few of her own pieces to Millers Village. Mark and Liebhard re-thatched the roof and built in a stube, as Mark loved the smokeless air of his parents' house. Klaus was included in all the work they did so that he could learn.

On the Sunday morning before the wedding, Lena and Greta walked up to visit Lady Elena, as was their custom. This was always a happy visit, and eagerly anticipated by Emerlind. The teenager had settled in finally, and had become very attached to Lady Elena, but she missed Greta. Lady Elena's form was still very maidenly, although everyone now was aware of her condition. She was healthy and happy too. Shortly before noon, Lena and Greta took their leave so that they could be home in time to prepare dinner.

As they walked through the fields toward Millers Village, they were hailed by someone behind them. It was Reiner. He slowed his horse so that he could walk with them. Lena saw frown lines on his face, a most unusual occurrence. Whatever troubled him, he was not willing to discuss before Greta. They walked along, catching up on the week's news.

When they reached the mill, Lena told Greta she could run down to her house, check on the animals, pick the eggs, and see if there were greens in her garden for the pottage.

Reiner had sat down when he first entered. Now he got up and paced. "Where is Liebhard?" he asked.

"He will be visiting his parents. His mother is still quite distraught about Mark. She tiptoes around and is quiet as a mouse when Mark is anywhere near. She is angry with Liebhard. He should be home shortly. What troubles you, Reiner?" she asked, dropping the "Sir" as she and Liebhard usually did when he was visiting.

"Well....I got a letter." His face clouded.

"Do you want to wait until Liebhard comes and tell us together?"

"Yes, I think so," he said, and sat down again. Lena poured some beer for him. He watched her as she moved about her kitchen. She had grown used to this, and it did not trouble her. His feelings were what they were, and he was the gentlest and most loyal of men. For his part, it was one of the few wistful times he allowed himself.

"We were up visiting Lady Elena this morning. She seems very well. And Emerlind is developing into a pleasant young lady."

"Yes. That is another strange part of my problems," Reiner responded enigmatically.

The door opened and Liebhard entered. He did not look happy either, but his face warmed when he saw Reiner.

"Reiner, your visit will help my temper," Liebhard said.

"I hope so. Is your mother still angry?" Reiner asked.

"Yes. This will be a long cold time, I think. Mark must get his stubbornness from her!" he quipped.

"Liebhard, Reiner has received a letter, and that is why he is in a low mood today," Lena interjected. She poured some beer for Liebhard, and returned to preparing dinner.

"What a letter. My father wrote. Can you believe that after almost fifteen years he has deigned to remember he has a second son? And almost as though not a moment has passed he presumes to tell me what to do!" He jumped up from his chair, very angry.

Lena stepped up to him and touched his arm. "Reiner, please read the letter to us." He looked down into her eyes, calmed down, sat down and pulled the letter from inside his tunic.

This first letter in fifteen years started by berating Reiner for his disobedience. Sentence after sentence described his father's dissatisfaction with his son. One sentence then mentioned that the Archbishop of Mainz had described Reiner's success with the salting project as exemplary. No praise followed from his father. Instead he commanded his son to return to the estate, that there was a widow nearby who had land holdings that would expand the family's power, and that he owed homage to his father.

When Reiner finished, he dropped the letter on the floor, and rubbed it into the floor with his foot. "That is what I think of him."

Lena and Liebhard stared at him, speechless. They had hardly heard an angry word from him before this moment. Lena covered her cooking pot, pulled it away from the direct fire, and sat down.

"Tell us about your childhood," she said.

For a brief moment his eyes teared, Was it anger or sadness? Reiner leaned his head back, closed his eyes for a moment, and then began his story.

151

"My mother died of pleurisy when I was about four, I think. For a knight, a vassal to the archbishop, my father seemed to be home much of the time. We were three children. My older brother is three years older than I am. My sister was two years younger than me. We were all ill-treated by our father. Certainly, we were fed and clothed, but we were required to obey every small detail of what he wanted, or punishment waited. My older brother was a sullen boy, but who can blame him? He was thrilled to be sent off at ten years to be a page at another vassal's castle. I have not seen him since. I know he is alive, has a fief in the far east of the empire, near Bohemia.

My younger sister wilted more and more under my father's eye. He was thinking about to whom she would be married as long as I can remember. Years after I was sent to the monastery I heard that she had died about the time our father had arranged a betrothal for her. She was twelve. Why did she die? I have no answer. I have wondered if she just decided she did not want to live.

When I was eight, my father said I would be going to a Benedictine monastery near the Rhine River. I had not had the remotest notion before that moment that I was meant for the church. I had been looking forward to being sent away to any other fief, to get away from him. Can you believe that I was relieved to get away anywhere, even a monastery?

For some children, I am sure the experience of growing up in a monastery would be acceptable. It was all wrong for me. The abbot even wrote to my father and said he thought I would not make a monk, that I would be a man of action. My father came to the monastery, beat me and demanded the abbot make me into a monk. I think the abbot pitied me, but he tried to make me fit into that studious contemplative life.

When I was fourteen, I was meant to start taking my preliminary vows. Instead I escaped. I lived pretty rough for a few months hiding, travelling to my mother's cousin, who I knew was a bit of a wild man, but an enemy of my father. When I finally reached him, he thought it was a great joke that I had slipped from my father. He knew he could not support me outright, but he gave me a horse, all the equipment I needed and sent me down to another vassal far to the south who owed him a favor.

You know the rest of my story, more or less. I have been to Bohemia, the Piedmont, Rome, Sicily, even the land of the Ottomans. I have been in too many battles to count, seen many good men die. And finally, through great good fortune, Sir Gebhard brought me to help his brother. Here I am, content at last."

"But what did you mean about Emerlind being a part of this story?" Lena asked. Reiner laughed mirthlessly. "Lord Franz sympathizes with me about my father. I read that letter to him. I received it Friday. Yesterday, he asked to speak to me privately. He has hatched an idea that I should take Emerlind as my betrothed! He would like me to stay here in this part of the empire, which I would like too. But

Emerlind! She is a child! No, it is not the answer. Now I will have to disappoint him."

The three friends sat in silence for some time.

"Lord Franz will not be disappointed in you," Liebhard said.

"He is trying to help you," Lena piped in. She herself was troubled by every piece of information she had heard since Reiner arrived. He would never follow his father's command, but marriage to Emerlind? He would have to see that this might be an opportunity for him to settle at last. Her heart ached. This was not right! It was not right! She mentally shook herself. Reiner must choose his life. She wanted him to stay with them!

The passing clouds of these thoughts must have been apparent in her face, because Reiner suddenly stood up and came over to her. "I am not going to marry where my father wants, and I am not going to marry Emerlind."

The three continued to talk about Reiner, his father and Lord Franz until Greta came back. It was time for dinner, and Klaus came in as well. By the time Reiner prepared to leave later in the afternoon, his frown was gone and his mood was lighter. He gave Lena a kiss on the cheek, put his arm around Liebhard's shoulder, and he was off.

These were busy days in the fields. The meadows had been cut, the hay turned and the haystacks were complete. Some of the grain was nearly ripe. The growing season and the harvest had been good, and the rhythm had raised everyone's spirits. It was clear that the small population of the village could not keep up with the size of the fields and the maintenance of the village buildings as well as in the past, but they had managed quite well.

Mark's wedding day was a welcome break in the work. Many people from the manor village came down for the wedding festivities. Lord Franz and Lady Elena came too. Emerlind attended Lady Elena, but spent the whole afternoon with Greta and Klaus. Reiner was again in good spirits, and made everyone else happy too. Mark enjoyed himself immensely, and even managed to get his mother to smile at him. The dancing and eating went on until dusk, when Mark and Astrid were brought to the door of their house. Astrid's boys were going to stay with Klaus in his room, which Lena thought would be a long night for her family.

After almost everyone had gone home, Reiner came into the mill with his friends. He was happy this day because Lord Franz and he had spoken about his suggestion about Emerlind. Franz accepted Reiner's reasoning. He admitted that he had made the offer more as a means to keep Reiner here than as a good match for either Reiner or Emerlind. He also had assured Reiner that the young girl knew nothing about the discussion.

Village life settled down peacefully. Mark spent half days with his stepsons harvesting at the manor village. Lena found that Astrid was a welcome neighbor and sister. She did no gossip but was friendly and happy to accept help when she needed it. Liebhard had decided how he would expand the barn. He had bought three ewes and would build a box stall for them at the far end of the barn. He also made a separate coop for the chickens up against the barn, and bought a dozen additional hens. With the return of Jake, they had also needed an extra stall.

CONSPIRACY

About a week after the wedding, Lord Franz sent a message to Lena and Liebhard, asking them to come up to the manor. With some curiosity, they rode over to the manor village. Lena did not see Lord Franz as often now because the growing season had been busy. Reiner was just returning with the two young squires, Rudi and Conrad, very hot in their half armour, having practiced military tactics on horseback. He hailed his friends happily, dismissed his young charges, and took off his armour with Liebhard's help. They told him Lord Franz had asked them to come up. The three entered the hall, and were immediately met by Lord Franz and Lady Elena.

"Let us go up to the solar," he said cryptically.

When they had all sat down, they waited expectantly. What could Lord Franz be planning? He stood up, pulled out a paper, and then began to tell them its contents.

"Sir Manfred has been forced by his father to agree to come to Katzenberg, to the count's court. In this letter, copied by the count's scribe and sent to us, Sir Manfred has demanded certain safeguards. He wants a mounted guard to come to his father's fief, and ride with him to Katzenberg. He demands safe conduct. He asks that the guard be sent in a timely manner so that he will arrive at the count's royal court the first of September."

This announcement drew exclamations from everyone, irritated by the demanding tone of the knight. Lord Franz raised his hand for silence.

"Sir Manfred refuses to be tried in a court. He demands trial by combat. He says that he will meet any knight in sword combat on foot who would stand as champion for Lady Clara, be it family, friend or hired knight."

Everyone spoke at once. This was not a surprise, but all those present were angry at the way Manfred presented his wishes.

"Has Lord Frederick found a kinsman who can bring this combat to Sir Manfred?" Reiner asked.

"No one has been found. I believe the Abbot has some small hope of finding a defender, or hiring someone. I myself am considering if I will take her defense," Lord Franz said.

"I would like to meet him," Liebhard interjected. "I would break his back with these two arms—even against his sword."

Sir Reiner put his hand on Liebhard's shoulder. "I know you could. But in the law, you cannot meet him. Only someone of his rank can meet him."

"Lord Franz, please read exactly what Sir Manfred said about who he would agree to do combat with," Reiner asked. He was now standing on the other side of the sitting area, opposite Franz. Lena looked up at him, aware that his tone was purposeful.

Lord Franz looked at Reiner closely too. He opened the letter, found the spot, and began to read.

I will accept only trial by combat to defend myself against this outrageous charge. I will fight any kinsman of this lady, any friend who might dare to come forward, or even a hired knight if such can be found. And I will fight this challenger in sword combat, on foot, to the death to prove my innocence.

All had been looking at Lord Franz, but when they turned to Reiner, they saw almost a new man. He had begun to smile slowly. It was not a friendly smile. He stood squarely, put his hands on his hips, and murmured, "I am that friend who will come forward." Amid cries from everyone, he continued, "but you must all assist me in one thing. This must be a secret until the very moment the combat starts."

"What are you thinking?" both Franz and Lena said at the same time. They caught each other's eye, and Lord Franz understood for the first time one reason she had been so tormented about marrying Liebhard.

"Sir Reiner, why? Don't put yourself in this danger," she begged, tears standing in her eyes.

Liebhard took her arm gently and turned her toward him. "Lena, support him. This is what he wants to do."

Lena coughed a ragged sob, gained control of her tears, but continued to tremble with anger and fear.

Reiner's heart swelled with love for her at that moment. But he did not fear Manfred.

"I told you when he hurt you that I would kill him. I know you were shocked then, and you are shocked now. Now he will be killed. He has committed a capital offence. He has murdered a lady. I know Manfred's measure. I know his fighting ability. I do not fear him. He would never readily agree to fight me. It has not occurred to him that I would be the challenger. However, he has said in his own words that he will accept any friend of the lady who comes forward.

You wonder why I want this to be a secret. My challenge will be most successful if he does not know until the moment I come forward in combat that it is I who will fight. In this way he will have no chance to ponder or plan how best to meet me." Reiner had thrown his head back slightly as he spoke, and he seemed so powerful, undefeatable, so mighty, that everyone drew in their breath.

"Reiner, I know Manfred's sword ability. He is young and powerful. Are you sure of this?" Lord Franz asked.

"Lord Franz, I have sparred with him many times. I have watched him. I am older. I am experienced. This is not conceit on my part. I can defeat him. I will kill him." Reiner answered. He felt a strange release, a freeing of bonds, as he spoke. What had occurred in his own thinking he was not sure, but his sense of self-worth had risen like a tidal wave within him.

"I will support you completely, Reiner," Lord Franz said, crossing the room to take him by the arms. Liebhard gave him a bear hug. Lady Elena leaned up and kissed his cheek, though her eyes were round with anxiety. Lena, the last to approach, put her forehead on his chest, which took his breath away.

"I am sorry. I am frightened for you. But, Sir Reiner, I believe in you completely," she whispered.

"Lord Franz, you must write to Lord Frederick and to the abbot. Tell them to keep secret that we have found a champion. Do not say who, but say you are confident the champion will defeat Manfred. Perhaps they can even help by letting the story fly that they have found a champion among the abbot's people. We also need them to demand that the traditional rules of trial of combat will apply: no armor except sword and shield, only leather or linen clothing, no head covering."

"I will write today," Lord Franz said, smiling conspiratorially.

"Let's sit down and do some planning," Lord Franz said. When everyone was seated he said, "First, I think we five must all plan to go to Katzenberg. Lady Elena must go as Lady Clara's nearest friend and main accuser; and I must go as her husband. Reiner, you will be my knight, and Liebhard will be your squire. Lena, you will be Lady Elena's maid."

"Is that allowable, Lord Franz? We are just free tenants of yours. Can we take such positions? " Lena asked.

"Your position will not be unusual at all. Liebhard will be presented as a substitute squire needed because of the great loss of life in the pestilence. Usually a squire would have to be of the knightly class, wouldn't he, Reiner?"

"I have met many squires and even some knights who are from free man or tenant class," he answered, and smiled at his giant of a friend. "You will have to learn some simple tasks before we arrive in Katzenberg. And I think we will dispense with a sword for you. That might be stretching the question a bit too far."

"We have, what, eleven days to prepare? We need to think about clothes. Reiner is your sword in good repair? You might want to look at mine and my father's. And our shields too."

"You are very thoughtful. My sword is what I will use, but I will look at your chain mail, if I may, in case Manfred insists. My chain mail has seen too many battles to be in good condition. I have a leather tunic and leggings I will wear."

"Let's go now to my father's room and down into the cellar, and we will look over what we have. Liebhard, you must come too. We will need to outfit you with the right kind of long knife and a quarterstaff." With that the men left the room, their minds full of weaponry.

Lena and Lady Elena had both sunk onto chairs. They sat in silence. Lena was aware that Lady Elena was uncomfortable and did not dare to speak.

"It's all right, Lady Elena. We three have a very close friendship. But in the end, only one conclusion could happen. Sir Reiner is a knight. I am a miller. I could never have been more than a kept woman to him. We have not spoken of any of this. Liebhard, Reiner and I are friends deep and forever, and we know how each of us feels. Liebhard is my loving husband. He is not jealous of Reiner. He is sad for him, as am I."

"I cannot understand completely. I am sad somehow too," Lady Elena said, and sighed. "Sir Reiner is an admirable man, but had until today a touch of melancholy. This afternoon he is like a power unleashed." Lena nodded in agreement.

"So, we must think about clothes. Your blue dress, the one you wore on your wedding day, will be perfect. We will need to make a proper wimple for your head though. A kerchief will not do. And you will need some simple necklace. Do you have something?"

"I have a small cross on a leather cord," Lena answered. I have a pretty blue glass brooch from my mother that can be made into a pendant. I am not sure if she had a chain for it." She heaved a sigh at the thought of her mother.

"When you come up tomorrow, please bring what you have. We will look through my things and Clara's and find something suitable," she laughed. "Let's go to my room now and look for a head dress." The rest of the afternoon was spent trying various head covers. They finally settled on one of Clara's, which would have to be enlarged slightly. Lena's leather shoes were quite good, and her stockings were fine.

When the men came back into the solar, all discussed the problem of Liebhard's clothing. He was so very large compared to the two knights, that none of their tunics would fit him properly. Lena and the lady decided that they would take his best blue tunic and sew ribbon on its edging, as well as do some needlework around the neck and sleeves to dress it up. They decided they would sew him some new colored leggings, as knights seldom wore the brown and black leggings that peasants did. His leather shoes would have to do, but his leather belt would be improved with silver studs along the top and bottom. Franz was able to find an old loose hat from his days as a squire which Lena would enlarge by opening the seams.

"I think we have thought through the clothing and weapons. Lena, you had better plan to spend time up here with Lady Elena every day to work on manners of a lady in waiting." The women laughed and made plans. "Reiner, I will take over the training of Rudi and Conrad until we are ready to leave, so that you can spend time with Liebhard, going over training," Lord Franz said.

When the group broke up, Reiner invited himself down to dinner with them at the mill. Their conversation was subdued as they rode to Miller Village. Liebhard and Lena remained unsure what was behind Reiner's decision. After they had dismounted and taken care of the horses, Reiner asked if they would walk with him along the river. This was a novel idea for them, this day, a late summer harvest day, but they agreed. The fieldwork was well in hand.

They walked along in expectant silence for some time, until they came to a wider part of the path. Reiner stopped, and suggested they sit here to talk. Lena sat on an old stump, Liebhard sat at her feet. Reiner sat opposite them on a fallen log.

"Since I took the leap into my future by running away from the monastery, I have had a life I chose, but it has not been easy. With no family support, I have not been in a position to advance, to gain a fief. I have served as a warrior, a guard, and a member of a large retinue. I think I would say I have been buffeted along by chance. One day I will tell you about some things you do not know. Suffice it to say, I expected nothing in my future but to live out my days.

By the luckiest of chances, Gebhard needed at least one experienced man to come with him to help his brother. The count had a good account of my abilities, and chose me. From the first day, I knew I had arrived to a place and to people who I could respect and who valued me. Lord Franz has given me great responsibilities and has expected that I could do them. You two have made me feel that I can accomplish nearly anything, that I can overcome any obstacle. You have all given me your complete trust.

It is hard to explain, but I feel like my chest, my body is expanding. I feel like I have a new lightness in my step. In the morning when I wake I expect the day will be good, not just survivable.

When I heard Manfred's demand, I felt as though I was asked to come forward. Not by any of you, but by my own voice within me. And it is strange, but I almost feel like I see that this is my way forward. I am climbing, and the way is growing easier.

I ask that you do not fear for me. I draw strength from your confidence in me. Please do not lose faith in my ability."

Liebhard jumped to his feet, lifted Reiner off the ground in a great bear hug.

"I cannot even tell you how much confidence I have in you! It is too large."

Lena, who was still sitting, took in all that Reiner had said. She realized too that she had seen this growth in confidence, this ability to take on every new task. She got up and put her arms around him.

"These are tears of joy for you mingled with my own weakness, Reiner. I have always felt you were capable of great things. When you first came you had a veil of melancholy about you. It is gone, isn't it?"

He kissed her hair lightly before he pulled away from her. "Thank you for those words. I have needed to hear them from you."

Lena thought of Lord Franz and suddenly laughed. "You know, Lord Franz did the same to me as we have done to you. He demanded such incredible things of me and did not think for one moment I could not do them. He bullied me when I said I could not. Remember, Liebhard, when he demanded I go out and get Smoke?" She then told Reiner in detail the story of Smoke's arrival, and soon was describing her squabbles with Franz over his wounds, his collection of fees, his ideas about sheep, and other stories. They all laughed together, but praised the young lord's enthusiasm and trusting nature.

These stories fleshed out for Reiner that strange relationship between Lord Franz and Lena. It was not a relationship of lord and peasant, or a physical attraction. It was not a relationship of unequals. He could see in his mind's eye the two ranting at each other in her mill kitchen. In an odd way they were almost like family members; loving, irreverent, trusting of each other. She was a strong, unique woman, but she had blossomed into her full potential because of Franz.

As they walked back to the mill, Reiner began to explain to them some of the manners and ways of acting that would be expected of them. He cautioned that Lena be silent about her position as a miller, and that she not admit she could read. He mentioned little things like not speaking unless spoken to, not looking directly at knights or lords, or just looking fleetingly. He suggested that Liebhard start now to walk only behind Reiner, unless he was asked to do otherwise. The litany of things they should practice had gotten quite long by the time they got to the mill.

At the door, Reiner beamed at them. "Now let's forget all of that while we have dinner!"

After dinner, Reiner and Liebhard walked out on the village path, practicing. They took out their horses, Liebhard being directed how he should serve his knight. The other villagers were quite curious, particularly Mark. They could not be told everything, but they were told that Liebhard would be acting as Sir Reiner's squire, and Lena would be acting as Lady Elena's waiting woman, and that they would be traveling to Katzenberg at the end of August. This set the village abuzz. Astrid's sons and Klaus walked along, copying Liebhard. Soon there was too much laughing for Liebhard to learn anymore. Late in the afternoon, Reiner forced himself to go back to the manor.

The next week was crammed with necessary chores followed by hours of training and practice. Lena's blue brooch was matched to a chain of Lady Clara's. Lena and Lady Elena secured the help of two village women to work on Liebhard's tunic and leggings, and on Lena's wimple. Lena spent hours working on her manners as a waiting woman. She liked being with the lady, but in her heart she was very happy that she was not really a waiting woman. She found it inferior to her own ideas about herself.

The day finally arrived that they must travel to the count's castle. Because Lord Franz did not want Lady Elena to be overtaxed in her condition by a rough hurried ride, they decided to leave just after dawn. Pisces was to be Liebhard's mount, as a serviceable charger for a squire. Lena decided to ride Jake rather than the priest's horse. Jake had recovered from his months of ill feeding and care, and she found him an enjoyable horse to ride. They planned to arrive two days before the combat, so as to spend as little time in the castle as possible. Rudi and Conrad were left to mind the manor, with Mark coming up at night. Franz had deemed Lena and Liebhard passable in their roles, but did not want to push their chances. Arriving in the evening, they would have one full day before the day of the combat.

From the very first, Lord Franz wanted them to play their roles. This meant that Franz and Reiner lead the group, followed by Lady Elena and her maid, Lena, with the squire, Liebhard, bringing up the rear. He led a pack horse with their needed armor and supplies. Franz set a quick walking pace, which he and Reiner estimated would get them to Katzenberg just an hour or so before the gates closed for the night.

For Lena, every new vista brought her a little farther from her home than she had ever traveled. What was clear to her and the others was that the countryside was still suffering from the ravages of the pestilence of the previous year. Many fields lay unworked. Few workers were harvesting at what would have been a normally busy time. In fact, they saw surprisingly few people on the road during the morning. Most of those they saw were tradesmen with carts and pack mules.

They stopped for a meal at midday, and allowed Lady Elena time to rest. She insisted that she was well and they should not stop on her account, but Lord Franz insisted. Lena, as the waiting maid, opened the food baskets and cider jug and passed the food around to everyone. Although they could not help chuckling at each other occasionally, to the passersby their group probably looked like what it was pretending to be.

They mounted and continued on their way. By midafternoon many more travelers could be seen on the road, going to Katzenberg or coming out of the city. By late afternoon, the road toward the city was teaming with people, all intending to reach the city before the gates closed. They began to meet a few knights that Lord Franz knew, and one or two who knew Reiner. Lena tried to ride along quietly and subdued, but all of the sights around her made her want to exclaim. To actually see all of these people moving about like ants, each with his own purpose was beyond anything she had imagined. She looked back at Liebhard several times and saw he felt the same.

Finally they reached the gates of the town. The town spread out below the castle itself, so they had some distance yet to travel. The gate keepers spoke with Reiner a few moments and then they were allowed to go on toward the castle. Every square inch seemed to be built up to Lena's inexperienced eyes. The houses all crowded in upon each other. Where did people grow food she wondered. It was all mysterious to her and wondrous. They travelled slowly through crowded streets, Liebhard going ahead, telling people to make way, while Reiner now rode behind to protect the ladies.

It was nearly dusk when they came to the castle gates. Lord Franz spoke a few moments with the guards, and then they entered. He stopped Brutus and in a commanding voice called for the stable men. Quickly two young boys came forward and held the horses. Liebhard had jumped off Pisces and helped Lady Elena dismount, while Lena was left to dismount on her own.

As the horses were led away, and instructions given for their packhorse bags to follow them into the castle, Lord Franz, took Lady Elena's hand and led her to the building entrance. Lena followed behind a few steps as she had been trained, with Liebhard following Reiner, and directing the two young servants who toted their belongings. The steward came out hurriedly and profusely welcomed Lord Franz, who was a vassal to the count. He directed servants to lead them to their chambers and announced that supper would be in an hour.

Lady Elena and Lena were brought to a room which was already occupied. They would be sharing with another lady, her waiting lady, and one of the countess' young waiting women. The other women were just dressing for supper. Lady Elena introduced herself to the other lady, who told her who the others were, without actually introducing them, which Elena did for Lena as well. Lena checked their bags as they were brought up, and Lady Elena directed her where to put them and what to unpack. Within a short time the other inhabitants left, and Lena and Lady Elena were able to relax a bit.

"How are you feeling, Lady Elena?" Lena asked. "It has been a very long day for you. Do you think you are up to supper? Maybe I can get something from the kitchen for you."

"I feel well. It was not too hard a day. I think I will just lie down for a few minutes while you unpack. I am glad that we can be next to each other here. I hope you will not be too uncomfortable," motioning to the floor mattress where Lena would sleep.

"Not at all. My eye is a little tired though. I am going to put my patch on to make it work hard. I hope we will not have too late a night."

"Let's use my condition as an excuse to come up early after supper."

About a half hour later they dressed and went down to the hall. Lord Franz and Reiner had been watching for them. Someone else was there, Sir Gebhard! He beamed at Lady Elena and slid a teasing eye toward Lena. He had apparently been apprised of their little deception. Lena saw that Liebhard stood soberly behind them.

"Lady Elena, sister, how happy I am to see you," he took her shoulders and kissed her on both cheeks. As he touched her second cheek he winked at Lena and whispered, "You are a very appealing waiting woman, Lena. Can I pretend you are unmarried?" Lady Elena and Lena could barely control themselves from bursting into laughter.

Lord Franz came forward and formally took his wife's hand. Sir Gebhard, as his brother and a vassal in his own right, followed behind. Lena walked behind him and sat behind Lady Elena. She knew she would be told later where she might sit. Sir Reiner had gone to a lower table, followed by Liebhard. A few moments later, the steward came forward and told Lord Franz where his squire and waiting woman could sit, which was back against the wall on the far side of the hall.

As everyone was beginning to sit at their places, Lord Frederick entered with Abbot Wenzel. The steward rushed to meet them, and brought them to sit at the count's table. Lord Fredrick saw Lord Franz and bowed. The abbot looked over, nodded, and they sat down.

The supper was long and noisy. Lena and Liebhard were not used to the din and were careful not to speak too much. They had sat down next to each other, as if almost by chance. The food was rich and abundant, far more variety than they had experienced. As they were finishing their meal, and Lena was hoping they could soon go to their beds, a servant delivered a note to her. It was from Reiner, and very simple. He asked that Liebhard come to him, and that she go to Lady Elena. They got up and did as directed.

Abbot Wenzel was seated at a chair pulled up between Lord Franz and Lady Elena. As Reiner and Liebhard came to their table, Abbot Wenzel said to Lady Elena, "When you have finished dining, I request that your party come to the count's chapel. I would like to lead you in a quiet prayer for Lady Clara's soul."

Lady Elena, bowed her head and nodded. The abbot stood up and gave the smallest nod to Lena, but his eyes actually twinkled. He liked this ruse. After he had walked away, Lord Franz gave orders for the group to go to the chapel.

About ten minutes later, they were all gathered in the chapel, including Lord Frederick and Sir Gebhard. Liebhard closed the chapel door and stood guard so no one else could enter. For a few minutes they actually did follow the abbot in prayer. Then he asked them to explain their plan.

Lord Franz turned to Reiner. "Reiner leads us in this and he will explain." The abbot's eyebrows went up as he waited expectantly.

"My lord abbot, and Lord Frederick, I have said that I will be Lady Clara's champion. I want to see justice done, to see a woman slayer slain. I know Sir Manfred, I know his fighting ability, and I know him as an egotistic young man. Without boastfulness, I can say I can defeat him. We have decided not to announce to him that I will be his adversary until the moment of combat. This will give him no time to prepare to face me."

The abbot studied Reiner. Lord Frederick came forward and embraced the knight. "You do us great honor and kindness. It has been clear from the beginning that my family had no knight to meet this murderer."

The abbot leaned forward. "Can you say from your heart, from your very soul, that this is not overweening pride?"

Reiner bowed his head, then looked up into the abbot's eyes. "When I heard Manfred's demand for a trial by combat, it was almost like a voice within me that said I must champion Lady Clara." He spoke so softly and gently, his voice was barely audible.

The abbot stood up. "Kneel before me. I will give you my blessing." Reiner went down on his knees and bowed his head. The abbot made the sign of the cross over him and prayed. It was a very solemn moment for all of them. He touched Reiner's shoulder and told him to rise.

"Tomorrow Sir Manfred arrives. Lord Frederick and I along with Lord Franz will be asked to come forward to witness his arrival and to listen to the terms of the combat. I understand from the count that the combat will be at two hours after dawn the next morning. I will not be able to speak to you as I would like during these days, or acknowledge that I know you. Perhaps we will meet later and Lord Frederick and I will be able to thank each of you."

Everyone was greatly moved by his kind words, since their experience had led them to believe that he was a hard if fair man.

Lord Frederick came forward and thanked each one of them. He grabbed Reiner by the forearms and kissed his cheeks. Tears stood in the old man's eyes. He turned, joined his brother-in-law, and left the chapel.

Reiner seemed lost in thought as the others all talked about this moving evening. He roused himself. This was real. This was a new door he had stepped through, yet it all felt right. He had chosen this. He watched all of his friends, caught Liebhard's eye and smiled. Liebhard smiled broadly and grabbed him by the shoulders.

"I salute you, brother!" he said. If Lord Franz or Lady Elena was surprised by this familiarity, they did not show it.

Reiner saw that Lena's eyes were wide with anxiety, but proud of him also. Here were his two closest friends, one so enthusiastic and one fearful for him. The day after tomorrow all of this would be behind them. For just an instant a small shudder of fear went through him. He mentally shook off the passing thought. He would be able to defeat Manfred.

That night, after everyone had found his bed, Reiner lay awake. Liebhard was on a floor mattress next to the bed he shared with Lord Franz. Another vassal and knight slept in the other bed in the room. From the regular breathing he surmised all of the others were asleep. He normally fell asleep within minutes of crawling into bed. This night was different. He sensed that his companions already unconsciously treated him differently. They pinned their hopes on him. They trusted him to succeed where they could not. Thinking back over these wonderful months since he had met Lena, Liebhard, Franz, and even Gebhard and Lady Elena, his heart swelled at the trust they had placed in him. He could not have been at this junction in his path without them. They had given him hope. They had made him believe in himself again.

Perhaps he could find a way to bring Giorgio here….No he must not get ahead of this test. He thought about his son. He would be three, going on four. He had received a message in May from the abbess thanking him for his recent gift. She said Giorgio was a good active boy, who loved to play with the other boys but did not talk very much. She had written that he was well grown, tall for his age, with blue eyes and copper gold hair. Reiner turned over. He yearned for his son.

The next morning Lady Elena purposely stayed in bed until the others had finished dressing and left the room. Lena lay silently beside her.

"Good, we have the room to ourselves now," the lady said. She sat up. "Are you well, Lena?"

"I had a little trouble falling asleep, but then I slept until the others rose," she answered, getting out of her bed and rolling up the quilt and mattress so that they had more room.

Lady Elena got up, and Lena helped her change into the other dress she had brought. They would be spending time during the day with the countess, so she also put on her best wimple and a beautiful necklace she had worn the day Lord Frederick and the Abbot had come to their castle. Lena dressed in the same clothes she had worn the day before.

As they came down the stairs, they were happy to find that Gebhard was waiting for them. He greeted Lady Elena warmly, and led her into the hall. The rest of their party were already together at the table, where less than half the places were taken—many had apparently broken their fast earlier. Good mornings were made as would be expected, since other people were within earshot. Lady Elena turned and told Lena to sit beside her, as she might need some help with the dishes. They all ate fairly quietly, except for Gebhard, who found many little ways to tease them about their ruse.

Lady Elena, who was not amused by his persistence, asked him to tell her about his fief.

"Ah, an arrow well shot," he responded. "I can say that my brother had things in hand. The loss from the pestilence last year was not as bad as at your fief or

Millers Village. I believe we lost one in four. I was not hit hard by loss of craftsmen. My old priest survived. You might think this makes me quite pleased. Yet I would rather be here, at the count's castle, serving him. Or if not that, I would be happy to serve you, Franz, at your land. I can run my fief, but it does not satisfy me. I miss the camaraderie of the count's court too."

"Perhaps you should get to know the bishop's court better, try to make yourself needed there. Then you might put a man in charge at the fief and be more at the center of action," his brother answered.

A silence followed as each thought about the conversation. This was broken by Lord Franz's suggestion that they walk through the count's gardens.

The brothers walked on either side of the lady, leading the way through the garden entrance. Reiner fell in step with Lena, while Liebhard took his position behind all of them. The gardens were extensive. They passed large kitchen gardens on the left and entered a formal walled meditation garden. Lena gasped despite herself, never having seen such a highly manicured, beautifully designed combination of flowers, shrubs, and fruit and ornamental trees. Reiner smiled at her response, but looked away. The gardens were certainly good, though not of the caliber he had often seen in the Italian states, and not as highly ornamental as those one saw in the Ottoman lands. He was surprised that he felt nostalgic for all those places he had been and experienced. At the time, his life had often seemed a drudgery through which he must live.

By the time they reached the fishpond, very few other strollers could be seen. The pond brought a whoop from Liebhard, and Reiner had to turn and order him to be silent. Liebhard gave him a crooked grin but nodded. The others had all stopped, so Reiner motioned Liebhard to follow him, and they walked to the water's edge. The pond was teaming with fish.

"A fishpond like this is common at larger castles. You can imagine how many mouths they have to feed day after day. A pond like this can produce quite a stock of fish, especially these rough fish we see here," he gestured as he spoke softly to Liebhard. Liebhard was bursting with interest and had many questions, but Reiner put his finger to his lips. "We will talk about it later."

The two walked back up to the path to the others and the group resumed their walk. They walked the whole circuit of the pond. By then it was time for Franz to join Lord Frederick and Abbot Wenzel in preparation for Manfred's arrival. Gebhard excused himself as well, wishing to find old friends of his among the count's retinue.

Sir Reiner took his place next to Lady Elena. Lena now walked with Liebhard. They found it hard not to talk about all they saw. When they were back in the castle courtyard, Reiner stopped and said in a low voice, "I think I will take Liebhard with me out of the town somewhere so that we can do a little weapons practice. I want to be sure I am seen by a few as possible. Perhaps we can find the steward and he can escort you to the countess?"

"Yes, I had an invitation from her last night to join her today," Lady Elena replied.

Reiner hailed a servant and in no time the steward arrived to lead the lady and Lena off. He watched them go, noticing again how well Lena held herself. She could easily pass for a gentlewoman. He sighed.

"Liebhard, call for our horses. Then go up to our rooms and get my sword and your quarterstaff. Bring our shields too. I will wait here." Reiner raised his eyebrows as he said this and Liebhard suppressed a chuckle. It was hard for the two of them to act like master and servant.

While he waited, one or two knights he knew passed by. He conversed with them but tried to give the impression that he was still in temporary service to Gebhard, and had attended Gebhard's brother to Katzenberg on some business. Since he had been at a lower level of service for the count, no one seemed surprised.

Once mounted, they rode out as knight with his squire. Finally the town was well behind them. Reiner looked over at Liebhard and sighed, laughing. "Now we are free to be ourselves for a while. I hope you do not mind working with me a bit with my sword though. Your quarterstaff will get a bit beaten up, but I want to practice my strokes."

They reached a stretch of land from which they could see in all directions, so that they would know if anyone saw or was able to overhear them. They tethered the horses and walked out to a fairly level spot. At first Reiner worked slowly, to give Liebhard a chance to learn what to expect. He need not have worried. Liebhard was quick and he was accomplished with the quarterstaff.

"How do you know this combat so well?" Reiner asked. He was breathing faster than he had expected. Liebhard was quite a challenging combatant.

"Mark and I practiced most days. We also practiced with knives when we had a chance," he said, standing nonchalantly, feet apart, with the quarterstaff upright in front of him, both hands holding it. Reiner noted that such a stance was imposing, and could be menacing to an opponent who was uncertain.

"What prompts you to take that stance?" he asked.

"Oh, my father taught us that. It is kind of a trick. It looks as though you are standing, unprepared. But really, you are using the staff to center you so that you are ready to spring either way. If you hit to my left, I am already poised to go that way."

He then moved in slow motion both ways to show Reiner what he meant. It was a simple and very exciting piece of fighting Reiner had not seen.

They spent several hours practicing, taking many breaks to discuss tactics. It was early afternoon when Reiner stopped and suggested they had exercised enough.

They sat down and shared some cider Liebhard had brought in his saddle bag. Not once had Liebhard brought up the combat the next day.

"You do not ask me about how I will fight Manfred tomorrow," Reiner said.

"You know how you will fight him, Reiner. I can teach you nothing. I know that you can defeat him. I know you," Liebhard answered simply. He had been looking off into the distance, but he sought out Reiner's eyes.

"How have I been so lucky, finally, to have such friends as you and Lena?" Reiner said, leaning over and patting Liebhard's shoulder. He heaved a sigh and forced down a rush of strong feelings. He thought for a moment that he was going to cry. Every feeling had been so elevated since they had arrived at the castle. He mentally chided himself to settle down. Emotions were dangerous in combat.

Meanwhile, Lena and Lady Elena had been introduced to the countess and her ladies in the countess' rooms. About a dozen women were there, those sitting were the noble ladies, while the waiting women stood. Lady Elena was shy at first, and stiff, but then one of the other ladies came forward to say she knew Elena's mother. Lady Elena seated herself next to this woman, Lena taking her place behind her. This friend of her mother's said after only a few moments, "I see that you are with child. Are you well enough to travel like this?"

Lady Elena may have been startled and embarrassed by this, but she laughed lightly and said, "You are discerning. I have enjoyed excellent health, and have no trouble travelling at all."

This exchange prompted conversation from all of the ladies, leading to much discussion about children, and several hours passed easily before it was time for all of the ladies and their servants to leave to prepare for supper.

Liebhard and Reiner returned to town by late afternoon, and went to their room. About an hour later, Lord Franz came in accompanied by his brother Sir Gebhard. The brothers had been looking for them.

As they were alone, they were able to speak freely, and Lord Franz told them about Manfred's return. "He came riding in with his guard, sitting on his horse like some conqueror. He wore his armour, all polished and glistening. It is clear that he sees himself as one falsely accused, but will win victory because he is invincible. He gave proper homage to the count and other dignitaries who are here. He barely bowed to the abbot or Lord Frederick. Now that I know he is a killer, I see him with different eyes, but to someone who has never seen him before, he appears as the image of a powerful knight."

He stood without bowing his head as the charges and judgment were read against him. He did not disagree with the terms of the combat, so it will be the traditional form of only leather or cloth clothing, sword and shield, no head covering. His only question was to ask who his challenger was. The count said the champion of Lady Clara would appear at the time of combat. Sir Manfred looked annoyed at this, nothing more. He fears no one."

"Did his family attend him?" Reiner asked.

"His father came, because the interdict required it. His brother did not," Lord Franz answered. "We were surprised to see that several of his father's retainers accompanied them though. Sir Gebhard has tried to investigate and to find out why they are here. They have been very closed mouthed. We are concerned that malice is planned."

"We must go down to supper soon. I think that Manfred will be there, with his father. I am not sure where the count will seat him, but probably at the head table on his side opposite Lord Frederick and Abbot Wenzel. We will be arriving late, and will be separated as last night. Reiner, I think we should not talk at all tonight in the hall. We do not want Manfred's entourage to guess anything. Do you agree?"

"I do. Liebhard and I will go down to the far end as soon as we enter, and I will sit at the bottom of the retinue table."

When they reached the hall, Lord Franz joined his brother, who had already led Lady Elena to their places. Lena was already at the far end of the hall. Each member of their group saw when Manfred entered. Two of the count's knights escorted him, as he was a man upon whom sentence had been given, even though he was a knight. Manfred's father was a man in his late prime, not as old as Lena's father had been when he died. He bore himself well, but anger and anguish marked his face. The retainers were seated several tables away from Sir Reiner.

The meal was surprisingly quiet and short, since everyone was aware what the next day would bring. The count and countess rose and after they left, the hall emptied. There was no chance for any private conversation for any of them in their rooms, as others with whom they shared rooms had also returned there after supper. There was nothing to do but declare sleepiness, and go to bed. None of the party expected they would sleep well, but as it happened only Lena and Reiner lay awake. She was able to finally put aside her fears and drift off.

Reiner lay down, knowing he was too excited to sleep immediately. He tried not to think about the combat. He did not want to over think how he might fight. He tried to suppress the extreme anger he had felt when he saw Manfred. He had not known Clara, and although he consciously wanted to champion her, in his heart he wanted to see the man dead mostly for his action against Lena. Anger would not help him fight well. He thought about Liebhard, about the ruse he had taught him. Liebhard had stood there so casually, all the time ready. It was his stillness that had caught Reiner's attention. This would be quite effective during the combat, he thought as sleep finally came to him.

When Reiner woke after dawn, he could hear from his breathing that Liebhard was awake. He touched the big man's arm and motioned to him. They quietly dressed and left the room together to relieve themselves.

"Let's go down to the hall. We will break our fast as early as possible, while few are up," he said.

"What about weapons? Do you want me to go back and get them now? Liebhard asked.

"No. I think we will go back to the room after breakfast to talk to Lord Franz, if we do not see him before."

The two walked down to the hall, squire following knight. Only a handful of people were there, and some food was just being brought from the kitchen. Liebhard sat at the bottom table, not far from Reiner. Each ate a solitary breakfast.

Somewhat later, Sir Gebhard entered with Lord Franz. They barely nodded to Sir Reiner. They had nearly finished eating when Lady Elena and Lena arrived, but Lena stayed at their table with the lady. The hall was now filling with others. Lord Franz sent a note to Reiner to leave soon and meet him in their chamber. Reiner motioned to Liebhard, and the two left the room. Manfred had not appeared.

Some minutes later, Lord Franz entered the room where Reiner and Liebhard waited.

"In about an hour, the count has said that the blast of a horn will announce that the combatants are to arrive. We intend to be there some time before that, and will be seated with Lord Frederick and Abbot Wenzel. When you hear the horn, you will find Gebhard waiting for you just inside the hall. He will go before you to the ground set for the combat. It is already cordoned off, as you saw, in the meadow just below the castle wall. We will have your horses waiting just outside the hall, for the short ride down."

They talked for a time, making sure they had forgotten nothing in their plans. Then Lord Franz left.

"It's just the two of us now and waiting," Liebhard said quietly. Reiner was glad of Liebhard's presence. He was calm and steady. Reiner took this moment to review in his mind the terrain at the battle site. They had stopped and walked over it the previous afternoon when they came back into the town. It was part of the area that the knights used for weapons practice including mounted combat. The area was nearly barren of grass and tamped down by frequent use. It was fairly level. Since no rain had fallen for several days, it was more likely to be dusty than slippery. It was a good site.

Reiner took out his leather jerkin and leggings. The leather leggings reached just over his knee, and were worn over his leggings. He pulled the jerkin over his tunic. It had cuts and mars on it from earlier battles, even several stains which must have been blood. He looked at his sword blade one last time, just as they heard the sound of the horn. They gathered up their weapons, Liebhard carrying his as a sign of his position.

In the hall they found Gebhard waiting. As they mounted, he said, "We will ride out just beyond the entrance and wait for the signal from my squire that Manfred is already at the site. Then we will ride out. He will not see you until you walk into the area, as it is now surrounded by stands where the onlookers are already seated."

Lena sat behind Lady Elena, who sat next to Lord Franz, just behind Lord Frederick and Abbot Wenzel. The count sat just below them to the left. There had been a buzz of conversation among the people already in the viewing stands until the horn sounded. A nearly complete silence fell. Moments later Manfred walked in, wearing a new looking well cut leather jerkin and leather leg covers. His head was bare and his copper hair rustled lightly in the wind. He looked splendid, she had to admit. He strutted about, looking for his challenger.

THE HERO

A raised din of conversation announced the approach of someone from outside the stands. Then a complete silence fell as Reiner walked in. He too wore leather, and it looked battle tried and worn. His bronze hair was pulled back loosely and tied at his nape. He stopped near the center of the combat circle, stood in an open stance, the tip of his sword touching the ground, held vertically with both hands at its hilt. He looked casually at Manfred but said nothing.

Manfred's complete surprise was palpable. "What is this? You cannot be a challenger. You are not family or friend." His voice rang out in the silence.

Abbot Wenzel stood up. Every eye turned to him. He opened a paper and read in a strong commanding voice Manfred's own words:

I will accept only trial by combat to defend myself against this outrageous charge. I will fight any kinsman of this lady, any friend who might dare to come forward, or even a hired knight if such can be found. And I will fight this challenger in sword combat, on foot, to the death to prove my innocence.

The count stood up. "You have heard the defendant's own words. He will accept any challenger."

The crowd buzzed and then went quiet. Manfred looked with burning hatred at Reiner. With his sword held up, he walked a few steps toward Reiner, seemed to stop and with lightning speed, struck at Reiner with a huge stroke from the right arcing down toward the left. Reiner, from his apparent defenseless stance had moved so fast that he was able to bring his own sword down behind Manfred's, propelling the younger man sideways so that he almost lost his balance. He saved himself from falling by thrusting his sword into the ground.

172

As he tried to free his sword, he half turned toward Reiner, expecting another blow, only to find the older knight looking at him oddly, half smiling. He had returned to his nonchalant position with sword between his legs. The crowd burst into laughter.

Now Manfred was an angry bull. He was a powerful, angry bull. His next sword stroke came from the left, just as he got his sword freed from the ground. Again, Reiner caught the sword from behind, speeding it to the right, Manfred with it.

Twice tricked, Manfred stood just a moment, sword held in his right hand. This time he struck straight down at Reiner's bare hands, which were again resting at the top of his sword in the same relaxed pose. Reiner jumped back like a cat, bringing his sword up hard against Manfred's downward thrust. Manfred lost his two-handed grip, barely holding on to the hilt with one hand as the sword rose straight up in the air. The clang of sword against sword had been deafening.

Reiner used this moment to strike Manfred's raised sword on Manfred's right side. This turned Manfred slightly to the left, making the only stroke available for the young man a backhanded stroke, which Reiner easily parried as he jumped back. Manfred pursued him with wild rage. The next five minutes was titillation like a heavy bull chasing an agile cat.

The weight of the swords and the speed of the action were taxing to both men, and their strokes became slower and less forceful. Manfred was expending added energy trying to catch Reiner.

Suddenly, the game changed. The cat attacked. Instead of jumping back as they struck swords, Reiner pressed Manfred with a second fast stroke. Manfred began to use his shield arm in defense, leaving just one hand to power his sword strokes. Round and round they went, like the cat whipping the bull.

By now, sweat was running down the faces and arms of both men. Manfred's loose hair was wet and matted to his face and neck. Their chests heaved. Then, oddly, Reiner took again the nonchalant stance with sword between his legs. Manfred could see only red. He charged forward, but Reiner easily jumped aside, delivering a sword cut to the back of Manfred's left leg. Blood streamed down his calf.

The stunned Manfred somehow managed to react immediately. Reiner's left side had been exposed briefly. Manfred brought up his sword, scraping along Reiner's ribcage, cutting through the leather. But he too had exposed himself. Reiner delivered a deep sword slice into the young man's neck.

Manfred toppled to the ground, amid startled cries from the crowd. He lay there, blood gushing from his throat. Reiner, blood trickling down his side, looked up at Lord Frederick. He said in a ringing voice, "Lady Clara's murderer is slain." The onlookers fell momentarily into a stunned silence.

At that second, Liebhard was at his side. He took his sword and shield. Reiner put his hand on Liebhard's shoulder. It was not possible for the onlookers to tell if he was leaning on the huge man for support as they walked off the field. People had started to come out of the stands, many onto the field. Lord Franz had jumped down, reaching Reiner's other side. Somehow Gebhard had managed to get Lena down to the field, and she ordered them to get Reiner to sit on a stool that someone brought. He virtually collapsed onto the stool, which frightened all of them. With Lord Franz, his brother and Liebhard standing around her to form a shield from the view of others, Lena carefully lifted the leather jerkin. The cut was six inches long and had touched the bone on two ribs. Why so much blood, she wondered? It must have cut much deeper before it hit a rib. Somehow, Lady Elena forced her way through, gagging at the sight, but holding out her shawl. Lena took it and tied it tightly around Reiner's torso. All the while he had watched her face. She did not appear appalled. It was not too bad, then.

"Let's get him to the horses. Liebhard, you lift him onto Pisces, and put me behind him. Let's get him back to Lord Franz's chamber as quick as we can." Once they heard her orders, they all responded immediately, They mounted, with Liebhard taking Reiner's charger. They all rode carefully but quickly out of the arena, crowding around Reiner so that few even had a glimpse of him. The retainers of Manfred's father were milling around the slain man, but one or two tried to follow Reiner's group on foot. They had fallen far behind by the time they had Reiner in the castle courtyard.

Liebhard was off and beside Pisces in a moment, lifting Reiner off and carrying him like a child up the stairs. Lord Franz asked the knight who was there to please leave for a few hours, and their group all crowded in. Lord Franz helped Lena take off Reiner's jerkin and tunic. Lena called to Liebhard to run down to get her vinegar, clear lard, linen bandages and some loose wool.

"What do you think, Lena?" Reiner asked. His voice was clear and he was not coughing.

"You have lost quite a bit of blood." We need to stop the bleeding. What do you think of my tying it closed with stitches?" She could not think of any other way to close it.

"I have seen that done in Ottoman lands," he said.

"Lady Elena, find some very strong thread or string and the biggest needle possible. Lord Franz, can you find a servant and ask them to send up hot clear broth and cider?"

A short time later, Liebhard was back, and held Reiner still while Lena cleaned around the wound, which was still oozing blood. When Lady Elena came back, Lena took the needle, held it over a candle, threaded it, and asked Franz to hold the sides of the wound closed. Threading through the live skin was frightening, though Reiner steeled himself to hold still. Lena made three ugly but tough stitches. Blood still seeped out, but slowly. She sat back and look at it. What else could she do? She carefully rubbed lard on the wound, laid a clean linen patch on it, and with

Franz's help they rapped linen around Reiner's torso, going once over his shoulder to keep it in place.

They all sat back, looking at Reiner, who had closed his eyes. Now he opened them. They were clear. He took Lena's hand and closed his eyes again.

"Lord Franz, do you think you can force the steward to move your roommates? Then maybe Lady Elena and I can move in here with you tonight. Liebhard, will you help Lady Elena bring our things to this room?"

When the broth and cider were brought up, Lena said, "Reiner, Reiner, wake up. Now you must take all of this broth and cider." He opened his eyes, Liebhard propped him up, and Lena helped him drink the broth, then the cider. He gave them a smile, and then either fell asleep or fainted. Lena covered him with a quilt, but remained sitting on the bed beside him.

Within an hour, all of them were settled in the same room. Lord Franz, Lady Elena and Gebhard had gone down for dinner and brought back food for Liebhard and Lena. They said they had been asked many questions in the hall about Reiner's wound and congratulated all around for his magnificent fight. The count sent his surgeon, but Lord Franz forestalled him, saying the Abbot had already sent his doctor, who had treated Reiner. He then told the Abbot's doctor the reverse. Lord Frederick himself came, and sat with them for a short time. Lord Franz assured him that Reiner's wound had bled profusely but was now under control.

All afternoon Reiner slept. At supper time, once again, Franz and Elena left to dine and assure all that Reiner was not badly injured. While they were gone, Lena asked Liebhard to get more broth and cider. She had kept her same position beside Reiner as he slept, and leaned her head back against the wall now, closing her eyes for a moment.

She must have dozed, because she thought she heard her name. It was Reiner. "Lena. Lena." He put his hand on her arm, and she was now wide awake. She leaned forward, fearing he was delirious.

"Lena, where is everyone?"

"It's alright. Lord Franz and Lady Elena have gone to supper. Liebhard is getting you more broth."

"Listen. It is not all right. We should plan to leave tonight if possible."

"It is not possible. You have not even passed any water. Until you do, I know that you are still weak from blood loss."

"Listen to me. If I die, the combat will be inconclusive. Manfred will not be proved a murderer. It is in his family's interest that I die, so they are not shamed. That is why all of the family's men are here. They have a strong motive to attack— to kill me in any way. The sooner we leave, the less time they have to think about when to act. I can travel. I will be safer by far on a horse than here."

"Your wound will surely open again!" she worried, unconsciously taking his hand and pressing it against her heart.

"I know you fear for my safety. Please listen to me. I know I am right. We will have to leave before the gates close, or at worst as soon as they open in the morning."

She looked at him, holding his eyes with hers. He had so much more experience in matters like this. She was perhaps too trusting. Could he withstand a day long ride? He was a strong, tested man.

"When the others come back we will talk. It will be up to you and Lord Franz. I will support you, but I am frightened for you." Realizing she held his hand against her, she laid it on his chest, placing her own over his for a moment.

Liebhard returned with broth and cider. Lena, now on the alert, smelled both carefully, even touching them to her tongue. They were untainted. Liebhard at first watched her curiously, but then asked, "What's this? What has happened?"

Lena looked at Reiner. He explained to his friend what he had already told her. Liebhard was quick to make some suggestions.

"I know where our horses are in the stables and our gear. I can get them ready and in the courtyard myself whenever I need them. The stable boys know me now, and would not be surprised. Maybe Gebhard could hold them while I carry you down. Lord Franz and the ladies could carry all or our belongings."

Reiner managed a smile at his friend. "You are full of ideas. Good ones."

When Lord Franz and Lady Elena returned, the group held council. Lord Franz only needed to hear Reiner's thoughts before he immediately agreed.

"I will wait an hour or two and then write a note to the count, saying that because you are well enough to travel we are considering leaving sometime during the day tomorrow. That way, even though we leave at the crack of dawn he will not be surprised. It also allows very little time for news of our departure plans to spread. I will send a note to Gebhard now, asking him to come here to talk with me about an important matter. We will need his help."

As he began to write his notes, the rest packed and made a few plans. Reiner also whispered to Lena that he needed to urinate, so she and Lady Elena stood outside the door for a few moments while Liebhard helped him. The lady was amused when Lena explained how important this little event was.

As early as possible, they all lay down to sleep. As usual, Liebhard was awake long before anyone. He touched Lena's shoulder before he quietly went out. She woke the others, lit candles, and helped Reiner take as much cider as he could drink. She checked his bandage and was pleased to find no seepage during the night. Just as she finished, she heard a light knock on the door and Gebhard came in.

"All ready? I am going down to hold the horses," his eyes glistened with excitement and concern.

In a moment Liebhard was there, picking up Reiner. The others followed silently, Lena walking out last, after surveying the room, blowing out the candles and closing the door. By the time she reached the courtyard, everyone else was mounting. Reiner had been placed on Pisces, who was smooth and gentle. The horse left for her was Reiner's charger. She paused for a split second, but Reiner said in a low voice, "He will give you no trouble, just act confident." This reminded her of Lord Franz's comment about meeting Smoke, and she smiled as she got on the horse which Gebhard held for her. He spooked just slightly at her different touch, but settled down as they went through the open gates. The guards gave them a wave of farewell. They walked silently down the streets of the waking town, and reached the gates with no trouble. The guards had not yet opened the gates, but responded immediately to Lord Franz's command. They were out and on their way.

Lord Franz set a quick trot pace. He rode beside Lady Elena so that Lena and Liebhard could ride on either side of Reiner. The three friends talked very little, but Lena and Liebhard were highly aware of Reiner swaying in his saddle. Several times he caught himself before he fell asleep. Before they stopped at noon to rest, Liebhard had had to steady him several times.

At noon, after Liebhard lifted Reiner off Pisces, he laid him on the blanket Lena had spread out. Lena had noticed his tunic had blood marks on it, and when she raised the tunic was discouraged to see that the linen was wet with blood. She and Franz unwrapped the bandages. The stitches had held. The jarring was just too much to keep the wound from moving. They carefully re-bandaged the wound.

Lena sat back on her heels. "Reiner, this is a lot of blood loss. Are we halfway, Lord Franz?"

"Maybe a little over halfway. We should be home in about four hours."

"I wish we could stay here for a day or two. Reiner, this is dangerous for you to ride on."

"I think I can make it. Are you saying you think I cannot?"

"Please don't assume I know so much about this. The blood loss is frightening. You are strong and determined. I think you will make it but your recovery is going to be harder."

"Let's ride then. We must go faster—only safe when we get to the manor…" he said with as much enthusiasm as he could muster.

They ate a worried lunch, Lena plying Reiner with as much cider and hot water as she could make him drink.

Lord Franz, who had been quiet during the lunch, turned to Reiner and said, "I think we should tie you into your saddle. What do you think?"

"Yes. Feet into stirrups and hands to saddle," the injured man said. He was pale and very tired.

Liebhard carefully lifted Reiner up and held him while Lord Franz devised a way to tie his feet, and then his hands to the saddle.

"How does that feel, Reiner? Is it too tight anywhere?"

"It's good," came the short reply.

They started off gingerly at a fast trot, and for about two hours Reiner was able to stay upright. Then he started to lose consciousness and sway forward in the saddle.

The fields were lush on both sides of him as he rode. He saw him running along through the tall wheat. He was waving. He smiled at him and beckoned him to come, but he stopped waving. He started to cry. He kept riding his horse forward. He had to go on. He stood and watched. Sister Cecilia came and put her arm around him, but he kept crying. He kept riding away, he had no choice. Now when he turned he could barely see Giorgio.

"Stop, everyone," Lena said. "He is unconscious. Liebhard, please untie Reiner's hands. Let's leave his feet tied. Can you lift me up behind? Lord Franz, you will have to lead Reiner's charger, so Liebhard can manage the pack horse and help me if I have trouble." Everyone did as she asked, now aware that Reiner was no longer conscious.

"What do you think, Lena? Lord Franz asked, worriedly.

"Let's step up the pace. Pisces has an easy gallop. The faster we can get there the better," she said bravely.

Reiner floated into semi consciousness now and then, feeling warm and happy. He half understood that he was being held from falling by one he loved. The warmth of her breath on his neck, the feeling of her body behind him and both arms around him was like a cocoon of security.

The fields were waves of gold, rye and oats ready to harvest. The horses were trotting briskly. He looked over at her and caught her eye. He smiled and she smiled too. But she was crying, wasn't she? He realized he should be sad too. Then he took her arm: she was holding it up against her breast. He took it in his hands lovingly. He had beaten her. He would kill him. Her skin on her arm was ivory flushed pink, with a bewitching curve as it went under the sleeve of her shift. He felt her forearm and wrist but there was no break. Her wrist was delicate.

Her body against his back was warm and caressing. Where was her horse? Her arms were around him for some reason. It was delicious to feel her there. He caught himself before he fell down, as he stared down at Manfred. He felt happy and lightheaded. It was so dark, but surely it was mid-day? He was so wet on his left side. He was sweating from the fight. Where was Manfred? He was not in the ring anymore. It seemed like they were going in circles. He was dizzy. He should get down. His feet were stuck. He would never be able to finish the combat like this.

Not one word was spoken during the rest of the trip. They galloped into the courtyard in the middle of the afternoon. Max came running, and held the horses. Rudi and Conrad hurried out of the hall, and helped Liebhard untie Reiner as they were told cryptically about the combat and return home. Liebhard eased him down into his arms. Lena slid off the horse and ran ahead to call Oona. After giving her several requests, she went into Reiner's room where Liebhard had laid him. The bandages were soaked with blood. Everyone came in, and Lord Franz helped Lena remove the bandages. Tears streaked Lena's face. Lady Elena sobbed.

"Now, steady, everyone," Lord Franz said. "Lena, the stitches are still intact. Let's bandage him up again. We have to keep him totally quiet. Out, now, everyone, except for Lena. No, Liebhard we may need your help." Rudi and Conrad were reluctant to leave Reiner, and stood in the doorway watching as Lord Franz and Lena worked over their teacher.

They carefully cleaned his body of all the blood, rebandaged him, and lay him back. He had not regained consciousness. They sat a while with him, and then Lord Franz left, saying he would check back in a few hours.

"I am going to stay here with him. I will try to feed him all the liquid I can."

"Lena, I am going to ride home to check on the children and the livestock. I will come back tonight so you can get some sleep," Liebhard said. He came up behind her, bent down and kissed the top of her head. "He will make it."

The young squires would have sat with her all the time and she let them stay for long periods, seeing their worry. Reiner woke up about an hour after they had re bandaged him, and was able to drink some liquids. He was very pale, even his lips were pale. He had no fever, but he was extremely weak. As Lena was telling him about their arrival, he dozed off again. The same pattern continued throughout the night. He got no worse, but fell asleep within moments of waking up. He was so still that at times she touched his face to be sure he was alive.

Liebhard came after dark and stayed until dawn, so she was able to sleep for a few hours.

She was so worried she would not be on time. She ran and ran, but could not seem to get any closer. She started crying, but that was silly, because now she could not see where she was going. Then she heard someone laugh. She woke up. She was lying at the bottom of the bed, curled up. She raised her head. Reiner was looking at her.

He had been looking at her for some time, not wanting her to wake. Her hair was like a stream out behind her head, shining, soft and lightly curled. She held her hands loosely fisted in front of her face. Occasionally a frown would cause light frown lines to appear between her eyebrows. Her shift was askew from her restless sleep, pulled far down in front so that the soft curve of her breast was visible. He was so pleased to have her there.

"Oh! You are awake!" She jumped up and came around the side of the bed, happy and relieved. She put her hands on his cheeks and kissed his forehead. "We have been worried to death!"

Reiner looked up at her, pleased to be kissed. He was so very tired. He was very thirsty and had to relieve himself, both good signs, he knew.

"Is Liebhard here? If he is not, I am afraid you are going to have to help me," he said, throwing back the quilt.

"Oh. Try to move very slowly so you don't disturb your wound. Shall I get Lord Franz or Rudi or Conrad?" She was suddenly very embarrassed. She should not see him bare, she thought.

"Come on, it is just something everyone has to do," he chuckled weakly. "If I am not shy about it, you should not be."

Lena closed her eyes a moment. She was being silly. She got the chamber pot, placed it near the bed, and helped him sit up and close to the edge of the bed. The rest he was able to do himself. She kept her eyes slightly averted. When he was finished, she helped him to lie down again.

"Now you must drink. I have cider or cool broth"

"What about some hot water with honey?"

"Drink what I have here and I will ask for that," she responded.

"Broth then, Mother," he said, smiling. "You are kind of a dragon, you know."

"You are much better, I think," she answered, holding the cup up to his mouth. He took it and drank himself.

""Done. Now can I have hot water with honey? I have a hunger for it."

Lena laughed happily and went to the kitchen with the new order, and for a request for some cooked eggs and cheese. Reiner was on the mend.

An hour later, when Reiner fell asleep, she found Lord Franz, told him Reiner was much better, but to ask Rudi and Conrad to sit with him during the day. She went home later in the morning, sponged off all of the blood which seemed to have spattered all over her, changed clothes and washed her hair. She was so glad to see Greta, do her chores, anything that was ordinary and every day. Liebhard and Klaus were out cutting the last of the grain with the other villagers. She pulled together a dinner basket for them and walked out to the fields.

Liebhard saw her from a distance. He waved, called Klaus, and they both came off the field to Lena. As they ate, Lena told Klaus about all of the sights they had seen, about Reiner's magnificent battle, and about his wound. Liebhard had already told him parts of their experience. He was very excited to know as many details as they could give him. He also wanted to see Reiner. They decided the children and Liebhard would come up to see the invalid after they came in from the fields.

Lena went up to watch Reiner after she got back from the field. He slept almost the whole afternoon. The young squires were in and out, wanting to help, until Franz took them off to practice with swords. When Reiner woke up he was very thirsty and needed to relieve himself. No seepage was coming through the linen from his wound. He had no fever!

Reiner was sleeping when Liebhard, Klaus and Greta arrived. They walked in and sat down, making just enough noise to wake him. He smiled. In fact he lay there smiling at them for a few moments. He had survived. He had won. He had killed the murderer. He felt so comfortable with himself. Then he sat up carefully with Liebhard's help, Lena putting pillows behind his back, and he greeted them.

Klaus, surprisingly, came forward and hugged him, gulping back a sob. Reiner was his hero. He wanted to hear all over again, from Reiner himself, what had happened. Reiner sat for a moment, and when he started to talk, he described first how Liebhard had taught him the trick of standing with weapon between hands, tip resting on the ground. From there he described every detail, almost every sword stroke. It was almost enough for Klaus, who was enraptured.

Lena let them stay another half hour, but then shooed them home so that Reiner would sleep. After they had gone, she plied Reiner with as much liquid as he could drink and got him ready for sleep.

"I will stay here again tonight, but you are doing very well. Tomorrow night I think we can just arrange for Rudi and Conrad to look in on you once or twice during the night. You are going to have to be very cautious, Reiner, about moving your torso, bending over too far, picking anything up, especially with your left hand, for many days, maybe weeks. When the wound looks like it is closing well, we are going to have to take out those stitches too."

Reiner had listened to all she said and knew that her plan for him was good. He was happy he was mending well, but sad too. To be her sole interest these last days had been satisfying to him.

"I have you to thank for being alive today. There is no one to whom I would rather owe such a debt. You saved me."

Lena was embarrassed by his high praise, but wanted him to know how much she valued what he said. "You are my beloved friend. I would have taken your place if I could have." She leaned forward and kissed his cheek. He took her chin lightly with his right hand and kissed her gently on the lips. As he took his hand away, he smiled. Lena, leaned back, stood up, and went to take her place in a chair beside the bed.

"Go to sleep now," she said quietly.

The next morning, after she felt sure Reiner was recovering well, she rode home to the mill. She spent a homely morning cooking and cleaning with Greta. They walked out to the fields, where almost all of the harvesting was complete, and ate the packed lunch with Liebhard and Klaus. Lena told them about Reiner's rapid recovery. They would all visit him again before supper, they decided.

Liebhard was sitting next to Lena, and when he leaned across her to reach the cider, his arm touched her breast. She was jolted with sexual excitement and looked up to see that it had registered with him too. It had been at least a week since they had been together. He gave her a bold smile and she smothered a giggle. Tonight could not come too soon.

Reiner was having a rousing conversation with Rudi and Conrad when they arrived. The squires stayed during the first part of their visit with Reiner. It was almost festive. Greta ran off to see Emerlind a bit later, and the three teenagers went out to walk in the village, no doubt to pester a couple of pretty girls. Lord Franz came down when he heard they were visiting.

"Has Reiner told you he received a letter from Abbot Wenzel?" he asked after they had greeted each other. "He has not told me yet what the Abbot wrote." He added.

All three turned to Reiner. He smiled sheepishly and toke a fold paper out from under his pillow. "The abbot writes that he will visit here in about a week. He is coming personally from the archbishop of Mainz to reward me for my combat. He does not suggest what this reward might be, so we are all in the dark. He also writes that he will be on a mission to Trier, so he will be stopping here only for a day or two."

"Will Lord Frederick be with him?" Franz asked.

"He does not say. It is a brusque letter. Much the same way as he talks, not wasting breath on what he considers as inconsequential," he said.

"I am glad that he shows you this honor, Reiner," Lena interjected.

"And I received even a stranger letter yesterday. Lord Franz you did not know that my father wrote again." The warm smile had left his face. "If it had not angered me so much, I might have laughed at its contents.' Now he drew out a second letter. He looked around at them and then read the letter aloud.

This second letter from his father started again with a sentence commanding Reiner to show the respect due to his father. What followed was cloying. He said that Reiner's fame as a fighter, and as the savior of Lord Franz's fief had spread far and wide. He said that he was like his father and his ancestors in his bravery. Now it was time for Reiner to return to the loving bosom of his family. When he finished, he pretended to spit on the letter. Everyone sat in embarrassed silence.

"Needless to say, I will not reply to this letter either. You may think I am cruel to not forgive my father. I cannot. I do not honor him."

After a long silence, Lena spoke up. "We would perhaps all feel the same as you do, if we were in your position. Maybe someday in the future you will come to think differently. He has some good in him: he must have."

"There are people in this world, Lena, who are basically bad, cruel, or selfish. You look for the good because you have seen mostly good."

Liebhard leaned forward. "Reiner, you forget Dieter."

Reiner was taken aback. He reached for Lena's hand. "I am sorry. You are right."

Lena managed a smile. She did not like to see this unforgiving anger in her friend. Not long after this conversation, they gathered Klaus and Greta and made their goodbyes. Lena promised she would be up the next day.

After they had eaten supper, done some sewing and repairs, it was time for bedtime. Klaus and Greta went off to their beds. Liebhard reached for Lena, and pulled her gently into his lap. They kissed and caressed each other until Liebhard lifted her up and they climbed the stairs. He walked behind her caressing her buttocks. They undressed in the light of a single candle, and as Lena pulled up her shift, Liebhard reached out and cupped her breasts.

"Oh!" she said involuntarily. Her breasts seemed a little sensitive. He did not take his hands away, but slowly and gently fondled her.

"LENA!"

"What?"

"Don't you notice your breasts are a little larger? And your nipples. Are you pregnant?"

She ran her hands through his soft hair as she thought about her last flow. She was overdue by two weeks. She was not always regular. Had she felt differently? Not really, but her breasts were sensitive just now. She laughed as she felt her desire rising with his every caress. "You might be right!"

Liebhard picked her up and laid her on the bed, his hands moving down the length of her body. She was so highly aroused she started to moan. She could not stop pressing her body up to his. She thought she would lose her mind, her excitement rose and rose. They could not seem to get enough of each other, making love a second time before they nestled together and fell asleep.

She woke at dawn when he climbed back into bed. He kissed her lovingly. They lay together contentedly for a few minutes before she threw back the quilt and got up. She reached for her shift, but as she raised her arms, Liebhard was behind her, cupping her breasts again. He kissed her neck, licked behind her ear. He sat down on the edge of the bed holding her in his lap, nuzzling her. Then he kissed her lips and raised her off his lap.

"I think I am crazy with love for you sometimes," he chuckled.

"I too," she said softly.

When Liebhard and Klaus came back from the field, Klaus went with Astrid's boys to try to catch some fish in the river. Greta, Lena and Liebhard walked up to the manor to see Reiner. They found him playing a board game with Rudi at the hall table. He looked rested and in good spirits. After their greetings, Greta ran upstairs to find Emerlind. Rudi went off to find Conrad.

"Well, you two, you look exuberant. What has happened?" Reiner asked presciently.

The couple laughed, embarrassed but happy.

"Does it show that much?" Liebhard asked. "Well, we might be expecting our first child. Not completely sure yet!"

Reiner laughed and congratulated them. He reminded himself that this day was bound to come. It caused a tiny ping of pain in his heart, which was far outweighed by his friendship for them. He leaned his head back, and decided it was time to tell them his own secret.

"I have wanted to tell you many times something about me. I have a son."

"What?" they both said at once, amazed at this revelation.

"Tell us about him, Reiner!" Lena said excitedly. She wondered if this was the reason he had seemed so melancholy when he first arrived.

"Giorgio is almost four. I lived with a young woman in northern Sicily. She was from a trading family in the town near the lord I served. She was free born, like you. We never considered marriage because of our different status, and I don't think we really loved each other in that way. When she became pregnant, we were brought into reality. Her father, who had turned a blind eye to our relationship, had every intention of finding a husband who was a merchant. When Giorgio was two, he was able to arrange a match, and Angela was willing, even eager, to be established as the wife of a townsman. She easily gave up our son to me.

I was able to place him with an old woman I knew, and she cared for him well. I saw him almost every day when we were not called into some skirmish or battle. Then my lord died, and his retinue was broken up. I was told I would serve his cousin, the Count of Sponheim. It was with a heavy heart that I realized I would have to find a place for Giorgio so that I could take my new position.

I did not want to be too far from him, certainly I could not leave him as far away as Sicily. I finally decided I would bring him as far as Augsburg. That is where my first lord had his fief. I was there several years, and knew the area. On the way to the count's, I stopped at the Benedictine convent. The abbess was kind. They have several "orphans" there, all illegitimate like Giorgio. She agreed to take him, and I pay a yearly fee to her. Sister Cecilia, who cares for the children, writes to tell me how he is.

"Tell us more about him," Lena said.

Reiner's face shone with happiness as he described his son. Then he said, "My hope is that I will be able to bring him up here to be nearer me. You can see now why I hope to receive a large gift from the archbishop."

"Why did you not tell us earlier? We will be happy take him to live with us!" Liebhard said without a pause. Lena nodded in agreement.

Reiner's face turned red with joy and surprise. He had not even considered this possibility.

"You must think about this more. It would be much to put on Lena's shoulders if she is going to have your own baby soon."

"We do not need to think about this, Reiner. You are like family to us. We will be his aunt and uncle. And when you decide his future, when he is older, we will support you," Lena answered.

"Why am I so blessed to have you as my friends?" Reiner asked. He tried to lean over to hug them, but Lena jumped up and pushed him back, giving him a hug.

"Don't forget your wound!" She commanded. The men laughed, and Liebhard patted Reiner on the back.

"Well, that's settled, then. When will you go to get him?" Liebhard asked.

"You cannot go for weeks, Reiner. You will have to be able to defend yourself, which means you have to get your strength back." Lena said.

"Yes, Mother. I plan to get well quickly, and be very careful that I have no setbacks. I will write to Sister Cecilia though, and advise her of my plans," he mused happily.

Lena went up to visit Lady Elena before they left. Lord Franz was with her. Lena told them that they should ask Reiner about the news they had just heard. She laughed and refused to tell them more, so they followed behind her down to the hall. When they heard Reiner's secret, they were just as surprised as Lena and Liebhard had been, and interested to hear that Giorgio would be coming up to live with Lena and Liebhard. They were not told Lena and Liebhard's news yet.

At supper that evening, Lena told Klaus and Greta that she had a surprise for them. She told them that Reiner's son Giorgio would be coming to live with them. They were amazed and full of questions. Klaus was old enough to have heard about a child being born out of wedlock, but Greta found the idea hard to understand. They tried to keep it simple, but explained that Giorgio would be like one of their own family, like a nephew come to live with them.

It was threshing time in the villages, and everyone worked long hard hours. It was also time to start the harvest of winter vegetables from the small house gardens. Lena and Liebhard were also busy with the regular cycle of milling every few days. One of them tried to go up to see Reiner every day. Finally, about a week after they had learned Reiner's secret, Liebhard came home with news that Abbot Wenzel was expected the next day.

Reiner was impatient from the moment he woke up. He had dressed in his best tunic, and wandered around the hall and courtyard. Lord Franz came down and waited with him. They walked down to the village and back. Finally a young boy came running up to say that the abbot's retinue could be seen in the distance. Thirza was sent up to tell Lady Elena, who came down with Emerlind.

Abbot Wenzel entered the yard, Lord Frederick at his side. The retinue that followed was larger than Reiner had expected, until he remembered that the abbot was going on with a mission to Trier. There were six knights with several squires and three additional monks. All were greeted formally by Lord Franz and Lady Elena.

Abbot Wenzel turned to Reiner. "I greet you warmly, Sir Reiner. I am pleased to see you are recovered well." He took the knight's two hands and held them between his. Lord Frederick came forward and holding his forearms, kissed him on both cheeks.

All of the visitors were invited into the hall. The abbot as usual, wasted no time asking that they have a private meeting with Reiner. Lady Elena led the abbot, Reiner and Lord Frederick up to the solar. Meanwhile, Lord Franz entertained the retinue while Oona and Thirza hurriedly prepared for a much larger group at dinner than they had expected.

Once the abbot was seated, he again praised Reiner. "Your battle was epic. I have never seen the like. The archbishop was extremely pleased and asked for a description of your prowess several times."

"The archbishop has been interested in you since he heard of the salt processing. He has asked me to convey to you his wish to grant you a fief in his holdings. It is a large fief, recently vacant, east of Mainz. You will not be surprised to hear that it has two salt mines. This fief, I have been told, is at least twice the size of Lord Franz's here. He will also give you new amour and a horse of your choice. In addition, the archbishop has given me this to give to you." He pulled a leather pouch from his robe and handed it to Reiner, who was overpowered with sentiment by the bounty the archbishop showed to him.

"We of Carla's family cannot compete with such bounty. We have this to give to you, but we wish to know if there is any service that we can offer to you?" He gave Reiner yet another pouch, which the knight took, but barely noticed, after he had heard the abbot's last words.

"I am humbled and pleased beyond words by these many gifts. Your last words have almost caused my heart to stop. They are very timely. May I tell you something about myself, so that you will understand?"

The abbot and Lord Frederick leaned forward with interest. They by now were ready to expect anything from this singular knight.

"In my youth, I was led by thoughtless passion. I had a son from a woman out of wedlock. She was not of the knightly class. I have put my son Giorgio into the care of the nuns of a Benedictine convent in Augsburg. My friends, who you know, Lena and Liebhard, have agreed to take him in and care for him until I have decided his future. I wish to bring him here as soon as I can. I had thought that when I was well I could do this. It would be a great kindness to me if you could have him fetched and brought here."

The abbot actually chuckled. "You are human, as we all are! Lord Frederick and I can easily do this." He turned to his brother-in-law. "I hope you agree?"

"With all of my heart. Can we send one or two of our present retinue now?"

"Yes. Sir Reiner, we will send one of my best knights and his squire tomorrow morning to fetch your son. It is pleasing to us that we can fulfill your request. But let us not forget the archbishop's fief. You will accept it, I hope?"

"I am honored by his offer and will offer myself as his vassal as soon as I can travel to Mainz."

The three men stood up and the abbot asked after Lena and Liebhard, since he had not seen them when they arrived. He asked if they might come up so that he could greet them. Reiner went down and asked Lord Franz if he could send for

Lena and Liebhard to join them for dinner, and then asked the lord and lady to come up to listen to his news.

The rest of the day was joyful for everyone. Lena and Liebhard arrived in their best clothes, were greeted warmly by Clara's family, and overjoyed to hear all of Reiner's news.

The abbot and Lord Frederick grilled Reiner's conspirators about every aspect of their activity after the combat. The abbot was amused about the white lie Lord Franz told about the care Reiner received by the count's doctor. He and Lord Frederick were brought to the edges of their chair by the description of the group's stealthy escape from the castle, and the near death of Reiner by loss of blood.

After they had been told all, the abbot said, "I have heard that a ballad is now being sung about your epic combat. I have not heard it, but I trust you will as you travel east to your new home."

Reiner was embarrassed to hear this piece of information. He felt overwhelmed at all the changes that happened to him in these last weeks. He remembered the strange sensation he had had when the question of a challenger against Manfred had come up. His life and expectations had been turned right side up in these past few months. It was as though he had lost his balance in his old self and must leap to a new bright unknown. Everyone around him here was so happy for him and he knew he was happy too, but his emotions were jumbled.

After dinner, the abbot introduced Reiner to the knight, Johan Ostbach, who would be sent to Augsburg to fetch Giorgio. He was a young man, and had a gentle demeanor, which pleased Reiner. He had been concerned that his son would find this strange transition difficult, and wanted the best person possible to be his surrogate for this trip. Reiner told him about the convent, Sister Cecilia, the abbess, and particularly about his son. He told Johan that he would have a letter and gift for the convent ready in the morning before the knight left.

It had been expected that the abbot and Lord Frederick would rest during the afternoon; however, they asked if they could be shown the salt mining operation. Since Reiner was not allowed to ride yet, Lord Franz agreed that he and Liebhard would take their guests out to the site. All of the retinue were eager to go as well. When they had left, Lena stayed with Lady Elena, Emerlind and Reiner.

The women were full of questions for Reiner, questions about his future that he was really not able to answer. He told them what he could remember of the area where his fief was. He knew it to be even farther east than his father's land. He estimated that it was easily three or four days of hard riding from Lord Franz's land.

At a lull in the conversation, Lena brought up the subject of Reiner's stitches. "We really have to remove these. The sooner the better."

"And there is no time like the present."

"I am not sure I can do it alone. I have not looked at your wound for a few days," Lena said.

Lady Elena reminded them that she was squeamish about wounds and blood, which they all remembered and chuckled about. She and Emerlind went upstairs to the solar.

Reiner turned to Lena. "Can you do this by yourself?"

"I have no experience in this. I am going to get a small pair of scissors or clipper and some clean linen and lard in case we need it. I will bring it into your room."

When Lena came back, Reiner was sitting on his bed, but had not removed his tunic. "I am sorry, but I still have a weakness when I try to raise my arm."

Lena smiled and carefully helped him pull his tunic up over his head. Now when he was sitting before her, healthy, bare to the waist, she was embarrassed. He had a powerful though lithe physique. She leaned down, touching the edge of his scar. His body twitched and shivered.

"Oh! Did I hurt you?" she asked.

"No. I am well. You touched me," he answered tersely.

It was clear that his body had responded to the very touch of her fingertips. She continued touching only the scar, blocking out as well as she could the undercurrent for both him and her. She carefully snipped off the knot on the stitch that was in the best healed area. Holding the scissors, she placed the string on the blunt side of the blade edge and pressed her finger hard against the string. She gave a tentative pull. There was a little pucker of the skin on the other side of the scar, and a drop of blood. She knew she had some movement.

"Get ready. I am going to tug," she said. She gave a sharp quick pull. The string popped out. A few drops of blood came out. "That was better than I expected," she said.

Reiner said, "Well done!" It had hardly hurt, to his surprise.

Lena cut the second knot. This one was a little more challenging, but came out after the third sharp pull. The blood seeped out, but quickly stopped.

The third knot was in an area that was slightly red and puffed. She cut the knot off, but did not try to remove it.

"I want Lord Franz to look at this and pull it. He always has the right solution to every problem," she said.

Reiner had been in a moment of sweet reverie. As Lena had worked, he could feel her breath on the bare skin of his chest. Now that he knew he was leaving, his perception of her had become sharper, like trying to press every aspect of his feelings for her into his mind. In a few weeks he would not be facing these constant temptations that her presence brought to him. He closed his eyes so that she could not see what lay there.

Late in the afternoon, the salt mining tour was finished and the party came back to a festive evening of food and drink. It was after dark by the time Lena and Liebhard mounted their horses for the ride home. The children were already in bed, so they were very quiet entering the mill. Liebhard lit a candle from the embers in the fireplace, and led the way up the stairs. They made love tenderly and almost tentatively. They were very happy for their own hopes, but the fact of Reiner's approaching departure made the future also seem reduced.

As they lay together in each other's arms, Liebhard spoke. "I will miss him so. Besides you, he is the only friend I have ever had."

Lena had nothing to add. He had so clearly expressed what they were about to lose.

The following morning as Abbot Wenzel's group was still organizing their departure, Reiner found Sir Johan and his squire already in the courtyard, waiting for him. He handed his letter and a small pouch to the young knight. They briefly discussed the route he would take.

Reiner said as they mounted, "I will hope to see you in three weeks' time, maybe less. You may find you have to ride slower on the way back."

"Put you mind at ease, Sir Reiner. We will bring your son back safely," Sir Johan responded, and saluted him before they trotted out of the courtyard.

A short time later, Abbot Wenzel's group had gathered, said their farewells and were on their way to Trier. Lord Franz and Sir Reiner stood together, watching them leave. The young lord turned to Reiner. "Now you have to work to get strong again. I will be a careful task master, since Lena is not here to make sure you do not overtax yourself," he said, and smiled at his friend.

Reiner had been thinking about this himself, and they discussed how he should recover. They called the squires and did some careful slow motion sword work with Reiner. In just minutes he was weak and sweating. Franz laughed and told Reiner the story of his walk to Anna's, and how the women had shown him he was not as well as he thought.

After Reiner had rested, Rudi brought out Reiner's charger. Rudi had been given the task of exercising the horse daily, so the animal was calm and easy. Franz and Rudi helped Reiner mount, and at first Rudi led the charger. Reiner found that the movement of the walk did not trouble him at all, and took the reins. He continued to walk the horse in the courtyard and then down the road, the young squires walking beside him. When he came back and was helped to dismount, he was a little dizzy.

"That's enough for today, Sir Reiner," Franz ordered.

Each day they did more. Working with his heavy sword was very taxing for Reiner, so he switched to a quarterstaff, which he carried around for hours in his left hand, raising and lowering it. He used it when he fenced with Rudi or Conrad. The boys rode with him down through the village every day, going a little farther each time.

By the end of a week, he mounted with no help and could carry on a fair combat with the quarterstaff. The next week he carried his sword, lifting and lowering it, although this he could do only for a short time. He started riding at a slow trot without any trouble. He rode for miles with the young squires, even galloping once or twice without harm.

A week and a half after Abbot Wenzel left, Lena and Liebhard were happily surprised to see Reiner ride up to the mill. They hurried out, but he had dismounted before they could help them. He laughed happily.

"I hope I am in time for dinner?"

"How good to see you!" Lena said. "And looking fit!"

Reiner handed his reins to Liebhard's waiting hands and received a not quite gentle slap on the back.

"Lord Franz must have learned his treatment of convalescents from you. He is a stern master, but I must admit a good one," he said to Lena. "I've missed your visits up to the manor, but I am glad you stopped to see me when you were milling," he said in a half complaint.

They went into the mill. Dinner was not quite ready, so they had time to chat. Reiner told them about Lady Elena's insistence that she oversee a new suit of clothes for him. She offered him a choice of fabrics, took his measurements, and brought up two seamstresses from the village to help with the work. He was to have a new dark red highly embroidered tunic, a new fine linen shirt, and dark blue leggings. The widow of the tanner was working on a new belt for him, one that was engraved and studded.

"I have also been thinking that Giorgio will need new clothes. Before you say no, remember he is my son, and I want to pay for his needs." What followed was much quibbling about how much coin Reiner would be allowed to give them. He had more gold than he had ever had in his life, and he wanted to give them what seemed like an extravagant amount for the needs of his son. Finally Liebhard threw up his hands and surrendered. They would accept what he offered.

The next hours were spent in pleasant conversation as they ate. When it was time for the knight to ride back to the manor, Liebhard insisted that he ride with Reiner. The two friends saddled their horses and mounted, talking about nothing important, but knowing they were enjoying one of their last times together before Reiner left.

PARTING

At the beginning of the third week, Reiner started to ride each afternoon with the young squires on the road toward Katzenberg, hoping to see the knight returning with his son. He worked himself hard every morning to get his strength back. He could now wield his sword well enough for a short period. Rudi and Conrad loved to take turns opposing him, but by now he was stronger than they were, and could disarm them at will. He rode over to see Lena and Liebhard each day they did not come up to the manor village. One or both rode back with him.

The nights were hard. He lay awake thinking about his son. He would see him for only a few weeks before he would have to leave. How was he now? Would he know his father? When he finally managed to find sleep he experienced strange nonsensical dreams involving chases and fights that were in fantastical settings, falling and falling, being lost in dark woods, and many times woke wet with sweat. He woke early each morning, before dawn, and was so restless he could not go back to sleep.

Just shy of three weeks, he rode east on the road to Katzenberg once again with Rudi and Conrad. He stopped and sat on his horse, searching the horizon. There in the distance, he saw riders. He watched as they came closer. It was two riders with a packhorse. The boys saw the riders too and asked Reiner if it was them. He nodded, his eyes glistening with tears. He set his horse to a trot, the boys joining him. The distance closed rapidly.

"Sir Johan, welcome! Giorgio!" The little boy sat in front of Johan, his eyes big. Reiner could not tell if the boy remembered him. He did not want to frighten him. He turned his horse and rode alongside Sir Johan. He put out his hand and gently patted his son's head.

"I have missed you every day. I hope you were happy with Sister Cecilia. I am so glad that you are here."

Giorgio reached up to his father's hand above his head, and patted his father's hand. It was such an unusual gesture, even comical, that Reiner chuckled.

"Do you want to ride with Johan the rest of the way or would you like to ride with me, your daddy?" He almost wished he could take the question back, seeing the little boy's hesitation. But then, like a miracle, Giorgio pointed to him and said, "Daddy."

Reiner reached out his arms and Johan lifted the boy, putting him into Reiner's arms. He gathered his son closely, but not wanting to frighten him, placed him in front of himself on his horse, all the while talking to him, asking him if he remembered the many days last year that they had ridden together like this. The child did remember something of that ride, because he put his little hands on his father's hands and pretended to hold the reins, as he did before so many months ago.

The others fell behind slightly to give Reiner some privacy with his son. They rode in the same formation into the courtyard. Lord Franz heard the many voices and came out quickly. Lady Elena followed in a few moments. Reiner dismounted, gathered his son in his arms and introduced him to the lord and lady. The couple made much of the little boy, and he leaned shyly against his father's shoulder.

After Reiner had settled Giorgio in their room and sat with him showing him his belongings, the boy relaxed enough to be curious about the hall and the people there. Reiner brought him out and talked with Lady Elena, allowing Giorgio to investigate. He walked about looking at everything and everyone, returning to Reiner or Johan every few minutes.

When supper was served, Reiner held his son on his lap, and they ate from the same trencher. Before the meal was over, the little boy's eyes were drooping, and then he was asleep. Reiner got up slowly, waved goodnight to everyone, and took his son to bed. He undressed in the near dark and lay down with his precious treasure. He thought his heart would burst with happiness.

The next morning he woke and lay happily next to Giorgio. The boy had snuggled close to him for warmth. He waited patiently until he heard some noise from the kitchen and when Giorgio started to move restlessly, close to wakefulness.

"Good morning Giorgio. How is my son?" he asked the boy.

It was still hard for Reiner to understand what the boy said. He mixed some of his words from Sicily to the language he had spoken in Augsburg. Finally he worked out that the boy needed to relieve himself and was ravenously hungry. They were joined at breakfast by the young squires and Sir Johan. Later Lord Franz, Lady Elena and Emerlind came down. The squires had great fun entertaining the little boy with silly tricks.

After breakfast, Reiner told his son they were going to visit the boy's aunt and uncle. He was very curious that he had an aunt and uncle and wanted to go right away to see them. Reiner called for his horse and soon they were off, on their way to Miller Village. As they neared, Klaus saw them. He waved and turned to run to the mill. Reiner could hear him calling his mother.

His shout brought Liebhard out from his brother's house, where he was helping Mark with some carpentry. Meanwhile Lena came out of the mill. His two friends hurried forward to greet Reiner and Giorgio.

Lena came up to the horse, reached up and touched Giorgio's cheek. "Oh my love, I am so happy to see you! I am your aunt Lena." She was snared by the boy's eyes. They were identical to his father's in form and color. They were the same limpid deep pools. She could see his father in the boy's features. His hair was now gold, but she thought he would be darker as he grew up.

Liebhard came up behind her, reached up and shook the little boy's hand. "I am your uncle Liebhard. Let's get you down." He lifted the boy off the horse, held him high in the air, and gently twirled him. He brought him down to his chest and hugged him. Giorgio had giggled as he was twirled, and he seemed happy to stay in Liebhard's arms as Reiner dismounted. He had tears of joy in his eyes.

"Dada cries," Giorgio blurted, almost crying himself.

Liebhard hugged him and kissed him. "He is so happy you are here at last! We are so happy too. Okay, now you are down," he said as he put him on the ground. "Time to meet the rest of your relatives."

Lena took Giorgio's hand and went to Klaus and Greta, each of whom kissed him and hugged him. Klaus told him he was a blacksmith and would show him his smithy later. Other villagers had by now arrived and made much of the little boy. Reiner watched, his heart full. His son would have a secure happy life here though Reiner could not stay here with him.

The morning sped by and soon they were eating dinner in the mill, a building that captivated the little boy. He ran up and down the stairs, pointing at everything. Greta was like a little mother hen, following him around, somehow understanding what he asked and answering him.

Lena, Liebhard and Reiner watched and laughed. They talked too about how they would settle the boy. Reiner wanted to keep Giorgio with him at the manor until it was time to leave. He asked if it would be all right if he brought Giorgio down each morning, and came by in the afternoon, stayed for supper and took the boy home in the evening. All agreed this would work.

In a moment of silence, Lena leaned forward. "Reiner, his eyes are the copy of yours. I see you in his features, but exactly in his eyes." Reiner looked into her eyes as she spoke and she thought her voice would falter. She realized that it was his eyes that had drawn her from the first.

The next two weeks followed the pattern that Reiner had requested. By the end of that time he was nearly back to his former strength, though he admitted to Liebhard that he would not have been able to defeat Manfred at that moment. He knew he was well enough to travel. His new clothes were ready, and Giorgio was settled. He did not want to leave yet. He tarried. Then his summons came. A knight and squire arrived to travel with him to Mainz. The archbishop expected him to return with Sir Wolfram, the seasoned knight who came.

The following morning, Reiner and Giorgio arrived at their usual time. Reiner was dressed in his new clothes. When Lena saw him, she cried.

"You must leave today?" she asked.

"The archbishop has sent me an escort. I must obey," he said shortly. Her tears made him feel like he would lose control of his emotions. He did not want to frighten Giorgio. He dismounted and lifted his son off the horse, trying not to act any differently than he had any other morning.

"When I return to the manor, Sir Wolfram, the knight who was sent, would like to leave. I wish to see everyone here who has been so kind to me all these months. Perhaps you can take Giorgio with you and Liebhard and I will walk about the village,"

"He is over at Mark's already," she answered, taking Giorgio by the hand. "Come with me Georgi, we have to go to see how many eggs we can find this morning."

Reiner watched them until they had disappeared into the hen coop, before he turned and crossed the road to Mark's home. Mark and Liebhard were working in the new room and greeted him as he entered. Liebhard looked at his clothes and put his hammer down.

"Your summons has come," he said.

"Will you go around with me to see everyone before I leave?" Reiner asked.

Liebhard nodded. It was the first time Reiner had seen his friend on the verge of tears.

Throughout the next hour, the two friends sought out all of the villagers. They walked back to the mill when they had finished, Liebhard with his arm around Reiner's shoulder.

"I do not want you to leave," Liebhard said, packing into those few words the breadth of his love for his friend. "Go in to see Lena. She will be brought very low by this."

Reiner entered the mill. Lena was sitting alone at the table, her head on her arms. She looked up, her eyes filled with tears. He went around and lifted her up, pulling her against him. They stood embracing each other, not speaking, only the repressed sobs shaking their bodies.

"Lena," he whispered. "I... You know. Take care of my son."

"My heart is breaking," she said. "I will love Georgi as my own. You know. Go out and bring him back up to the mill. He is down with Greta at the blacksmithy. I will come out when I can."

Giorgio saw his father coming and ran to him, grabbing his hand and pulling him along to where Klaus was working. Klaus and Greta had long faces: they now knew he was leaving. He embraced them both, and he, Greta and Giorgio walked back up to the mill. Lena was there, her eyes red but the tears had stopped. Liebhard held his horse by the reins.

Reiner squatted down in front of his son. "You are so lucky Giorgio. Now you have two names, Giorgio and Georgi! Georgi, I must take a long trip now. I am going away to visit a great lord. He has given me many gifts, and I am going to thank him. You will stay with Lena and Liebhard. I will miss you every day." He took the boy in his arms and held him close, kissing him many times. He picked him up, and handed him to Liebhard.

Reiner mounted, looked down at the three loves in his life. "May God protect you from all harm. I will try to come back next summer."

He set his horse into a low levade, raised his arm in salute, turned and galloped away.

Later Lena wondered how she and Liebhard had been able to go on so normally with daily life after Reiner left. The black empty space of his absence changed even their relationship with each other. It was as if each wished to cry alone. They cared for their children, loving Georgi both for himself and because he was Reiner's son. They were able to be joyful that they would soon have a child. They hardly mentioned Reiner. It was a wound that needed to heal.

Reiner's first letter to them in late November came as a needed balm. He clearly missed them, but he was satisfied in a way that made them happy for him. He found his fief in good order. He had been allowed to choose two young knights and three younger men from among the archbishop's retinue to serve him. The salt mines were not toxic and had been extremely underutilized by the previous vassal, who had been ailing and who had not understood the salting process. Reiner had the mines producing well. He wrote that he had copied Lena's ideas of short workdays, large numbers of workers, and fair pay, all of which worked. His fief had suffered minor loss of life during the pestilence, though he had lost a few people in the past months. He had the service of an old knight who had been with the fief for over a dozen years, which had helped him understand his lands. He had met the young widow that the archbishop had suggested would be a good match for him, and he thought they could have a good marriage. They would wed after Christmas.

Like a water spring that had been opened, Lena and Liebhard talked of Reiner every day. They would mention something he said or did, or remind each other of some story or quirk of his, or wonder how he would have approached a problem.

Lena went up to ask Lady Elena if she would write a letter to Reiner for her. The young lady's pregnancy was now quite advanced, but she was well. She was eager to do what Lena asked, and said she would like to include some of her news in a letter as well. Lena first told Reiner about Georgi. Just four, he thought he could do everything Liebhard and Klaus could do. Liebhard had taken over the work of running the salting process, and had taken Georgi with him once or twice to see the place. He liked to feed and tend the animals, but wanted a dog most of all. Lord Franz had promised him that he would have a dog one day. Lena told Reiner that she felt well, and expected her baby in May. Klaus, who had turned thirteen, was very interested in the younger sister of the baker in Lord Franz's village. Mark and Astrid had a new baby girl, as did Lars and Margit. She teasingly wrote that there must be something in the cider they made that was causing this rash of births. And she wrote that they all missed him very much.

Both Franz and Elena enclosed letters with hers, and they were sent off to Reiner.

A new priest came to Lord Franz's village before Christmas. He also came to Miller Village to say mass at Christmas. He baptized Lord Franz's son in late January. Lady Elena had had a long labor, and Lena stayed at the manor for two weeks during that time. Lord Franz had acquired a new young knight and a squire, and had decided to retain both Rudi and Conrad, who were now squires themselves. He had also enticed additional families to his village from other areas because his salting gave him money to pay them to come.

Between running the salt mines, milling, and their children, Liebhard and Lena were as busy as they had been the previous year. Mark helped with both the salting and the milling. His sons were old enough to work in the salting too, which would help to pay their dues to Lord Franz.

Reiner wrote again in late January to tell them that he had wed Lady Helene of Bodenfeld, a fief near his own. She was a widow a few years younger than him. As the only daughter in her family, she had a good dowry. She had lost both her husband and her daughter to the pestilence. He did not describe her, but said she liked to hear his stories of his time at Lord Franz's fief, and he hoped they could meet her one day. He sounded content.

Every month or two, letters were exchanged between the friends. News was sent back and forth. From each side, there was a wish for more news.

By late April, Lena had to give up almost all of the mill work. She was told by everyone that she was going to have a big baby, which surprised no one, considering Liebhard's size. Liebhard teased her happily about how she waddled, but made her laugh even though she was annoyed. By mid-May, she thought there was no way she could be comfortable lying down, sitting or standing. When her time came, Anna came, shooed Liebhard away and helped her. To her surprise, the delivery of her big baby son was easy. She thought she would die of happiness.

Liebhard smothered her with kisses, and could hardly give up his son long enough for him to nurse.

"What shall we name him?" Lena asked Liebhard. They had skirted this subject, not wanting to challenge fate.

"I want to call him Reiner. Do you think our Reiner would mind?"

Lena laughed a little at the circular question: older Reiner now or young Reiner when he grew up?

"I think he would be happy to have our son as his namesake," she answered, and reached over to kiss her loving, doting husband.

Reiner was a big satisfied baby, who slept well within a few weeks. Greta now had a very full life. She still minded Georgi closely, but loved to take care of her new baby brother. She still found time to run up to visit Emerlind, especially since there was much conversation about possible husbands for her, and Greta feared she would lose her soon.

Lena had Lady Elena write a letter for her to Reiner. She told him of their new baby boy and how dotingly happy they were, that Liebhard was a big softhearted spoiler of the baby, holding him all the time, wanting to take him everywhere. She told him that the baby's name was Reiner, and they hoped he did not mind.

A letter came back very quickly. He was overjoyed for them. He loved the fact that they had named the baby after him. He gave them the news that Helene too was expecting a child. He also said that he hoped to be riding in that direction in midsummer to investigate salt sales with the Archbishop of Trier.

Reiner had indeed been overjoyed for them. He read Lena's letter, laughing to himself, cherishing every word about his son Georgi. He read parts of the letter to Helene, and she smiled to see his happiness. He had told her something of his history, and she knew how much these two people, Liebhard and Lena, had helped him through many hard times, and that they cared for his son.

Reiner had landed well on his feet in his new space. It seemed that almost all of his years of hard endurance had prepared him to take on the challenge of his fief and his commitments to the archbishop. He had not been in a hurry to meet the young widow that the archbishop wished him to marry. He felt he could not have anyone new close to him yet. He yearned for his son, Lena and Liebhard.

He had met Helene at a fete at another fief in early November. She was extremely shy and appeared almost fearful of meeting him. Instantly he wished to put her at ease. His care and sensitivity opened her personality to him. He found that she was a thoughtful though sad young woman. She was quite pretty. He met her at her father's estate the following week and they agreed to marry. It was a simple uncluttered understanding. They knew they could make a good, even happy, life together.

FRIENDS

It was a hot day in late June. Lena had thrown on her oldest short sleeved linen dress, nearly white from many washings. She had just seen Greta off to take Georgi and Reiner over to Anna's for a visit. Liebhard, Klaus and all the men were in the fields. She had not combed her hair and had barely covered it in the morning, so that it hung loose around her shoulders. She stepped out of the mill, on her way to work in her garden patch.

"Lena!"

She turned to see the most splendid knight riding a magnificent black bay charger in shining trappings, followed by several retainers and a servant leading a heavily laden pack horse. The man was so beautifully dressed that it took her a moment to realize it was Reiner.

He jumped off the horse as she put down her basket, and they rushed to each other. They embraced ecstatically, so happy to see each other. Reiner picked her up and twirled around. He leaned back from her slightly and looked down into her eyes.

"All these months. So many changes. Yet it seems like we were together just yesterday." He felt in his heart a basic change: Lena was now his friend without the great heavy weight of desire. That had mellowed to a sweet memory. "I have brought gifts for you and Georgi," he said as he motioned toward the pack horse.

Lena looked into those deep eyes that she loved. She stepped back from him and took his two hands, brought them up to her lips. "I am so happy for you Reiner. In your letters we saw that you had landed on your feet. Come. Greta has taken Georgi and Reiner up to Anna's. Bring your beautiful new horse. Georgi will want to ride it out to the fields to see Liebhard." She kept his hand in hers as they walked up the road.